D0139843

EDUCATION IN A DIGITAL WORLD

WITHDRAWAL .

Drawing on a wealth of theoretical and empirical work, *Education in a Digital World* tackles a number of pressing questions, such as: How are 'global' trends in educational technology refracted through national policies and processes? How exactly are educational technologies linked to issues of global economics and the fortunes of national and international economies? To what extent are digital technologies implicated in the commercialisation, marketisation and commodification of education?

These questions, and others, are addressed throughout eight wide-ranging chapters, which consider topics such as the national policy strategies of countries across North and South America, Europe and East Asia, the educational technology portfolios of international organisations such as the United Nations and Microsoft, as well as the role of education and technology in international development and the on-going efforts to provide 'one laptop per child' across low-income regions and countries. Through these examples Selwyn develops a detailed analysis of education, technology and globalisation, drawing together arguments and debates from various academic perspectives. Written in a detailed but accessible manner, this is an essential book for anyone wishing to gain a better understanding of the role of education and technology in contemporary globalised society.

Neil Selwyn is Reader in the Department of Culture, Communication and Media at the Institute of Education, University of London, UK.

EDUCATION IN A DIGITAL WORLD

Global Perspectives on Technology and Education

Neil Selwyn
INSTITUTE OF EDUCATION – UNIVERSITY OF LONDON, UK

Routledge
Taylor & Francis Group

NEW YORK AND LONDON

LB
1028.3
.S38884
2013

HARVARD UNIVERSITY
GRADUATE SCHOOL OF EDUCATION
MONROE C. GUTMAN LIBRARY

First published 2013
by Routledge
711 Third Avenue, New York, NY 10017

Simultaneously published in the UK
by Routledge
2 Park Square, Milton Park, Abingdon, Oxon OX14 4RN

Routledge is an imprint of the Taylor & Francis Group, an informa business

© 2013 Taylor & Francis

The right of Neil Selwyn to be identified as author of this work has been
asserted by him in accordance with sections 77 and 78 of the Copyright,
Designs and Patents Act 1988.

All rights reserved. No part of this book may be reprinted or reproduced or
utilized in any form or by any electronic, mechanical, or other means, now
known or hereafter invented, including photocopying and recording, or in any
information storage or retrieval system, without permission in writing from the
publishers.

Trademark notice: Product or corporate names may be trademarks or registered
trademarks, and are used only for identification and explanation without intent
to infringe.

Library of Congress Cataloging in Publication Data
Selwyn, Neil.
Education in a digital world : global perspectives on technology
and education / Neil Selwyn.
p. cm.
Includes bibliographical references and index.
1. Educational technology—Cross-cultural studies. 2. Education and
globalization—Cross-cultural studies. 3. Computer-assisted
instruction—Cross-cultural studies. I. Title.
LB1028.3S38884 2012
371.33—dc23
2012001506

ISBN: 978-0-415-80844-6 (hbk)
ISBN: 978-0-415-80845-3 (pbk)
ISBN: 978-0-203-10817-8 (ebk)

Typeset in Bembo
by Taylor & Francis Books

CONTENTS

PREFACE

Digital technology is now a prominent feature of education provision and practice in many countries and contexts. Mobile telephony, internet use and other forms of computing are familiar, everyday tools for a sizable proportion of the world's population. Billions of personally owned digital devices are in frequent use, and billions of others are used communally in shared, public settings. Governments of nearly every country in the world now have established policy agendas that seek to encourage and support the use of digital technologies in schools, colleges and universities. Digital technology is a topic that is of significance to a global educational audience.

Yet while this is now an internationally important field of study, many academic writers and researchers remain surprisingly uninterested in discussions of the forms of educational technology that are situated beyond their own familiar boundaries. This is especially the case for academics working in Anglophone countries (myself included), where global awareness of educational technology often goes little further than the academic educational technology literatures from the US, Canada, Australia, New Zealand and the UK. Besides these familiar settings, the occasional reports from 'other' countries that one may come across are seen usually as marginal additions to the field. The 'international imagination' of many English-speaking educational technologists is therefore fairly unadventurous and largely monocultural. Is the use of computers in Chilean schools essentially the same as in Chicago? Are online learners in Mali are doing pretty much the same things as they do in Melbourne? After all, are we not living and working in a 'one-size-fits-all' global village?

Clearly this is *not* the case and, if pressed, many Anglophone writers and researchers would concede that they are less aware than they should be of the diverse educational technology issues and debates that are of importance outside (over)developed Euro-American contexts. The unfortunate inability of many native English speakers to become proficient readers and speakers of other languages means that great swathes of educational technology discussion and debate remain out of sight and out of mind. As a result, many of the issues and concerns that are of importance outside the English-speaking regions remain at the periphery of the field. One of my intentions in writing this book was to push some of these issues further into Anglophone educational technology discussion and debate. Educational technology is certainly a field in need of an expanded global consciousness.

Significantly, then, this is not a book whose perception of the term 'global' is confined to over-developed regions such as the US, Europe, Australasia and East Asia. Indeed, educational technologists would do well to take heed of Divya McMillin's (2007, p.9) criticism of the media and communications literature – when arguing that "the generalisation of US and UK experiences to the rest of the world is a growing source of embarrassment among scholars". In the same spirit, the present book has been written in response to the clear need for a more inter-nationalised and comparative analysis of educational technology. This is a book that focuses deliberately on the state of education and technology in Africa, South America, South Asia and the Middle East as well as the more documented cases of Europe, North America and East Asia.

Another motivation for writing this book is my on-going desire to develop analyses of educational technology that are more socially attuned. Despite the best efforts of a few critically minded scholars, there is still a distinct reluctance amongst educational technology writers and researchers to think about the connections between digital technology use and the wider world – i.e. what takes place beyond the immediate context of the technological artefact and the individual user. I have long believed that any analyst interested in engaging with the topic of educational technology should focus on the 'bigger picture'. This entails asking a wide range of awkward questions. For example, what are the connections between digital tech-nology and the politics of education? What connections are there between the use of digital technology in education and matters of economics and economy? How is educational technology connected with the many cultural formations and social relations that constitute 'society'? This book, then, is a modest attempt to identify and explore some of these connections – especially as they appear to be taking shape at international as well as at subnational levels.

While I had always assumed that my writing was reasonably sympathetic towards these 'bigger picture' issues, my early preparations for writing this book left me quickly aware of my previous failures to think properly about the connections and disconnections between educational technology and what can be simplistically described as the 'global' arena. Even having finished the book, the more that I read about 'other' contexts and countries then the more I become aware of the (dis)-connections between educational technology and local contexts and settings. Looking back on my earlier experiences of encountering educational technology around the world it is now obvious, for example, that observing the use of laptop computers in a Seoul high school raises a completely different set of issues from observing what appear to be the same devices being used in high schools in inner-city São Paulo or, indeed, in a classroom in rural Wales. Further sets of differences are apparent when one reconsiders the national policy programmes and agendas in each of these education systems. The use of any 'digital technology' device in any type of educational setting in any country is therefore a complex knot of issues, interests, actors and agendas. This book is an attempt to at least begin to make better sense of this complexity.

Perhaps unsurprisingly, one of the key themes that emerges throughout this book is the importance of 'context' – not least the need to address carefully the local, national *and* global contexts of educational technology. As such, this is a book that ends up considering a range of 'global perspectives' rather than offering a singular 'global perspective'. In other words, this is a book that attempts to recognise the diversity and heterogeneity of technology use around the world rather than peddling a globalist account of a unified technology-driven world order. Each of the eight chapters take full account of the differences that exist between and within local contexts, as well as highlighting apparent global commonalities and similarities.

One final motivation for writing this book was a desire to reintroduce a political dimension into the academic discussions and debates that surround educational technology. All of the book's eight chapters have an underlying interest in the role of culture, politics, economics and society on the production and consumption of a range of educational technology products, practices and discourses. Crucially, I have tried to consider all of these issues at a 'micro' level as well as at a 'macro' level of analyses. This book therefore follows the maxim that thinking about the global requires that we simultaneously think about the local. As a result, this is certainly *not* a book that finds itself seduced wholly by rhetorics of globalisation, the 'end of geography', 'borderless worlds' and so on. Indeed, these are arguments and issues that the book seeks to challenge and critique whenever possible.

Despite the grand scale of all its aims and issues, I hope that the book nevertheless retains clarity in its overall analysis. While one of the main aims of writing this book was to problematise the universalising nature of the discourses that have come to surround technology use in education, it is important not to be overwhelmed by the scope and diversity of the issues that are under discussion. One of the dominant themes that emerges by the end of this book is that while the changes associated with educational technology may not be experienced as homogeneous processes across the globe, there *is* still a clear story that can be told about education and technology. As we shall see, this is a story that is as much as about the local as it is as about the global; and that is as much about ideology as it is about innovation.

Neil Selwyn
London, April 2012

ACKNOWLEDGEMENTS

I would like to thank the many colleagues and friends whose ideas, thoughts, suggestions and criticisms supported the writing of this book. In particular, a number of people were kind enough to read various parts of the manuscript and offer advice – these include Niall Winters, Will Farr, Carlo Perrotta and Enrique Hinostroza.

Much of the inspiration for this book stemmed from my experiences working with, and talking to, other writers and researchers around the world who share my interests in the area of education and technology. Even seemingly minor conversations with international colleagues when working away from the UK have helped my thinking on many of the themes explored in this book – often setting me off on various lines of enquiry and argument. In this sense, thanks are due to the following people (among others): Andreas Breiter, Mark Brown, Lin Ching Chen, Enrique Hinostroza, Kuo-Hung Huang, Ignacio Jara, Athanassios Jimoyiannis, Oystein Johannessen, Yngve Nordkvelle, Francesc Pedro, Morten Søby, Cathrine Tømte and Stefan Welling. Thanks also to Nicola Johnson and colleagues at Monash University who supported the visiting scholarship that coincided with the completion of the book.

I would also like to thank UK-based colleagues past and present with whom I have talked these issues through – not least Daniella Boraschi, Phil Brown, Peter Fairbrother, John Fitz, Michael Lightfoot, Martin Oliver, John Potter, Gareth Rees and Susan Robertson.

I am always acutely aware of the hard work that goes into the production of any book. So in terms of the writing and production of this book, I would like to thank all of the production and editorial team at Routledge – notably Alex Masulis and Anna Clarkson.

Most of all, I would like to thank Sophie for giving me the time required to write this book.

1

EDUCATION AND TECHNOLOGY

Developing a Global Perspective

Introduction

The on-going development of ever more powerful digital technologies is undoubtedly one of the defining features of the past thirty years. The pace and scale of recent digital innovation – in particular the growth of computing, the internet and mobile telephony – has prompted many commentators to describe digital technology as a key driver of societal development around the world. As Manuel Castells (2006, p.3) put it, "we know that technology does not determine society: it *is* society". For many people, then, digital technologies have led to a greatly improved era of living – the so-called 'digital age'. One of the many perceived improvements of this digital age is a reduction in the physical restrictions and 'frictions' of the 'real' world. Indeed, in the latter years of the twentieth century, there was much talk of a technology-led 'time-space compression', 'death of distance', 'end of geography' and privileging of 'virtual' arrangements over material arrangements. Digital technologies were seen to be supporting a redefinition of what it was to live and work around the world, echoing enthusiasms from the late nineteenth century for the 'new' technologies of the telegram, telephone and steamship. Indeed, the 1990s was a time of similarly breathless descriptions of a 'shrinking world' that was more connected and less divided than ever before. At the heart of all these recent changes was reckoned to be digital technology.

One prominent aspect of these claims was how change and remediation was supposedly taking place on a global basis. Indeed, twenty years on from the initial 'dot.com' boom of the 1990s, digital technologies still tend to be framed in terms that transcend local, national and regional boundaries. It has become common-sensical to imagine digital technologies as unfettered by the traditional limitations of countries and continents. This thinking has been evident in the metaphors used to describe digital technologies over the past thirty years, many of which imply an overcoming of global distance and space (e.g. the 'information superhighway', the 'worldwide web' and even the *inte*rnational *net*work). Other descriptions suggest a transcendence of the material world altogether (e.g. 'virtual reality' and 'cyber-space'). Recent discussions of the computing 'cloud' extend this logic further – evoking otherworldly visions of a ubiquitous source of computer power that exists around us regardless of our geographical location.

Of course, the on-going development of digital technology is associated with a number of more specific societal, economic and cultural changes. For example, the supposed ability of digital technologies to 'flatten out' hierarchies and introduce a 'hyper-connected' logic to the organisation of social relations has been welcomed by some commentators as supporting the (re)configuration of society along more dispersed and individualised lines (e.g. Friedman 2007). Even if we discount the more fanciful and idealistic aspects of some of these accounts, a large number of popular and academic commentators agree that the ever expanding 'connectivity' of digital technology is recasting social arrangements and relations in a more open, democratic and ultimately empowering manner. As Charles Leadbeater (2008, p.3) concluded:

> the web's extreme openness, its capacity to allow anyone to connect to virtually anyone else, generates untold possibilities for collaboration ... the more connected we are, the richer we should be, because we should be able to connect with other people far and wide, to combine their ideas, talents and resources in ways that should expand everyone's property.

Claims such as these lie at the heart of how many people perceive the 'digital world' alluded to in the title of this book. This is the prevailing sense that we are now living in a technologically re-ordered world – a world that is structured and arranged along significantly different lines than was the case even a few years before. There are clear articulations here with concepts such as the 'information age', the 'information society' and the 'post-industrial' era – ideas that all point towards the growing importance of the production and consumption of information and knowledge as key sources of power and competitiveness in the 'global economy'. Indeed, all of these concepts convey the common view that recent economic, social and cultural changes have been driven by – or at least shaped around – the on-going development of new computerised and telecommunications technologies (see Webster 2006). As Daniel Bell (1980) outlined in his description of post-industrial society, digital technologies are now "decisive for the way economic and social exchanges are conducted, the way knowledge is created and retrieved, and the character of work and organisations in which men [sic] are engaged". The focus of the present book, then, on *Education in a Digital World* corresponds clearly with these wider accounts of societal (re)organisation over the past fifty years – in particular the idea of there now being an intensified universal connectivity of information, as well as an apparently increased significance of knowledge.

Both these issues perhaps merit further attention before we progress further into more specific discussions of education and technology. With regards to the first issue of universal connectedness, it is worthwhile reconsidering Manuel Castells' description of the 'information society' and what he sees as the "networking logic of its basic structure" (Castells 1996, p.21). Although much criticised, Castells' description of the 'network society' rightly highlights the ways in which 'connective' features of technological developments during the 1980s and 1990s were paralleled by the corrective restructurings of capitalism and statism throughout this time, as well as by the rise of networked social movements such as ecologism. In all these ways, Castells draws attention to the increasing tendency of dominant functions and processes within contemporary societies to be organised around networks rather than physical boundaries. As he argued:

> Networks constitute the new social morphology of our societies and the diffusion of networking logic substantially modifies the operation and out-comes in the processes of production, experience, power and culture. While the networking form of social organisation has existed in other times and spaces, the new information technology paradigm provides the basis for its pervasive expansion throughout the entire social structure.
>
> *(Castells 1996, p.469)*

Crucially, Castells saw the growing organisation of society around dynamic networks as having led to a changed sense of space and time within many aspects of contemporary life. Castells described how societal arrangements were influenced more by the 'space of flows' (i.e. the movement of information, resources, objects or funding) rather than by the 'space of places' (i.e. their original location). This idea of a deterritorialised 'network society' has been illustrated ably of late by patterns of economic activity which appear to depend ultimately on global dynamics rather then any national influence (as was evident, for example, in the 'meltdown' at the end of the 2000s of global financial markets). Conversely, a deterritorialised networking logic can also be seen in 'global' social movements such as the 'smart mob' protests against various world economic summits throughout the 2000s, the so-called 'Arab Spring' popular revolts at the beginning of the 2010s, or even the persistence of decentralised terrorist networks such as *Al Qaeda*. All these examples illustrate the growing societal significance of the global transmission of information – for better and for worse. Thus while appearing to be concentrated at regional or local levels, most economic and political activity could be said to be determined ultimately at a global rather than local level of aggregation. As Castells (2006, p.4) reasoned, what may appear to be local activity must be understood instead as "diffused by the power embedded in global networks of capital, goods, services, labour, communication, information, science and technology".

In the eyes of many commentators, therefore, the primary significance of the information age and network society is one of globally networked power – in particular, globally networked *economic* power. This is certainly reflected in the 'network enterprise' of modern multinational corporations, based as they are on the networking of labour in the form of 'flexi-workers' and 'self-programmable labour' alongside the distribution of what Hardt and Negri (2005) term 'immaterial goods'. Indeed, economic commentators over the past thirty years have charted the rise of so-called 'immaterial' economies, built around global flows of 'weightless' products and services such as accounting, legal services, insurance, management consulting, training, marketing and software development (see Miller 2011). This new world economic order is seen to be founded upon globally networked processes that are fast-changing, flexible and based around ephemeral rather than material 'content'.

This, then, brings us to the second point of wider significance for this book – i.e. the ever-increasing influence of information and knowledge in contemporary society. Indeed, the spectre of the 'knowledge economy' could be said to underpin everything that has been discussed so far in this chapter (and indeed everything that will be discussed throughout the rest of the book). In simple terms, the 'knowledge economy' refers to the increasing significance of the production and manipulation of information and knowledge at the expense of the production of physical goods and services. As Chakravartty and Sarikakis (2006, p.22) argue, the 'knowledge economy' "symbolises a transition from the manual/machine-assisted production line of material things to an abstract, placeless interaction between human and electronic brains for the production of services". Following this logic, the production and distribution of knowledge and information is now a core component of contemporary economic growth and, therefore, changes in employment. As a consequence, the capacity of organisations and individuals to engage successfully in learning, training and 'reskilling' processes becomes an important determinant of economic performance (Pantzar 2001).

Indeed, the knowledge economy thesis implies that individuals and organisations face major educational challenges in adjusting to these new circumstances. Thus it is recognised by policymakers and employers alike that the nature of access to educational opportunities has implications not only for general economic competitiveness, but also for the employability of individuals and the consequent impacts on their standard of living. A dominant view has emerged in many countries and regions that the effective organisation of learning opportunities is a crucial driver of economic growth and – it follows – social cohesion. The emphasis on individuals within the knowledge economy model reflects a 'human capital' model where individuals participate in learning according to their calculation of the net economic benefits to be derived from education and training (Becker 1975). As Brown *et al.* (2008, p.132) reason, the essence of this human capital approach is that "income reflects the level of skill". Given the prevailing view of contemporary economic change as predicated upon knowledge-based forms of production, human capital theory sees individual workers seeking to participate in education throughout their lifetimes in order to capitalise upon the labour-market benefits that should result from skills renewal and development. In this sense, the main issue that individual citizens are required to address throughout their working lives is their ability to accrue the skills (and perhaps as importantly the associated certification and accreditation) required for success in the labour market. The main issue that governments are therefore required to address is the removal of the impediments or 'barriers' that prevent individuals from participating in education and training. As Andy Green (2003, p.87) reflects, "the impact of globalisation on the demand for skills and qualifications" over the past thirty years or so has been substantial.

The Significance of Education, Technology and Global Societal Change

As these latter points suggest, education is an integral component of the changing contemporary world. Whether described in terms of the information age, network society or knowledge economy, it is difficult to overlook the links between education, economy and society. The beliefs and values underlying most forms of recent education change and reform have therefore been simple ones – first, that a knowledge economy requires an information-skilled workforce in order to succeed, and second that the key to an information-skilled workforce is education and learning. As Roger Dale (2005, p.118) notes, the knowledge economy is therefore "intrinsically related to education". In these terms, education is positioned as a continuous concern – reflecting the ethos of 'lifelong learning' that embraces not only compulsory phases of schooling but also education and training throughout the life-course.

This, then, brings us to the core concern of the book – the significance of the use of digital technologies in these forms of education that underpin the digital age, information society and knowledge economy. From even our brief discussion so far, it should be of no surprise that digital technology is seen by most commentators as being an essential element of contemporary educational arrangements. Indeed, the educational controversies that raged throughout the 1980s and 1990s over whether or not learning about digital technology should be a core component of education (the so-called issue of 'computer literacy') have long since been resolved. Now there is widespread acceptance that digital technologies must play an integral role in the provision of all aspects of lifelong learning – from the integration of computers in school, college and university classrooms, to the virtual delivery of online courses and training. Digital technologies and media are also recognised as implicit elements of the 'informal' modes of learning that are stimulated by general interests, pursuits and hobbies outside the formal curriculum. In short, digital technology is now an utterly integral but wholly unremarkable component of educational conditions and arrangements around the world.

At this point, it is important to note that what is often referred to as 'educational technology' is not a single entity, but a diverse array of technological devices and technology-based activities and practices. In fact, many discussions of educational technology are focused only on a small number of the various forms of digital technology that are used around the world. Instead, educational uses of digital technology encompass the use of internet-connected computing devices such as laptop and tablet computers and 'smart phones', as well as the institutional uses of these technologies in the form of virtual learning environments, electronic smartboards and so on. These technological devices are used throughout educational systems to support a diversity of forms of educational provision from kindergartens to work-based training. Within the institutional contexts of school, college and university – for example – much effort is put into the use of classroom and campus-based technologies alongside the increasing use of 'blended' forms of online and offline provision of teaching as well as fully 'virtual' provision. Indeed, 'virtual schooling' is now a growing feature of school systems in North America and Europe. Virtual education is also a key element of the diversified provision of transnational 'offshore' higher education, where higher education institutions are providing international online education, partner-supported transnational programmes and even international branch campuses (see McBurnie and Ziguras 2010).

In all these forms, digital technologies are associated with potentially far-reaching shifts in the organisation and governance of educational provision. Commentators now talk about 'school 2.0' and the 'edgeless university' – reflecting the increasing fluidity and fragmentation of educational places and spaces. Conversely, in many regions of the world, digital technologies are being used to support large-scale forms of 'mega schooling' (Daniel 2010) – massively expanding access to education to populations who would otherwise be denied. There are, for example, a growing number of 'open' schools and universities where teachers and students are separated physically but educated collectively – from the Indonesia Open Junior Secondary School to the Open University of Japan. Latchem and Jung (2010) list thirty-three such 'mega-universities' in Asia alone, spanning from Israel to Macau. The scale of these reconfigurations of educational provision is considerable. The Turkish Anadolu University, for example, doubled in size between 1996 to 2006 and now caters for over 1 million students. Digital technology also lies at the heart of virtual consortia of traditional universities (such as the Korean Open Cyber University) and online brokers of courses from other institutions (such as the Syrian Virtual University). Also of significance here, is the technology-supported growth of private provision of education. Indeed, many of the initiatives described above include – at least in part – the involvement of an array of commercial interests. From the 1990s onwards, there has been notable growth in multi-billion dollar global educational media providers such as Pearson, Thomson, McGraw-Hill and the Apollo Group. Digital technology is therefore being used to support a diverse array of educational forms that are associated in turn with a diverse array of educational outcomes.

Of course, technology can be used to pursue forms of educational provision other than these centrally driven or commercially provided forms. For some groups of educators, digital technology is welcomed as a means of offering opportunities to move beyond the institutionalised provision of education altogether – allowing groups and communities of individuals to learn amongst themselves. This is reflected in the growing trend towards globalised forms of collaborative and self-organised learning – such as the online collaborations between educators and institutions to form 'globally networked learning environments' (see Starke-Meyerring and Wilson 2008). There is now increasing enthusiasm for the use of 'open courseware' and 'open educational resources' which are concerned with making educational materials available and reconfigurable online for no cost. There are now many examples of these open educational arrangements (see Conole 2012) – from large professional repositories such as the UK Open University's 'Open Learn' programme to volunteers from China and Taiwan translating open source materials from North American and European universities into Mandarin Chinese. In all these instances, high quality teaching and learning is no longer seen to be the domain of closed educational institutions and professional communities.

As all these examples suggest, education and technology is a broad topic that encompasses a wide range of forms and involve a wide range of interests. Yet despite its diversity, popular discussions of educational technology are disappointingly uniform. Indeed, the field of educational technology appears to generate a constant level of heightened expectation about the general ability of the latest 'new' technology to change education for the better, regardless of context or circumstance. Typical of this thinking, for example, is John Willinsky's (2009, p.xi) assertion that current forms of digital technology offer "the potential, on a global scale ... towards changing how and what the world learns". As the CEO of News Corporation (and investor in a number of educational technology companies) similarly reasoned: "In putting this creative force into schools we can ensure the poor child in Manila has the same chance as the rich child in Manhattan ... the key to our future is to unlock this potential" (Rupert Murdoch, cited in Willsher 2011).

Public proclamations of this sort exemplify the general belief amongst many powerful interests that digital technologies lie at the heart of fundamental educational change and renewal. One prominent discourse here is the notion of technology sustaining a genuinely worldwide rearrangement of educational access – in John Daniel's (2009, p.62) words, heralding "a tectonic shift that will bring the benefits of learning and knowledge to millions". The notion of educational technology as a global phenomenon is evident in the numerous celebrations of the ability of digital technology to allow educators and educational institutions to operate in 'borderless' and 'edgeless' ways, and for individuals to enjoy unprecedented levels of meritocratic educational opportunity. In an epistemological sense, digital technologies have been long associated with the 'de-territorialisation' and 'de-referentialisation' of knowledge, where knowledge has no boundaries and is free to travel around the world (see Readings 1996). For some critical educators, digital technologies are described as having the potential to support the development of cosmopolitan and communitarian forms of education, "powerfully contribut[ing] to the worldwide democratization, civic engagement and action-orientated social responsibility" of educators and educational institutions (Benson and Harkavy 2002, p.169). Other proponents are less specific but even more fulsome in their faith in the capacity of technology to support universal change. As Nikki Davis reasoned in all-encompassing terms: "If our society is to adjust to and avoid damaging turmoil, alienation, and the threat of disintegration, then the impact and potential of information and communications technology must be at everyone's fingertips" (Davis 2008, p.xxxv).

Education and Technology: The Need for a Globalised Perspective

These are all familiar and well-rehearsed portrayals of the place of digital technology within education. In much of the prevailing discourse, digital technologies are positioned at the heart of impending worldwide change and societal reorganisation, with educational technology assumed to be stimulating global transformations of education and learning. Whether this is the case or not remains a central concern of this book. Yet for the time being, it would appear clear that more time and effort needs to be spent thinking carefully about the issues implicit in these assumptions. In particular it seems that the discussions and debates that currently surround educational technology would benefit considerably from serious consideration of what is meant by these broad-brush allusions to the 'global', 'globalised' and so on. In other words, any serious discussion of contemporary educational technology needs first to be considered against the backdrop of what has become known as globalisation theory. Indeed, despite the obvious connections between educational technology and the wider global changes in society there has been surprisingly little attempt to link the prevailing arguments and assumptions about education and technology with what is known about 'globalised' society and theories of so-called 'globalisation' (although see Buchanan 2011). It is to this subject that we must now turn our attention.

While used frequently in popular, political and academic debates, the concept of 'globalisation' is an often ill-defined and inconsistently applied term. Indeed, as John Urry (2002) describes it, the term 'globalisation' belies a 'confusing mixture' of various disparate and conflicting issues and agendas. In an everyday sense, the notion of globalisation is used most often to refer simply to a vague notion of "increasing connectedness of human activity across the world" (Unwin 2009a, p.15). Yet in a more focused sense, the economist Theo Levitt popularised the notion of 'globalisation' during the first half of the 1980s to describe on-going global changes with regard to production, consumption and investment. In these terms, at least, it is difficult to argue against the recent historical significance of globalisation. Yet as the considerable debates that have taken place in the wake of Levitt's initial work suggest, we certainly should not accept the globalisation thesis as a given. Instead, it is perhaps most helpful to approach globalisation as a contested concept.

It is here that we can turn to Colin Hay's distinction between the notion of globalisation as *discourse* and globalisation as *process* (see Hay and Rosamond 2002). In these terms, much of what we discuss in this book refers to globalisation as discourse – i.e. how the abstract idea of general globalised change is used as justification for more specific actions. This reflects the Foucauldian notion of discourse as the historical and cultural production of systems of knowledge and beliefs which is shaped, and shapes, our behaviour (Foucault 1981). This perspective highlights the role that 'globalisation' can play as an imaginary in contemporary educational technology – i.e. as a vehicle for all sorts of ideological agendas. This raises questions over the ways in which notions of 'globalisation' and 'globalised' aspects of society such as educational technology are described, how these descriptions shape what we do and do not see in educational technologies and, then, influence how these educational technologies are ultimately used and treated in society. It is therefore important to ask what such 'stories' omit (and therefore imply as insignificant) and question the assumptions presented to us as 'fact'. Furthermore, examination of globalisation as discourse can help reveal the structures of power and real shaping concerns behind the ostensibly bland, corporate face of 'globalised' society. These are all key themes that we shall return to throughout the book.

That said, in order to understand the significance of globalisation as discourse, it perhaps makes sense to first consider the tangible forms of globalisation as *process* – i.e. in terms of apparently global products, policies and outcomes. Most definitions of the processes of globalisation centre on matters of space, place and time, as well as the movement of people, ideas and information within them. Perhaps the most-straightforward description is offered by David Held and colleagues, who describe globalisation as:

> a process (or set of processes) which embodies a transformation in the spatial organisation of social relations and transactions – assessed in terms of their extensibility, intensity, velocity and impact-generating transcontinental or interregional flows and networks of activity, interaction, and the exercise of power.
>
> *(Held* et al. *1999, p.16)*

Central to this description is the movement of 'flows' of ideas, information, practices, institutions, objects and people interacting with local populations and local contexts. Allied to this notion of global flows, then, are the various terrains, routes and conduits along which these movements take place (what Held refers to as spatial organisations). Here then, the notion of 'scapes' can also be used to refer to a wide array of means of transportation of people, objects, and information. As Held's description also implies, it is important to consider how these various 'scapes' are organised through networks – both within and across different societies (see Urry 2002).

The highly networked nature of these processes is evident in Arjun Appadurai's (1990) description of different global flows and scapes that underpin contemporary society. These include flows of people (what Appadurai refers to as 'ethnoscapes') such as global workers, business travellers, students, tourists and migrants relocating to other nations. Appadurai also points towards flows of ideas and practices regarding government and institutional activities (what he refers to as 'ideoscapes'), the global movement of trade and capital ('financescapes') and global flows of media content ('mediascapes'). A final component in Appadurai's model is the transportation technologies that facilitate these movements of people, goods, ideas and information. These 'technoscapes' range from the shipping container to the wireless internet connection. In all these ways, globalisation therefore implies a number of potential changes to social organisation and social relations. These include an internationalisation and liberalisation of practices and processes underpinning the increasingly unrestricted exchange of information, ideas, objects and people between organisations around the world. These changes also include the dissemination of objects and experiences around the world on a 'de-territorialised' basis where social space is separated from physical place or location.

While useful, these descriptions still tell us little about the nature of the products, policies and outcomes of the processes of globalisation. In this sense, Levitt's original description is useful in reflecting the fundamentally *economic* nature of the concept of globalisation. Indeed, when using the phrase 'globalisation' most people are – at least implicitly – referring to the growth of economic globalisation over the past forty years or so. As far as many commentators are concerned, the globalised nation of the economic sphere is all encompassing. Regardless of geographical location or social background, most readers of this book will be aware of recent changes in international trade, global patterns of consumption and the outsourcing of production to other regions. If nothing else, these changes are typified by the growing importance of multinational and transnational corporations in everyday life – described by Rizvi and Lingard (2010, p.28) as "the single most powerful force in creating global shifts in economic activity". Indeed, the activities of corporations such as Wal-Mart, Exxon Mobil and Citigroup could be said to be shaping the world in which we live in increasingly interconnected and interdependent ways.

It is important, therefore, to distinguish between different elements of 'global' economic reorganisation. For example, it could be argued that the past forty years have seen a growing interconnectedness of economic markets and a creeping realisation of 'global common markets'. In industrial terms, for example, the production of goods and services now take place through worldwide production markets and international forms of trade and exchange. Worldwide demands for a sufficient 'global' quantity and quality of skilled labour is also of continued importance – not least the growing demand for high-skilled intellectual workers. In financial terms, the past forty years have also seen the emergence and dominance of worldwide financial markets. As all these substantial examples illustrate, economic globalisation needs to be understood as a multifaceted issue.

That said, any consideration of the contemporary significance of globalisation and the global also needs to look well beyond the economic. As Hirst and colleagues have argued, one of the appealing but infuriating aspects of globalisation as an area of investigation and debate is its all-encompassing character: "the term 'globalisation' seems to have an almost infinite capacity to inflate – so that more and more aspects

of the modern condition are increasingly drawn under its conceptual umbrella"
(Hirst *et al.* 2009, p.4). There are a number of other 'aspects of the modern condition' that therefore must be borne in mind throughout our proceeding discussions
of globalisation. One major domain to be considered is the sphere of *political* globalisation. Increasingly, political organisations around the world have been faced by
phenomena that have not been confined to – or easily addressed – within national
boundaries. Issues such as terrorism, the environment and climate, famine and other
humanitarian disasters have all merited multinational responses. One tangible outcome
of this has been a growing global reorganisation of legal and ethical affairs through
organisations such as the international criminal courts, international police and
'peacekeeping' forces (e.g. Interpol). Similarly, political governance and leadership
in a number of areas of policymaking and political control have been ceded to
'intergovernmental' and 'supranational' organisations such as the United Nations
and the European Union, as well as traditional world 'superpowers' such as
the United States who could be seen as acting on occasion as a *de facto* world government. In all these cases, politics would certainly appear to be an increasingly
internationally determined concern.

Other obvious aspects of globalisation beyond the economic include the
increasingly global nature of *cultural* change. This is perhaps most apparent in terms
of language – not least the growth of global forms of world 'Englishes', Spanish
and Mandarin as *linguae francae*. Also of significance is the rise of global and interrelated
forms of world religious ideas and practices, alongside other non-territorially-based
'world cultures'. For some commentators, this increased cultural 'hybridisation' is a
welcome element of contemporary life – leading to seemingly creative new global
forms and trends in spheres such as music, fashion and art. Mindful of the rise of
global media organisations and cultural brands such as Disney and Nike, other
commentators point more guardedly towards the tendency for "the artefacts of a
few dominant cultures to be spread much more widely across the world" (Unwin
2009a, p.15). Yet regardless of their desirability, such shifts and changes are clear
examples of the increasing interconnectedness and interdependence of peoples and
cultures around the world.

Of course, it is important to remember that while all these economic, financial,
political and cultural changes are certainly intensified and accelerated, they are not
necessarily new. It could be argued that many of the changes and phenomena
described above were in existence long before the latter half of the twentieth century. The key point to the globalisation thesis, however, is that these recent trends
and changes are unprecedented in terms of the extent of their scope, intensity,
velocity and impact. This is of course due to a number of interconnected factors.
On one hand, the structures supporting these recent intensifications are many –
including the rise of economic and military superpowers such as the US, USSR and
latterly China, as well as international economic and political responses (such as
the so-called 'Washington Consensus' during the 1980s). Yet perhaps even more
than these significant political realignments, however, it is crucial to recognise the

profound influence of the growth of digital technologies – not least computing technologies, telecommunications networks and the internet. Indeed, all of the recent processes of globalisation just described are entwined with the parallel development of information and communication technologies. In fact it may not be too far-fetched to state that many – if not all – of the recent 'global' changes and shifts described so far in this chapter are in some way reliant on digital technology and media – from the presence of US-led international armed forces in countries such as Afghanistan to the worldwide proliferation of the Disney brand. As Chakravartty and Sarikakis (2006, p.21) assert, digital technologies are both 'the nervous system' and 'the carrier' of many of the changes and shifts associated with the globalised information society.

In seeking to make sense of any aspect of contemporary globalised life, one therefore has to give careful consideration to technology-based processes and technology-based outcomes. Much of what has been just discussed in this chapter relates to technology-based processes, such as integration of the world economy and financial markets through telecommunications networks, the internationalisation of trade, communication and interaction through the internet, and so on. Much of what was discussed in earlier sections of this chapter with regard to work and employment also relates to technology-based (or at least technology-related) processes – not least the growth of technology-dependent employment and jobs. Indeed, as far as many commentators are concerned one of the most significant aspects of digital technology is the spectre of what economists refer to as 'technological bias' – i.e. the tendency that "at the same time that new technologies eliminate some jobs through automation they create new higher skilled employment and up-skill existing jobs" (Brown *et al.* 2008, p.132). In this sense, both technology *and* education are integral aspects of the increasingly globalised nature of contemporary society. It is against these wider concerns that the specific case of educational technology now needs to be considered.

The Significance of Education and Technology in a Globalised World

As should by now be clear, a strong case can be made for the centrality of digital technologies in the on-going globalisations of contemporary education. Indeed, contemporary education is entwined with a range of globalised processes that are predicated upon the use of digital technology. Education can therefore be seen as encompassing many of the issues outlined so far throughout this chapter – not least a confluence of digital technologies, ideas, institutions, knowledge and skills. One key issue that now needs to be addressed is identifying the global educational processes that digital technologies are most associated with and, most importantly, considering how can we gain a sense of the ways in which they are 'globalised'.

Of course, there is a growing body of literature on the globalised nature of education. As far as some authors are concerned, there have been a large number of undeniably international and transnational shifts in education (see, for example,

Waters and Brooks 2011). Indeed, in many cases, education is now considered to be an *almost* wholly globalised concern. As Jenny Ozga (2011, p.219) observes, there are many commentators who continue to:

> advance analysis in terms of the 'world institutionalisation of education' and who see the national context and international organisations as having only a minor mediating effect on the onward march of a world system. Local uniqueness is recognised, but it features as a rather quaint aberration in a standardising world.

While many other commentators (this book included) take a rather more nuanced perspective, growing numbers of scholars of education policy, sociology and economics have paid considerable amounts of attention to the globalised nature of education over the last thirty years or so. Even at the level of compulsory schooling, it is being increasingly argued that "education as an institution has become a global enterprise" (Spring 2009, p.10). This shift in perception reflects a number of notable recent trends. At all levels of education, for example, one can identify an increasing movement and mobility of students and educators – traditionally from 'East to West' but now increasingly in all directions. These trends are complemented by the setting-up of international schools, international curricula and international assessment regimes, as well as an increasingly fierce global competition between educational providers for student outcomes. Education provision around the world is certainly now subject to intensified international regimes of standardisation, scrutiny and competition – not least through comparisons such as global 'indicators' of educational 'quality' and 'effectiveness' in the form of the TIMSS and PISA testing regimes. The number of areas of global change within education are therefore substantial and far-reaching.

While many of the issues just listed are concerned largely with compulsory schooling, some commentators would contend that the globalisation of education has been particularly pronounced in the international marketisation and commodification of higher education. As Melanie Wilson (2010, p.182) contends:

> There is little doubt that the impact of globalisation on higher education has reshaped and continues to reshape the landscape of academia. Universities are increasingly more connected as global research initiatives become more commonplace; global university rankings influence university mandates and focus; global trade impacts publicly funded universities; and faculty and students can teach and learn in new globally networked ways. This changing landscape has challenged universities and colleges to revisit their *raison d'être*, all while remaining viable in this new global context.

If we reflect upon the many issues implicit in this quotation, then a number of important features of contemporary globalised education come to the fore.

Mirroring many of the concepts outlined earlier on in this chapter, Wilson describes contemporary global higher education as being a fluid and continuous process which is also more competitive for institutions and individuals alike. An individual is no longer assumed to be instructed for a fixed period of time in a fixed place – instead learning is framed as an individually centred and individually driven process. Moreover, the focus of this educational provision is seen to reflect the growing significance of the intellectually based *head* work of the knowledge economy as opposed to the manual *body* work of the industrial economy (Brown *et al.* 2011). As Betty Collis (2006, p.216) concurs, "know-why and know-who matters more than know-what".

As Wilson's description also implies, many of these changes relate to the nature of how education is now expected to be delivered. Most educationalists would agree that educational provision no longer needs to be bound either to the dominant institutional forms of the university, college or school, or to the dominant life-cycle of childhood to late adolescence and early adulthood. From a practical perspective, it is now received wisdom that education is a lifelong concern that should take place throughout society – reflecting the knowledge economy-related concept of 'lifelong learning' outlined earlier. From a more philosophical perspective, much of Wilson's description also reflects the on-going 'crisis of meaning' that institutions such as the university and school are undergoing in a world where national cultures and nation state are no longer significant, given their historical role as "the primary institution of national culture in the modern nation-state" (Readings 1996, p.12).

In all these senses, recent globalisations of education can be seen to present a fundamental challenge to established notions of what education is and what education is for. More substantially, these globalised practices and processes appear to be at the heart of significant changes to the nature and form of educational provision and practices. It is here, then, that educational technology can be understood to be of particular significance – a key element of how education is being re-orientated, realigned and reconstituted. Indeed, digital technology is a central element of all the areas of change outlined above – from the measuring and testing, to the marketing, delivering and consuming of education. If we cast our minds back to the various forms of educational technology highlighted at the beginning of the chapter – for example, the 'edgeless university' and 'virtual school', 'open education' and 'globally networked learning environments' – then it is easy to see how the promise of these new technology-driven educational forms offer a ready means of addressing the widely accepted and expected educational challenges of globalised change.

Towards a Critical Understanding of Education, Technology and Globalisation

This vision of newly globalised forms of education driven by economic, cultural, social and political change and supported by digital technology offers a comfortingly straightforward portrayal of contemporary education. Yet this simplicity of explanation belies the fact that many of the concepts, explanations and analyses outlined so far in this chapter are by no means as clear-cut and certain as they are sometimes presented. This is especially the case with the notion of globalisation. Indeed, as Rizvi and Lingard (2010, p.23) remind us, 'globalisation' is a "highly contested notion". As such it is important to retain a sense of critical distance and perspective when considering the actual significance of many of the ideas and arguments presented so far in this chapter – however forcibly and assertively they may have been argued. Indeed, it can be countered, for example, that terms such as 'globalisation', 'knowledge economy', 'information society' and the like are often used within educational debate in a decidedly empty manner – i.e. as labels and signifiers to lend a sense of gravitas, significance and urgency to otherwise contestable actions. In one sense, then, many of the discussions and debates of the globalisations of contemporary education and the associated role of digital technology could be accused of being little more than what Ellen Meiksins Wood (1997) rather cuttingly describes as 'globaloney'.

Thus having acknowledged the tone of current discussion and debate, it is important that we develop our own more appropriate and more measured take on the complex nature of – and complex relationships between – globalisation, global economics, education and technology. In particular, it would seem important to resist the temptation to produce too universal an analysis. For example, it is important to not overstate the case for the emergence of a wholly global economy, a wholly global tide of educational marketisation and decentralisation, or a blanket impact of globalisation on *all* economic, social, political and cultural aspects of education and society. Correspondingly, it is important not to overstate the irrelevance of national economies and domestic strategies of national economic management. As we shall remind ourselves at regular points throughout this book, it is especially important not to overstate the case and succumb to the notion of the 'powerless state'.

If we are to develop a more considered understanding of the globalisations of education and technology then a useful framework to turn to is David Held and colleagues' differentiation of three main approaches towards globalisation that have emerged within the social sciences since the 1980s. First is what Held identifies as the dominant view of globalisation within much of the social science literature as well as in popular, political and commercial accounts – i.e. the 'globalist' (often referred to as the 'hyper-globalist') perspective. Indeed, a globalist sense certainly pervades many of the arguments already considered in this chapter about education, technology and society. In more detail, a globalist stance sees most aspects of society as influenced by the rise of the global economy, the emergence of institutions of global governance and the development of global culture and civil society. In this sense, globalist accounts perceive the world as having entered a 'global age' defined by flows and scapes of capital, goods, services, people, technologies, information and ideas. Globalists point to the demise of the nation state as a dominant form of leadership and governance. Instead, the nation state is seen as having been super-seded by the rise of global markets and forms of international cooperation and interaction. These accounts are often unashamedly celebratory and optimistic – focusing on the benefits associated with global economic liberalisation, not least the growth of 'borderless' forms of 'denationalised' economic exchange.

There are, of course, many counter-arguments that can be levelled against the globalist position – not least that it tends to result in over-generalised and over-stated analyses. In particular, globalist accounts could be said to transfer unrealistic assumptions from the rich North onto other countries and contexts that are often different in terms of their economic, social or political circumstances. This is particularly the case with the globalist tendency to perceive the displacement of the nation state as a significant form of governance. Counter to this assumption, therefore, is the opposing perspective that the nation state is in fact *more* significant than ever in these contemporary globalised times. The 'sceptical' (or 'traditionalist') position to globalisation therefore contends that while the capacities of the nation state may have altered, they have certainly not disappeared. Sceptic commentators argue that what are celebrated as new forms of globalisation are in fact continuations of long-established patterns of internationalisation. While there may well be intensified relations between states and international institutions, it can be argued that nation-states and national governments remain the primary architects of their determination. Sceptic commentators point, for example, to a greater polarisation between sets of wealthy 'developed' and less-wealthy 'developing' countries, arguing that global shifts of power to less wealthy nations are exaggerated. Instead, all of the major changes over the last three decades or so can be said to have led primarily to the entrenchment of power within "the already advanced countries" (Hirst *et al.* 2009, p.3).

One of the key themes within the sceptical position on globalisation is the continued significance of the nation state in managing the deepening 'crisis' tendencies of capitalism. This trend was certainly evident in the response of different nation states to the post-9/11 'war on terror' and subsequent heightened political significance of countries such as Pakistan and Afghanistan. Similar arguments for the continued significance of the nation state are also evident in the responses of different nations to the global financial crises since the late 2000s and 2010s. As the 2010s progressed, so too did a number of other examples of national difference – not least the growth of populist left-wing national governments in Latin America, the resurgence of Russian independence from global forces and markets (most visibly in terms of its control of energy supplies), and the growth in Chinese and Indian reformations of the market economic model. All these examples point towards nationally framed and nationally fractious political situations in contrast to the globalist portrayal of a post-national world arena. Thus as Hirst *et al.* (2009, p.15) contend, "the burden of evidence still remains in favour of an inter-national economy (albeit now heavily overlaid by supranational regionalisation)" with national-level policies and national-level actors remaining sovereign. At best, then, any sense of 'global' transformation could be said to describe more accurately the converging nature of European, East Asian and North American interests, as opposed to the interests of all nations. In this sense, much of what is referred to as taking place on a 'global' level refers more accurately to the continuation of a structured 'centre-periphery' set of relations between a powerful 'core zone' of a wealthy minority of countries, and a rather less powerful and less wealthy majority.

The simplicity of these sceptical accounts is certainly attractive – especially to the more politically minded and pessimistically inclined social scientist. Yet the sceptical perspective can be criticised for presenting an overly dismissive account of some of the undeniably important processes and outcomes of globalisation highlighted throughout this chapter. At this point it is important to recognise that this distinction between globalism and scepticism is not intended to be a 'crude dualism' (Held and McGrew 2000). Instead, it should be seen as a spectrum within which most views of globalisation can be located. As such, a conciliatory position as described (and indeed as favoured) by Held and colleagues is that of the 'transformationalist' perspective. Here it is acknowledged that some forms of globalisation – both as processes and outcomes – are undeniably taking place, and are associated with some significant political, economic and social changes across some societies and regions. However, it is also acknowledged that these changes and patterns are *not* experienced across the world in a homogeneous form as a single 'condition'. Instead, the processes and outcomes of globalisation must be seen as uneven, disjointed and contradictory, and subject to various differences and imbalances in power between states, societies and communities. In providing an extreme example of this, Held points to the obvious fact that "political and economic elites in the world's major metropolitan areas are much more tightly integrated into, and have much greater control over, global networks than do the subsistence farmers of Burundi" (Held *et al.* 1999, p.28).

From the transformationalist perspective, then, globalisation is manifest as a form of 'global-stratification' rather than global-unification. Any global processes therefore need to be seen in terms of unequal and fragmented relationships where some states, societies and communities are enmeshed in the global order at the expense of other more marginalised actors. Thus, as Rizvi and Lingard (2010, p.24) reason:

> globalisation is an outcome of various structural processes that manifest in different ways in the economy, politics and culture. The globalised world is fundamentally heterogeneous, unequal and conflictive, rather than integrated and seamless. It is experienced differently by different communities, and even individuals, and is sustained and created by people and institutions with widely different histories and political interests.

This view of globalisation still recognises entities such as the nation state as key sites of determination. As Mok and Lee (2003, p.18) describe, "seen in this light, national governments are far from diminished but are reconstituted and restructured in the growing complexity of processes of governance in the context of globalization". This is particularly the case with public sector domains of society such as education. Indeed, from an educational perspective, the transformationalist approach has been pursued to good effect by commentators such as Phil Brown, Hugh Lauder, Roger Dale, Simon Marginson and others. As Marginson (1999, p.19) summarises, this approach sees globalisation as:

> irreversibly changing the politics of the nation-state and its regional sectors, domestic classes and nationally-defined interest groups. It is creating new potentials and limits in the politics of education. Its effects on the politics of education are complex … Increasingly shaped as it is by globalization – both directly and via the effects of globalization in national government – education at the same time has become a primary medium of globalization, and an incubator of its agents. As well as inhibiting or transforming older kinds of education, globalization creates new kinds.

Problematising Education, Technology and Globalisation

These latter debates and definitions therefore offer a solid and sensible basis for the remainder of the book. On one hand it seems clear that the perception of digital technology leading to a global transformation of education around the world is a deliberate over-simplification of what is a very complex set of arrangements. Despite the forcefulness of some of the descriptions and predictions presented at the beginning of this chapter, it makes no sense to follow a globalist agenda and attempt to produce a technology-focused account of a new unified 'global age' of digital education. It could, however, be argued that there is more sense in following a sceptical approach towards education and technology. Indeed, the likes of Andy Green have argued quite successfully that there has been little meaningful globalisation of education. As Green (1997, p.171) contends, although national education systems may have become more 'porous' and "become more like each other in certain important ways", there is "little evidence that national education systems are disappearing or that national states have ceased to control them". At best it could be reasoned that a more modest process of 'partial internationalisation' of education has occurred, involving increased student and teacher mobility, widespread policy borrowing and "attempts to enhance the international dimension of curricula at secondary and higher levels" (Green 1997, p.171). Otherwise, it could be said that a pronounced heterogenisation remains in terms of national – and indeed local – responses to global educational processes and imperatives.

While these rejections are certainly more persuasive than the globalist position, they are a dangerously dismissive position from which to commence our own analysis – especially as nearly twenty years of considerable social and technological change have passed since they were made. Thus while we would do well to avoid what Yeates (2001) terms a 'strong' version of the globalist thesis, it would be foolhardy to discount the possibility of there being *some* international change and possible convergence when it comes to education and technology. In this sense, there is certainly merit for the time being in continuing to take the issues raised by the globalisation thesis seriously. As even some generally sceptical commentators acknowledge, "while localities and national systems inflect the processes of globalisation differently and struggles are generated, convergences and homogenisation of educational forms and modalities, driven by monocultural logics are very clearly evident within and between settings" (Apple 2010, p.1).

Of course it is important to recognise at this early stage of our analysis that any changes that can be identified will be iterative and cumulative in nature. In rejecting the sceptical position we are not proposing instead that there is any identifiable global force for change when it comes to education and technology. Instead, we should simply acknowledge that there are a large number of changes in education (both minor and major) that could be said to be associated to some degree with the activities of a range of subjects of globalisation. Crucially, we need to acknowledge that these changes are not reducible to any one dominant 'effect'. Moreover, these changes should not be seen to be reducible to the interests of any one particular dominant organisation or subject. Yet on the other hand, many of these changes clearly do relate to the issues associated with globalisation discussed throughout this chapter. Certainly, then, one should not attempt to understand contemporary education without considering the issues associated with the processes and discourses of globalisation. Central to the concerns of this book, of course, is how digital technologies play a key role in all of these areas of global educational change. Yet we would be mistaken to think that all of these changes are driven by technology alone. At best, globalisation must be understood as a combination of "power relations, practices *and* technology" (Schirato and Webb 2003, p.1).

The aim of the remainder of this book is therefore simple – to bring all these concerns together, and to develop a detailed and critical understanding of digital technology in light of the wider global transformations of education. In order to achieve this, we therefore need to problematise many of the 'big' ideas and assumptions that we have been presented with in this opening chapter. This brings us back to Colin Hay's earlier distinction between viewing globalisation as *process* and as *discourse* – reminding us that very little of what is presented under the label of 'globalisation' is a matter of fact. Above all, then, it is important to acknowledge that notions such as 'globalisation', the 'knowledge economy' and 'information society' are simply "sets of value preferences" (Rizvi and Lingard 2010, p.32) – i.e. social imaginaries and ideological formations that present common (and often persuasive) understandings of how things 'should be' and 'will be'. Thus, as this book progresses, we would do well to resist the temptation to take every concept and every explanation that has been outlined in this opening chapter at face value. As Nicholas Garnham (2002) concludes, accepting unquestioningly the notion of something like the 'information society' does not "serve as a useful starting point" for any thorough social science analysis. Rather, the uncritical use of concepts such as these "merely and dangerously distracts – as is often intended – from the real issues" (Garnham 2002, p.267).

It therefore makes good sense at this stage of our analysis to treat the notions of the 'information age', 'knowledge economy' and 'globalisation' as 'problematic' – i.e. as useful means of highlighting clusters of issues for investigation and consideration rather than fool-proof blueprints for the future of the world (Lyon 1988). In this spirit, all of the ideas outlined in this chapter have proved useful in pointing us towards salient areas of questioning for the remainder of the book. In particular, four broad strands of the globalisation, knowledge economy and information age debates appear to be of overriding interest and importance – i.e. the *economic, political, social* and *cultural* aspects of educational technology around the world. In brief, then, our concerns as grouped under these terms are as follows:

- Economic: How exactly are educational technologies linked to issues of global economics and the fortunes of global economies? How is the human capital imperative for highly skilled workforces shaping the nature and form of educational technology around the world? To what extent is educational technology part of "an effort to impose particular economic and political agendas that benefit wealthy and rich nations at the expense of the world's poor" (Spring 2009, p.13)?
- Political: How are 'international' shifts in educational technology refracted through national policies and processes? How exactly are global issues received and acted upon at national and subnational levels? How are new (transnational) ideas and initiatives relating to educational technology layered over already existing strata of (national and local) educational discourses, practices and institutions? What are the different dynamics of interaction between the global, national and local levels? What evidence is there for a 'vernacular globalisation' of educational technology – i.e. the ways in which local sites and their histories, cultures, politics and pedagogies mediate (to a greater or lesser extent) the effects of top-down globalisation (Ngo *et al.* 2006)?
- Social: Where can educational technology be said to be socially or spatially uneven? Which countries, communities and contexts stand to gain most from educational technologies? How are educational technologies used in the poorest and least economically developed parts of the world? What is the role of individual learners and educators – i.e. are they simply passive participants or subjects of globalised forms of educational technology? What agency do individuals have and enact in their engagement with educational technology? What ideological agendas and values are attached to educational technology – i.e. to what extent does digital technology broaden, deepen and accelerate the commercialisation, marketisation and commodification of education?
- Cultural: To what extent does educational technology reinforce or challenge dominant global and local beliefs about teaching and learning? How are educational technologies shaped by global and local understandings of language or religion? To what extent is educational technology implemented in a culturally sensitive manner? To what extent does educational technology represent the imposition of a dominant culture – be it a homogeneous 'global culture', commercial culture or 'Americanised' culture?

Conclusions

All of the above questions are associated with questions of power – i.e. matters of who stands to gain most from educational technologies and in whose interests they serve. These then are the questions and the issues that shall form the focus for the remainder of this book. In pursuing these issues, we need to take a balanced and realistic view of the promises and the practicalities of educational technology. In other words, we must be mindful to develop an analysis that is neither overly celebratory nor overly cynical. At best, it is likely that the 'global story' of educational technology will be one of uneven implementation and unintended consequences. While associated undoubtedly with some substantial changes and shifts in educational provision and practice around the world, digital technology is also likely to reproduce, perpetuate, strengthen and deepen existing patterns of social relations and structures – albeit in different forms and guises. In this respect, then, it is perhaps best to approach educational technology as a 'problem changer' rather than a 'problem solver'. At best we should therefore approach globalisation in a transformationalist-inspired '*moderately* optimistic' approach (Busch 2000).

We now need to take our moderately optimistic intentions forward into the remainder of this book. This first chapter has established that educational technology is a key element in broader political, economic, social, cultural and historical contexts. It has also established that there are a wide range of actors in the shaping and implementation of educational technology around the world. These range from individual learners and educators, through to national governments, multinational corporations, supranational and intergovernmental organisations and all of the other infrastructural elements of the worldwide political order. All of these issues point to the complexity of the topic and task at hand. We should now therefore spend a little more time developing a useful, usable and (above all) understandable working framework for the remainder of this book. So how are we best advised to go about asking the questions and exploring the issues raised so far? The next chapter will now go on to develop the theoretical underpinnings of the book – both in terms of theorising education *and* in terms of theorising technology.

2

MAKING SENSE OF EDUCATION AND TECHNOLOGY

Theoretical Approaches

Introduction

The uneven growth of educational technology over the past thirty years is part of what Held and McGrew term the underlying 'puzzle' of globalisation – i.e. the "disjuncture between the widespread discourse of globalisation and the realities of a world in which, for the most part, the routines of everyday life are dominated by national and local circumstances" (Held and McGrew 2000, p.5). As was suggested in Chapter 1, while some aspects of education provision around the world may now appear to be more homogenised than before, the extent to which digital technologies have actually led to uniform fundamental changes in education is much less clear. In fact, nearly forty years on from the 'computer revolution' and nearly twenty years on from the subsequent 'internet revolution', it could be argued that education in most – if not all – societies remains as divided, unjust, unfair and unequal as ever. Even where educational changes have taken place, it is difficult to gauge any association with digital technology *per se*. Thus despite the globalist explanations that prevail, it would be fair to conclude that educational technology is certainly not a straightforward force for equal change around the world. Against this background, there is a need for a book such as this to move quickly away from overly general presumed 'effects' of globalisation, education and technology, and instead turn its attention towards the nuances and differences that characterise the actual (as opposed to the imagined) state of educational technology in our supposedly digital world.

One of the first steps in developing this more realistic account is to recognise the full range of involved interests in educational technology. As Chapter 1 has already suggested, there is a large number of different 'stakeholders' and interests at play here. These, of course, include all the familiar components of the 'education community' – schools, universities, teachers, students, academic researchers and so on.

Similarly, national governments, state organisations and other aspects of the 'policy community' also play important roles. Perhaps less obviously, educational technology is an arena where the actions of these local and national interests are entwined with the interests of 'supranational' and 'intergovernmental' organisations such as the World Bank, the International Monetary Fund, the United Nations and so on. Aside from these august institutions, education technology is also obviously dependent upon the actions of industry and commerce – not least the large number of multinational corporations and local companies involved in the development, manufacturing and marketing of IT products and services. These industrial and commercial actors are complemented by other private sector interests such as banks and financers, employers, philanthropic foundations and other commercial interests seeking to influence education for a variety of purposes. In terms of educational technology use in poorer nations and regions, it is also necessary to consider the interests of various non-governmental organisations, charities, donor agencies and other non-profit organisations. Clearly, then, any 'global' analysis of educational technology will encompass a large number of involved parties.

In order to construct a detailed account of educational technology along these expanded lines, we need to move beyond the established concerns and preoccupations of most other writers and researchers working in this field. This means doing more than simply asking abstract questions of how digital technologies *could* or *should* be used in educational settings, or speculating on the *potential* of technology to change learning. Instead, this means taking a deliberately critical approach that approaches the topic of education and technology in relational terms. As Michael Apple (2010) reminds us, the relational approach involves producing accounts that situate educational technology within the unequal relations of power elsewhere in society, within the realities of dominance and subordination, and within the conflicts that are generated by these relations. This is clearly a difficult step for many technology commentators to take. Yet instead of being distracted by our own (often privileged) personal experiences of digital technology we need to work instead towards understanding and acting on educational technology in terms of its complicated and often unjust connections to the larger society. In short, as Robins and Webster (2002, p.6) argue, we need to develop "a more sociologically grounded narrative of change". This, then, will be the approach that shall be pursued throughout the remainder of this book.

Education and Technology: The Need for Theoretically Informed Approaches

Given these intentions, we now need to develop a set of theoretical and methodological approaches suitable for the critical analysis of education, technology and globalisation. Of course, educational technology is not a field of academic study renowned for its theoretical ambition or rigour. At best, educational technology has developed into a field of study dominated by social psychological perspectives on learning and teaching, and thereby often overly concerned with matters relating to individual behaviours and individual development. The predominance of these concerns has led to a rather restricted view of technology use led by a common enthusiasm for social-constructivist and sociocultural theories of learning which, at best, offer a very localised understanding of the 'social' contexts in which technology use takes place. Despite regular calls for theoretical expansion and sophistication (e.g. Hlynka and Belland 1991, Livingstone 2012), educational technology remains a field that ventures rarely from these concerns. Indeed, it could be argued that even as it approaches a stage of 'middle-age' respectability, educational technology is an area of academic study that is stuck stubbornly in its ways – remaining in thrall to technicist notions of 'best practice', 'effectiveness' and proving 'what works'. In this sense educational technology remains a field of academic endeavour that is largely instrumentalist in its approach, with many writers and researchers concerned with the production of 'useful' but 'simple' accounts that make claims for digital technology and education regardless of social context. While this lack of theoretical grounding may be of little concern to the many educational technology practitioners 'on the ground' who continue to work successfully and profitably in the area, it presents a problem for addressing the social concerns of this particular book. Given the scope of the issues raised so far, there is a need for our proceeding analyses of education and digital technology around the world to take as considered and theoretically sophisticated an approach as possible.

With these thoughts in mind, this chapter will now go on to examine how the careful use of social theory can help develop richer understandings of the structures, actions, processes and relations that lie behind the 'global' implementation and use of digital technology in education. Of course, choosing a theoretical perspective or stance is largely a matter of personal conviction and belief. This chapter therefore makes no claim to there being one 'correct' reading of the issues surrounding technology and education (let alone technology, education and globalisation). Yet, it seems reasonable to assume that any attempt to make sense of the many forms of education and digital technologies to be found around the world will benefit from taking a broad approach to social theory. As such, there are a number of different theoretical approaches within the social sciences that may be of use – focusing variously on the contextualised and politically shaped nature of education and globalisation, as well as the socially constructed nature of digital technologies and education. In this spirit, we can first consider three potentially useful theoretical approaches to understanding the nature of education in the contemporary globalised world.

Thinking about Education and Technology

The Benefits of the Comparative Education Approach

There has been a long history of comparative analysis in the social sciences, stemming back to Durkheim's development of comparative sociology during the last years of the nineteenth century. As Novoa and Yariv-Mashal (2003) point out, the allure of the 'other' has been a longstanding interest of educational scholars – progressing from early twentieth-century interests in 'knowing the other' and 'understanding the other' through to later post-war concerns with 'constructing the other' and then most recently in 'measuring the other' (Halls 1990). Given this heritage, it is now recognised widely within the academic study of education (if not so regularly acted upon) that comparing different cases with each other can be of distinct advantage. This has prompted a continuing interest within contemporary educational scholarship in moving beyond examining two different cases and striving instead to undertake work that is 'implicitly comparative' (Phillips and Schweisfurth 2008).

Perhaps the main benefit that 'implicitly comparative' approaches bring to the study of education is to shift attention away from the Euro-American descriptions and analyses of education. This is especially the case with educationalists working from an Anglo-Saxon perspective. Here, the comparative education approach can encourage educationalists to engage with otherwise marginalised, non-English speaking traditions of teaching and learning, knowing and doing. As Phillips and Schweisfurth (2008) describe, comparative studies of education therefore allow English-speaking writers and researchers to:

- show what is possible by examining alternatives to provision 'at home';
- offer comparisons by which to judge the performance of education systems;
- describe what consequences may arise from certain courses of action by looking at experience in various countries;
- provide examples that allow them to see various practices and procedures in a wider context – throwing new light on what they know.

As this list suggests, one of the general advantages of the comparative education approach is allowing individual educational systems to learn from the experience of others and to understand better the nature of the problems that confront them – what can be seen as 'learning from comparing' (Dale 2005). Yet more useful still for the purposes of our own analysis is what Roger Dale terms 'explaining through comparing'. Here, the experiences of other systems are analysed not simply in an attempt to help improve education provision 'at home' or in a normative attempt to "prescribe rules for the good conduct" (Lauwerys and Taylor 1973, p.xii). Instead, comparative analyses are pursued with the aim of developing fuller understandings and explanations of the various re-articulations and re-scalings of education that result from wider political, economic, social and cultural shifts.

In this spirit of 'explaining through comparing' there are many issues that can inform our proceeding analyses of education and technology around the world. In particular, a growing theme within the comparative education literature has been that of exploring the significance of *context* at all levels and in many forms. The most successful recent comparative approaches have been those seeking to take account of "the historical, cultural, social [and] economic contexts in which educational phenomena are observed" (Phillips and Schweisfurth 2008, p.12). Moreover, as Bob Cowen (2006) reasons, as well as being concerned with the social embeddedness of educational phenomena within particular local contexts, the most successful comparative accounts are those that are interested in the concept of *transfer* between contexts – i.e. the movement of educational ideas, policies and practices from one place to another.

While not new, the emphasis now placed on context and transfer within the comparative study of education has certainly intensified in light of the globalised turn over the past thirty years. As Michael Apple (2010) reasons, any investigation of the apparent globalisations of contemporary education is now expected to pay particular attention to the bridges that exist between global and local contexts – thereby exploring exactly how 'meta-theoretical' considerations of globalisation are linked (or not) in practice to the rather less grandiose 'lived realities' of individuals, local institutions and local communities. In this respect, some of the most powerful recent comparative education analyses have been those seeking to move beyond disingenuous accounts of the seamless 'international transfer' of policies and practices and, instead, unpack the significance and dynamics of social, cultural and contextual differences as technologies are implemented in various settings and contexts. As Andrew Brown (2009, p.1144) concludes, the comparative approach therefore offers educational scholars:

> rich opportunities for the exploration of the effects of re-contextualisation, both as these technologies and associated practices move from one context to another and as the technologies themselves act as a conduit for the transfer of knowledge and the bringing together of individuals and groups, and their pedagogic, cultural and social practices. In the light of this, rather than address the local and global impact of digital technology [we need to] address a number of dimensions, and specific instances, of the educational use of digital technologies in a range of contexts.

In this sense, comparative education offers a useful opening framework for this book's specific enquiries – in particular outlining different areas of education worthy of consideration, and highlighting the forms and levels at which they are comparable. First, then, in terms of the objects of comparison, there are at least four main areas of 'education' that are of potential interest. As Dale (2005, p.142) describes:

- Educational practice: i.e. issues of who is taught (or more specifically, who learns through processes explicitly designed to foster learning). This includes questions of what is learnt, how and why, when, where, by/from whom, under what immediate circumstances and broader conditions, and with what results.

- Education politics: i.e. questions of how these things are problematised, decided, administered and managed. This includes questions of the patterns of coordination and governance that educational technology is subject to (e.g. funding, provision, ownership, regulation), and by whom, and following what (sectoral and cultural) path dependencies.
- Politics of education: i.e. questions of what functional, scalar and sectoral divisions of labour of educational governance are in place. For example, in what ways are the core problems of capitalism reflected in the mandate, capacity and governance of national education arrangements? How are the boundaries of the education sector defined and how do they overlap with and relate to other sectors? What 'educational' activities are undertaken within other sectors?
- Outcomes: i.e. questions of what the individual, private, public, collective and community outcomes of 'education' are apparent at each level of analysis.

These levels of questioning certainly appear to offer a considered and comprehensive 'way in' to addressing the use of digital technology in education around the world, distinguishing a range of issues that are central to the specific interests of this book. These include core questions of what educational technologies are being used, for what purposes and to whose benefit. Dale's list also raises key questions of the governance of educational technology, and the struggles and conflicts that surround it, as well as the linkages between educational technology and other areas of society such as economics and politics. Even Dale's disarmingly brief final suggestions for the analysis of 'outcomes' belies a complex of supplementary questions. For example, just what are the individual and collective, private and public outcomes of 'educational technology'?

Having identified these questions, we also need to be specific about the levels at which they are to be asked. This is an important, if contested, aspect of the comparativist approach. From the nineteenth century onwards, most comparative accounts were centred on the presumed importance of nation states and the study of national education systems. However, of late, there has been an increasing reluctance amongst comparative analysts to focus on the national level of description for fear of what Nancy Fraser terms 'misframing' what are now perceived to be increasingly 'post-national' problems (see Fraser and Honneth 2003). Prompted by descriptions of the declining significance – if not 'death' – of the nation state, some commentators contend that it now makes no sense to necessarily privilege national levels of analysis. Arguments of this sort have increased in light of the apparently internationalised context of globalisation, and assumed "growing commonalities across national contexts" (Phillips and Schweisfurth 2008, p.42).

Of course, these concerns are not specific to the field of comparative *educational* analysis. Indeed, a number of social science commentators have argued quite persuasively for the redundancy of cross-national and cross-cultural comparisons in the face of globalisation and its associated changes. As Peter Jarvis (2000, p.353) questioned in blunt terms, "why should we undertake comparative analysis at all in this global village?" In many areas of the social sciences, therefore, the 'methodological nationalism' that dominated fields such as sociology, policy studies and education during the latter half of the twentieth century is now considered to be of diminished value. Yet while there is clearly a need to be mindful of the changing role and capabilities of the nation state, it would be unwise to discount altogether the significance of the national context as a meaningful and important level of analysis. This is particularly the case in light of the sceptical and transformationalist accounts of 'globalisation' reviewed in Chapter 1.

As such, it could be argued that these latter concerns from the likes of Jarvis, Fraser *et al*. should be taken to warn against an *exclusively* national dimension to comparative research. As such there is still a place for comparison between nation states and countries while being aware of the need to also explore the 'dialectic of the global' (Arnove 2007). Indeed, while there are certainly many areas of society where the nation state may have less autonomy and power than it might have previously done (such as warfare, modern communications or the maintenance of national identity), nation states can be seen to retain a central defining role in terms of the domestic affairs of 'civil society'. Not least because of their relationship to territory and population, nation states and national governments therefore retain a powerful role in controlling and directing domestic social processes such as education – albeit in a manner that is mediated by other interests and agendas. Thus as Roger Dale (2005, p.123) reasons, "despite all the globalisation talk, by far the majority of education policy decisions are taken at national level".

There is, then, certainly still a place for 'methodological nationalism' in any account of education and technology – although we should be careful not to be exclusively national in our focus. We, therefore, need to return to the concerns outlined at the beginning of this chapter and pay due attention to the range of 'supranational' and 'subnational' influences and processes that are located beyond the national level. These too can be seen to set the agendas, shape the preferences, and set the rules that structure and bind the autonomy of individual nations. Some of these influences include transnational corporations, global capital, foreign exchange markets and intergovernmental organisations such as the European Union and the United Nations. Alternatively, other influences operate along societal rather than overtly economic lines. These societal frameworks are not centred on national boundaries *per se*, but instead are defined in terms of different political couplings (e.g. democratic or totalitarian), religious affiliations (e.g. Muslim or Christian) or even diasporic language groups (see Spring 2009).

While the power and influence of these supranational interests is of clear significance, we should also not overlook the importance of 'subnational', local issues. The scope of 'local' influences on what takes place in national contexts is also considerable – from the influence of local cultures, understandings and dialects, through to the material and physical characteristics of local settings, alongside the influence of local institutions and individuals. All these aspects of education and technology also require careful consideration throughout the remainder of this book. Any analysis of education and technology must also pay attention to the importance of individual perceptions and 'lived experiences' of education and technology. The ways in which digital technologies are likely to be understood and reacted to may also be influenced by previous educational arrangements and previous histories of technology use. Similarly, a number of non-human local issues are also of significance, such as local differences in space, topography and quality of physical infrastructure. In all these respects, educational technology must be understood as party to influence and interpretation by a complex of local, national *and* international interests.

The Benefits of the Political Economy Approach

While the comparative approach provides us with a rich framework for analysing education, technology and globalisation, other theoretical traditions are also worthy of consideration. In particular it is important that any analysis of educational technology does not become overly focused on *educational* processes and practices at the expense of considering wider economic and political influences. If we are to understand fully the dynamics of how globalisation influences an area of educational policy and practice such as educational technology, then we need to look beyond the traditional 'educational' concerns of curriculum and pedagogy, teaching and learning. In addressing the topic, our interest in 'education' is obviously broader than simply what goes on inside the four walls of the school, college or university.

Here, then, the political economy approach can be of considerable use in explaining the changing nature and form of education and technology in recent times. As its title suggests, the political economy tradition directs attention towards the mutual influence of political and economic interests and issues on society. As Vincent Mosco (2009, p.4) puts it, "the political economist asks: how are power and wealth related and how are these in turn connected to cultural and social life?" Political economy, therefore, highlights questions of production and consumption, the function of marketplaces and the role of commerce and commercial actors. Most importantly, it seeks to establish the links between these issues and the interests of national and global economic organisations. Political economy analyses can therefore offer an important reminder of the power relations between educational technology and economics. Of course, it is important not to be seduced into a total state of 'economism' where issues of economics and economy are allowed to overshadow all other issues. As Bernard Stiegler (2010, p.7) reminds us, for the political economist "the question is as political as it is economic". Therefore, the best political economy accounts aim to unpack what Stiegler terms 'the totality of social relations' between economic, political, social and cultural areas of life.

As implied above, the political economist tends to understand these social relations as being organised primarily around the operation of power. One of the key aims of the political economy approach, therefore, is to make explicit issues of power within society. Political economy analysts will often concern themselves with developing accounts of emerging and established hierarchies of power and providing explanations for their legitimation. As Robin Mansell (2004, p.98) reasons, "if resources are scarce, and if power is unequally distributed in society, then the key issue is how these scarce resources are allocated and controlled, and with what consequences for human action". In terms of education and technology, then, the political economy approach encourages an interest in the ways in which structures and processes of power are embedded within digital technology products and practices, as well as how the lives of individuals are then mediated by educational technologies. Key here are questions of domination, subordination and how the use of digital technologies in education contribute to the perpetuation of pre-existing – and often deeply rooted – inequalities. This suggests a strong focus on "the integration of corporations, states and classes around national, regional and even developmental divides" (Mosco 2009, p.107).

Some of the key insights to be gained from the political economy approach are the linkages between educational technology and the interests of capital and capitalism. Indeed, political economy commentators are traditionally interested in questions of production, consumption, work, labour, industry, marketing and commerce (Stiegler 2010). At one level, then, the political economy approach directs attention towards the machinations of the 'education industry' – raising questions of how the 'business' of education operates and the ways that particular forms of innovation (such as digital technology) are "recruited, put to work and traded upon" (Apple 2010, p.30). A political economy approach raises concerns over the commercialisation of technology-based education across borders and the state-approved (and even state-sponsored) liberalisation of educational technology markets to widespread global competition. It also raises questions over the associated internationalisation of authority as national educational authorities cede control and power over educational technology arrangements to regional alliances and authorities. The political economy approach therefore raises questions of how digital technology is implicated in educational circuits of production, distribution and consumption. For instance, what is technology's role in the privatisation of once 'public' institutions and practices, and the liberalisation of education markets? How is technology associated with the institutional extension of corporate power in the education industry? An underlying theme to all these issues is commodification – be it the commodification of educational content and consumption, or even the commodification of educational labour.

As all these issues imply, one of the key strengths of the political economy approach is its recognition of the breadth of actors and interests involved in an area such as educational technology – many of whom assume significant but often obscured roles in the global governance of education. The political economy approach therefore highlights the growing importance of transnational corporations and other private interests in the production, distribution and exchange of educational 'commodities' and goods. In this sense, attention needs to be paid to the recent vast expansion of the 'educational technology industry' with clear links to the integration of educational processes in the wider system of capitalism. Political economy therefore raises questions of the activities and agendas of classes not obviously involved in educational technology, such as "financiers, industrialists, technocrats and politicians" (Stiegler 2010, p.18). In the case of educational technology, the range and nature of these latter interests are certainly varied – from IT-related multinational corporations such as Microsoft and Cisco, through to large-scale general conglomerates such as Tata and ICICI with multiple economic interests throughout the production and service sectors. Echoing a theme that is implicit within the comparative education approach, political economy also highlights the ever-increasing role of intergovernmental organisations and supranational organisations such as the World Bank, the OECD and the United Nations. Underpinning such analyses are the linkages and power relations between all of these interests – not least the restructuring and reconfiguration of these private interests and public authorities into 'new institutions' such as global networks of government officials, private codes of conduct for corporations and action-orientated partnerships of NGOs, governments, corporations and other actors (Hale and Held 2011). As we shall see in subsequent chapters of this book, digital technology is now a key site of contemporary educational provision and practice where all these developments take place.

Aside from highlighting the complex of interests at play, a key strength of the political economy approach is its emphasis on history. Unlike many other forms of educational technology scholarship, the political economy approach certainly does not encourage a 'snap-shot' account of societal phenomena. Instead, as Robin Mansell (2004, p.98) describes, political economy engenders "an interest in the analysis of the specific historical circumstances under which new media and communications products and services are produced under capitalism, and with the influence of these circumstances over their consumption". With regards to educational technology, then, the political economy approach reminds us of the value of a concern for history in the face of apparently rapid technological development. Indeed, political economy encourages analysts to take a 'long view' of societal change – paying close attention to the relationship between history and current forms of social structure and reproduction. A key concern of contemporary political economy is the ability to gauge the extent to which we are in midst of distinct societal transformations and rearrangements of social structures and processes. Of course, in many instances, what appears to be profound societal change is often a subtle "deepening and extension of fundamental tendencies at work since the earliest days of capitalism" (Mosco 2009, p.27). In this sense, the political economy approach encourages examination of the continuities *and* the discontinuities between old and new forms of technology use in education. All these issues will be of key interest throughout the remainder of this book.

The Benefits of the Post-colonialist Approach

A third theoretical tradition that can add to our understanding of the complex issues that surround education, technology and globalisation is that of post-colonialism.

In many ways, the post-colonial perspective reinforces the critical and historical emphases of the political economy approach – making explicit the links between economic and political history, and patterns of unequal social relations and asymmetries of power that persist between nations and regions. This is achieved through an explicit focus on the historical relations that have shaped (and are shaping) the modern world. These include the European colonialisation of other countries since the sixteenth century, alongside more recent economic and cultural colonialisations of countries by so-called 'superpower' states such as the US, USSR and more latterly China. This sense of history can then be extended into examining the political aspirations of these 'subordinate' countries, and mapping their on-going shifts into post-colonial governance. The post-colonial approach therefore assumes an ever-changing world order – as evident in the increasing importance of distinct 'post-colonial formations' such as sub-Saharan Africa, militant Islam, East Asia and Latin America (Hoogvelt 1997). As such, the post-colonial perspective is often used within the social sciences as a means of looking beyond the inequalities of the present and past, and towards ways of addressing these inequalities in the (near) future.

While usually overlooked within discussions of educational technology, these issues are of obvious relevance to the varied implementation of digital technology in different educational settings around the world. For example, the post-colonialist approach makes explicit the linkages between capitalist economic interests and the fortunes of individual nation states and countries – issues which have a clear bearing on the deployment of digital technologies in educational systems around the world. In particular, the post-colonialist approach raises the issue of the possible continuation of the long history of 'traditional' colonialism through the dominant role of neo-liberal market interests within educational technology formations. As Held and McGrew (2000, p.5) describe:

> The history of the modern world order is the history of Western capitalist powers dividing and re-dividing the world up into exclusive economic zones. Today, it is argued, imperialism has acquired a new form as formal empires have been replaced by new mechanisms of multilateral control and surveil-lance, such as the G7 and World Bank. As such, the present epoch [marks] a new mode of Western imperialism dominated by the needs and requirements of finance capital within the world's major capitalist states.

As with the political economy approach, post-colonialism can help identify and expose the power relations that underpin the national and international imple-mentation of educational technology. These are, of course, complex issues. For example, although sometimes perceived in straightforward terms of "the emergence of a new empire based upon the hegemony of the USA" (Hirst et al. 2009, p.6), these new forms of neo-imperialism are increasingly evident in terms of the domination and subordination of the 'poor South' (i.e. 'Third world' states in Asia, Africa and

Latin America) by various configurations of the 'rich North' (Shafiul Alam Bhuiyan 2008). What exactly, then, are the connections between educational technology and the interests of North America, Western Europe, Japan and their constituent organisations such as the G-20 group of major economies, the International Monetary Fund and the World Bank?

We will return to these issues throughout our later discussions, alongside wider questions of (inter)national intent and agency. For example, often these unequal relations between countries are justified under wider discourses of 'modernisation' and 'development' and, as such, some of these relationships could be described as consensual rather than conflictory in nature. As we shall see in Chapter 6, for example, this would certainly be the position held by those interests seeking to bring educational technologies to poorer nations as part of international aid efforts. Indeed, digital technology and the wider connotations of the 'information society' have long been used in the continuation of the long-standing neo-liberal project of 'modernisation' where market-led democracy is presented as "a 'model' of development or progress that others can emulate" (Shafiul Alam Bhuiyan 2008, p.104). Yet the extent to which these arrangements are any less exploitative or unequal is unclear. As Hirst *et al.* (2009, p.6) contend, it could be argued that unequal neo-imperialist relations are actually perpetuated as the result of "a new strategy of unilateral action, building under its leadership transient 'coalitions of the willing' that vary in composition depending upon the objective at hand".

From this perspective, the use of digital technology in education is linked potentially with a number of issues that are of interest to the post-colonial perspective – not least the perpetuation and reconfiguration of patterns of dependency between countries. In particular, it could be argued that the so-called modernisation of developing societies through the increased use of educational technology perhaps makes them more dependent on the developed North – both for the technology itself and for the associated financial assistance. In focusing on and problematising these long-standing patterns and relations, the post-colonial perspective therefore introduces a number of questions relating to the role of technology in educational settings around the world. In this sense, post-colonialism offers a useful means of understanding the issues surrounding educational technology use in those countries and contexts outside the usual field of vision of the academic study of educational technology. The concerns and concepts associated with the post-colonialist approach can therefore support the 'renarrativisation' of our understandings of technology and education. In particular, post-colonialism can play the useful role of shifting attention away from the Euro-American concerns that tend to dominate the field, and towards the perspective of those formally colonised by European powers. The post-colonialist framework can therefore allow us to literally 'turn the world upside down' (McMillin 2007, p.183), to consider the 'not-spots' as well as the 'hot-spots' of the information society, and also to highlight the inequalities that persist within these settings. As McMillin (2007, p.3) concludes:

to work with a post-colonial framework means to understand the 'nation' as a heterogeneous space, one with uneven development, always under construction, and never complete. Rather than merely addressing the interconnectedness of north-south and centre-periphery dichotomies, a critical post-colonial position is engaged with the underlying problem of opening up critical spaces for new narratives of becoming and emancipation.

In addition to these insights, a further valuable addition that the post-colonialist perspective brings to our analysis of education, technology and globalisation is an emphasis on the pursuit of agendas for resistance, intervention and change. Indeed, the post-colonial rejection of the assumed superiority of Western cultures and agendas of progress and modernity is built around an implicitly radical agenda of seeking equality and well-being across the world. The post-colonial position is therefore useful in its interest in the formation of alternative forms of educational technology that could be considered more 'appropriate' – for example, technological arrangements that are based around the increased valuing of indigenous culture and language, or conceptions of learning that are privileged in other countries. Again, we shall return to all these themes as the book progresses.

Thinking about Technology and Education

Together, the approaches covered so far in this chapter already imply a complex account of education and society – enough to fill an entire library, let alone the remaining six chapters of this book. Yet, at this point we have covered only half of our stated brief of considering alternative theoretical perspectives on education and technology. Indeed, if we are to work with these sophisticated understandings of education, then we also need to work with an equally sophisticated understanding of technology. Here, it is worth also considering the critical theories of technology that have developed within the social sciences over the past thirty years. In particular it is worth reflecting briefly on the strengths of socio-technical approaches towards understanding the nature and form of technology.

Despite continued calls for improvement (e.g. Bromley 1997, Oliver 2011), it would be fair to conclude that most writing and thinking about educational technology takes a noticeably unsophisticated approach when thinking about the relationship between technology and the social. Many of the most popular – but also the most misleading – claims about education and technology (such as those considered in the opening sections of Chapter 1) tend to be based around deterministic assumptions that technologies possess inherent qualities, and are therefore capable of having predictable 'impacts' or 'effects' on whole countries, educational institutions, classrooms, teachers or learners if used in a correct manner. In its simplest form, then, such 'technological determinism' can be seen as a way of thinking about technology that assumes that technology determines social change. In its most extreme form, 'hard' technological determinism assumes that technology is the only factor in social change. While most people in education would feel uncomfortable in making such a direct association, many would perhaps concur with 'softer' forms of technological determinist thinking which assumes that technology has an influence (and often a strong influence) on social change. Thus, as Sally Wyatt (2008, p.169) observes, the idea of technological determinism continues to endure in most accounts of the relationship between technology and society:

> The simplicity of this model is a principal reason for its endurance. It is also the model that makes most sense of many people's experience. For most of us, most of the time, the technologies we use every day are of mysterious origin and design. We have no idea whence they came and possibly even less idea how they actually work. We simply adapt ourselves to their requirements and hope that they continue to function in the predictable and expected ways promised by those who sold them to us. It is because technological determinism conforms with a huge majority of people's experiences that it remains the 'common sense' explanation.

As Wyatt implies, there is a long heritage of technological determinism in popular, political and academic discussions of the 'effect' of technology on education around the world. A determinist way of thinking underpins the range of popular claims, for example, that internet use leads to an individualisation of learning. In fact, many of the enthusiasms for education and technology outlined in Chapter 1 appear to be driven by an underlying belief in technology as some sort of 'technical fix'. As Kevin Robins and Frank Webster (1989) observed, the history of education has been characterised by attempts to use the 'power' of technology in order to solve problems that are non-technological in nature. The history of education is also characterised by a tendency to ignore the often ineffective or unsustainable outcomes that arise as a result of technology use. As we saw in Chapter 1, there is little to suggest that much has changed in the twenty-five years or so since Robins and Webster made this observation. Indeed, this faith in the technical fix is pervasive and relentless – especially in the minds of the key interests and opinion formers of this digital age. As the co-founder of the influential *Wired* magazine reasoned more recently, "tools and technology drive us. Even if a problem has been caused by technology, the answer will always be more technology" (Kelly 2010, p.22).

Despite these common-sense proclamations, any serious account of education and technology needs to resist the assumption that any digital technology has the ability to change things for the better. While appealing to those people who want to construct bounded 'scientific' explanations and models, the dangers of these ways of thinking about the use of technology lie primarily in the simplistic conclusions that they lead towards. In particular, this way of thinking usually reaches conclusions that recommend the overcoming of 'barriers' or impediments within the immediate educational context, so that the inherent beneficial effects of technology may be more fully felt. This logic is illustrated in the frequent 'blaming' of individual educators or educational institutions for the failure of digital technologies to be used 'effectively'. Indeed, current discussions and debates about the use of digital technology in educational settings often continue to follow a decidedly externalist logic, 'treating new technologies as autonomous forces that compel society to change' (Nye 2007, p.27). Many of the claims and arguments presented in the opening sections of Chapter 1 were based around the assumption that digital technology is set inevitably to change various aspects of education on a global scale. As we later acknowledged in Chapter 1, this is clearly not the case. We therefore need to adopt a mind-set for the remainder of the book that reflects this disparity between the rhetoric and realities of technology and education.

There are many good reasons to attempt to move beyond a technologically determinist view of technology and education – not least because such thinking often leads to incorrect analyses and conclusions. If the relationships between education and technology are seen only in these 'cause-and-effect' terms, then the main task of any analysis of educational technology is simply to identify the impediments and deficiencies that are delaying and opposing the march of technological progress. This view is implicit, for example, in the increasingly popular proposals to dispense with the educational institutions or classroom teachers that appear to be impeding the benefits of technology in education. Technological determinism of this type leaves little room for manoeuvre, deviation or any other form of social agency in the implementation and use of technology. In short, it presents a view of technology and education where social actors are passive agents – simply reacting to technological developments in a cause and effect manner. As such technological innovations are seen to simply 'happen', leaving societies (and education) having to deal with the consequences and adapt as best they could to the new arrangements and new ways of being. At best, then, teachers, students, governments and everyone else involved in education are placed in a position of having to respond to technological change by making the 'best use' of the technologies that they are presented with.

Of course, we should remain mindful of the danger of setting technological determinism as a 'conceptual straw-man' (Winner 1993) and then finding oneself forced into a viewpoint where nothing can be said to be influenced by anything else. Indeed, as Raymond Williams (1981, p.102) warned, anyone resolved simply not to be deterministic faces "a kind of madness". To ascribe complete interpretability to any technology can be seen as an equally constraining and reductionist form of 'social determinism' where only social factors are granted any importance (see Potts 2008). In one form, this can lead to equally as misleading assumptions that technology is somehow 'neutral', malleable and 'one-way' – i.e. "one can use it without being used by it" (Beatham 2008, p.511). At best, then, we need to take a mutual shaping approach where technology both is shaped and shaping in a number of enabling and constraining ways. In this sense, technological development and technology-related change are therefore inherently entwined with social relations, structures and processes. As Slavoj Žižek (1996, p.198) concludes, technology and society are therefore mutually shaped and mutually shaping:

> the way computerization affects our lives does not depend directly on technology, it results from the way the impact of new technology is refracted by the social relations which, in their turn, co-determine the very direction of technological development.

This approach certainly provides more scope for what Wiebe Bijker *et al.* (1987) describe as 'open[ing] up the black box of technology'. In particular this perspective on technology allows for a better understanding of the influence of the local, national and international interests on the apparently 'global' forms of educational technology we have covered so far in this book. This moves us beyond the 'decontextualised' view of technology that is often pursued in the globalisation literature and serves only to "edit out the various forces and fields that both bring it into being, and deploy it" (Schirato and Webb 2003, p.47). Instead, this contextualised perspective leaves us able to identify these 'various forces and fields' and consider important questions of intent and agency. These include the exploration of how educational technologies are developed, implemented and adopted with specific purposes and practices in mind – not least the purpose of changing things and influencing society (Miller 2011, p.5). As John Potts (2008, n.p.) details, this way of thinking therefore offers a 'dose of social perspective' on how technologies are used in society, focusing on factors such as "social need, economic intention, political control, specific decision-making, the design of content: in a word, intention".

These ways of understanding technology are often described as taking a 'social shaping' perspective. Following this line of thinking, it is accepted that there can be no predetermined outcomes to the development and implementation of educational technologies. Instead, any technological artefact is seen as being subjected continually to a series of interactions and 'negotiations' with the social, economic, political and cultural contexts that it emerges into. As a whole, the social shaping approach therefore highlights the importance of recognising the social and interactional circumstances in which digital technologies exist and through which they attain their meaning(s). The strength of this approach to technology and education lies in its ability to allow a number of 'big questions' to be asked about technology that would otherwise be absent from the research agenda for education and technology. These questions include how individual educational technologies fit into wider socio-technical systems and networks, as well as what connections and linkages exist between educational technology and macro-level concerns of globalisation, the knowledge economy and late modernity. These approaches also offer a direct 'way in' to unpacking the micro-level social processes that underpin the use of digital technologies in educational settings. From both these perspectives, the principal advantage of the more socially nuanced theoretical approaches should be seen as their ability to develop a more socially grounded understanding of the 'messy' realities of educational technology 'as it happens'.

In approaching education and technology as a site of intense social conflict, these approaches can therefore allow us to move beyond asking whether or not a particular educational technology 'works' in a technical or pedagogic sense. Instead, these approaches allow us to address questions of how digital technologies (re)produce social relations and whose interests they serve. As such, the social shaping approach suggests that questions are asked about the large number of organisational, political, economic and cultural factors that pattern the design, development, production, marketing, implementation and 'end use' of a technological artefact in education. If we wish to gain a full sense of how and why educational technologies are being used in the ways that they are around the world, we therefore need to develop better understandings of how technologies are socially constructed, shaped and negotiated by all of these factors and all of the 'actors' that represent them.

Conclusions

Constraints of space notwithstanding, this chapter's brief consideration of the different theoretical perspectives available has advanced the case for taking a con-textualised and critical stance on education, technology and global change. Of course, while these theoretical approaches are important, we need to retain a sense of perspective regarding the strengths *and* limitations of social theory. Indeed, while maintaining a theoretical awareness it is worth remaining mindful of Manuel Castells' advice to 'wear one's theoretical clothes lightly' rather than displaying a dogmatic persistence to one viewpoint or approach. Indeed, Manuel Castells (2000) reminds us of the benefits of 'disposable theory' – recognising theory as an essential tool but also acknowledging it as something to be discarded when it outlives its usefulness in illuminating the substantive world. In these terms, any analyses of education and digital technology are perhaps best arranged around an assemblage of theoretical perspectives that can be used as, and when, they best fit. As Amin and Thrift (2005, p.222) reason:

> Theory has taken on a different style which has a lighter touch than of old. For a start, few now believe that one theory can cover the world (or save the world, for that matter). No particular theoretical approach, even in combi-nation with others, can be used to gain a total grip on what's going on. Theory-making is a hybrid assemblage of testable propositions and probable explanations derived from sensings of the world, the world's persistent ways of talking back, and the effort of abstraction.

We should therefore feel confident in taking different aspects of the theoretical perspectives reviewed in this chapter forward into our proceeding discussions. For instance, the comparative education approach confirms the need to move beyond the assumption that educational technology is a wholly homogeneous and unifying phenomenon the world over, and instead strive to make reference to what is happening elsewhere in terms of educational provision and practice. This perspective highlights the importance of context and the need for contextualisation – as Michael Apple (2010, p.195) reasons:

> one must be very cautious about appropriating the experiences of another country uncritically. Often, such 'recontextualisations' pull the reforms out of their context of intense debate that may characterise their development in the place where the policies originated.

Yet as the comparative education, political economy and post-colonialist approaches all remind us, our aim should not simply be to collect together an 'international picture' of education and technology but to consider the inter-relations between countries, regions and transnational corporations. We therefore need to construct different levels of supranational, national and subnational analysis of education and technology, and most importantly take time to consider the relationships between these levels. From the political economy and post-colonial approaches we can also take forward the idea that educational technologies are imbued with power relations between the many integrated interests involved in the 'business' of educational technology. This also highlights the importance of taking a historical perspective on the unequal power relations that persist between countries, and, most importantly, to make time to consider possible spaces for alternative arrangements, intervention and resistance.

Indeed, it is important to bear in mind throughout the course of this book that these critical approaches are not meant to be defeatist in their outcomes – the writing and reading of the book is intended to be a constructive rather than destructive exercise. The post-colonial approach, in particular, highlights the need to not simply decry the unsatisfactory state of the present, but also to consider opportunities and spaces for future critical action as well as critical scholarship. As such, the next six chapters of the book have been written in the spirit of offering an analysis that is able to point towards contradictions, controversies *and* the spaces of possible action. These intentions are implicit in our underpinning understanding of technology as being inherently socially shaped as well as being socially determining. Indeed, from the social shaping of technology approach, we can take forward the importance of developing a socio-technical understanding of education and technology – with a particular focus on establishing the specific interests that drive the agendas associated with the use of educational technology, and unpacking the relationships between technology and the different actors and interests implicit in educational technology use.

All of these perspectives certainly point to the need to seek to understand educational technology in terms of its complicated connections to the larger society.

All of these perspectives also point to the obvious complexity of educational technology and the likelihood that there will be *no* clear answers and *no* straight-forward analyses. Indeed, it worth reminding ourselves at this point of the inevitably contradictory and contested nature of the next six chapters. While we can be certain that education is not technologically determined, neither should we fall into the temptation of assuming that education is somehow party to a reductive form of economic determinism. Above all, we also need to take care not to overstate the coherence, power and achievements of the 'big issues' that we are tackling – not least capital and the neoliberal economic project. As John Clarke (2004, p.29) reminds us, we need to be suitably appropriate in our arguments and attributions:

> I want to insist on treating contradiction and contestation as integral elements of these processes. I want to argue that there are contradictions within and between the processes of globalisation, manifested in unevennesses, disturbances and encounters with old and new resistances and refusals.

So with all these caveats of complexity, contradiction and unevenness to the fore, we can now move forward into developing a set of inter-related accounts and analyses of the recent implementation and use of technology in educational settings the world over. We shall start with what is perhaps one of the most extensive but least discussed aspects of educational technology implementation and use around the world – the role of supranational and intergovernmental organisations. Just what are the linkages between educational technology and the activities and interests of organisations that are located above the level of national governments and nation states?

3

EDUCATION, TECHNOLOGY AND INTERNATIONAL ORGANISATIONS

Introduction

While the past two chapters may have warned against an excessively global level of analysis, this chapter will consider the international and transnational contexts of educational technology. In particular, this involves focusing attention on organisations and bodies whose actions and activities span beyond national boundaries. Key here, then, are the activities of multinational corporations – i.e. commercial enterprises that manage production and/or deliver services in more than one country. It is also important to consider the activities of supranational authorities – i.e. non-profit centralised authorities that are delegated power by various national governments to act on their behalf and in their interests. As the chapter will go on to discuss, a number of these organisations can be said to influence educational technology provision and practice around the world. Although the actions of these international organisations may not always be especially visible, they are nevertheless a crucial part of the educational technology landscape.

In considering the activities of these organisations, the chapter addresses the globalist assumption that the nature and form of educational technology is defined increasingly at international – rather than local or national – levels. As we shall see throughout this chapter, many seemingly localised examples of educational technology provision and practice have their roots in the extensive 'partnerships' that exist between international non-governmental bodies and private capital. We shall also see how the educational technology agendas of local institutions and agencies may be influenced by the activities and agendas of supranational state apparatus, international political regimes, multilateral organisations and economic blocks. In considering the influence of these international actors on the nature and form of educational technology around the world, a number of important questions are therefore brought to our attention. For example, how do international organisations deliberately set out to 'set the tone' and 'frame the problem' of educational technology? How do they influence and intervene in national policies, and what bearing do they have on local practice?

Of course the roles and responsibilities of these multinational corporations and supranational authorities are not straightforward. As was discussed in Chapters 1 and 2, educational technology is a complex intertwined set of processes that involve an array of intergovernmental organisations and multinational corporations. These processes are varied in nature, often being practical *and* discursive, financial *and* technical, political *and* cultural. Furthermore, the motivations and intentions behind each organisation's actions vary considerably, as does the dimension of their organisational power. In short, this is by no means a straightforward area of education and technology to describe. Thus while there are many ways that we could attempt to frame the proceeding discussion of the international shaping of educational technology, perhaps the easiest distinction that can be made is in terms of what can be loosely seen as 'public' interest and 'private' capital. As such, we can first consider the influence of intergovernmental and supranational organisations and then, second, the influence of multinational and transnational corporations.

The Role of Educational Technology in the Activities of Intergovernmental and Supranational Organisations

Intergovernmental and supranational political and economic groupings have long been important components of the global superstructure, particularly since the end of the Cold War at the beginning of the 1990s and the parallel rise of organisations such as the European Union in maintaining regional interests (see Stubbs and Underhill 2006). As such, the past thirty years has been a period characterised by the growth of a 'new regionalism'. Here groupings of nations have assumed a leading participatory role in global economics and politics, both in terms of trade and in terms of flows of capital (Dale and Robertson 2002). Now intergovernmental organisations (IGOs) proliferate the global political stage. These include high-profile organisations such as the European Union, the Organisation of Economic Cooperation and Development (OECD), the G-20 group of major economies, the League of Arab States, the Association of Southeast Asian Nations and others. Similarly a number of supranational organisations (SNOs) are also significant economic and political actors, such as the United Nations, the World Bank, the World Trade Organisation and the International Monetary Fund.

Although all primarily economic in their focus and political in their actions, the exact focus and role of these organisations varies according to constitution and history. For example, as an organisation established to represent and influence the interests of the developed economies of the world, the OECD has tended to work on behalf of the most successful and powerful elements of the world economy.

Historically, this organisation originated in the 1948 'European Recovery Programme' (commonly known as the Marshall Plan) which was put in place by the US to support the economic reconstruction of post-war Europe. This financed the founding of the 'Organisation for European Economic Cooperation', which in 1961 then became the OECD. As its history suggests, the actions of the OECD centre primarily on matters of economic efficiency and economic growth amongst already economically developed and wealthy countries. However, as with many international organisations, OECD's actions also place an emphasis on the importance of *extra*-economic issues, not least elements of social infrastructure such as education. Indeed, although different in their exact motivation and focus, most intergovernmental and supranational organisations could be said to now accord "greater importance to education than ever before" (Rizvi and Lingard 2010, p.131).

In forming agendas and perspectives relating to the economic and societal role of education, organisations such as OECD, World Bank and the like seek to play a number of different roles within the global economy and global polity. On the one hand, these organisations clearly seek "the control and orientation of international trade in their favour" (Dale and Robertson 2002, p.10), and therefore strive to act as significant agents in "both powering and steering the forces that make up global capitalism". In this sense, these organisations often operate as policy actors in their own right. This can involve practical interventions – for example, directly investing in programmes and initiatives, engaging in technical reporting and statistical work, acting as sponsors for academic research and hosting debate amongst networks of policymakers, researchers and consultancies. In a less direct manner these organisations often also seek to act as subtle 'spheres of influence' and 'back-stage' manipulators of global discourses about education (Rizvi and Lingard 2010, p.128). Thus as Jones (2009) observes, an organisation such as the World Bank could be said to play a range of roles in shaping educational policies, processes and practices, i.e.:

- shaping economic and social policymaking of governments around the world;
- being instrumental in forging policies that see education as a precursor to modernisation;
- serving as a major purveyor of Western ideas about how education and the economy are, or should be, related;
- being an influential proponent of the rapid expansion of formal education systems around the world – in particular, financing much of that expansion.

From a globalist perspective, these organisations could be argued to act as major contributors to the formation of a 'global culture' in education which works for a common good. However, from a more sceptical position these organisations could be argued to act as agents of the neoliberal project where "capital serves both as a prime driving force and as a model for its imitators or partners elsewhere" (Levidow 2002, p.234). From this latter perspective, although the educational motivations and interests of SNOs and IGOs are varied and extensive, many could be said to follow a neo-liberal, human capital perspective in terms of how "the world's wealthy nations need to educate their populations for competition in the global knowledge economy" (Spring 2009, p.58).

Yet from whatever perspective they are approached, it is important to understand the educational activities and agendas of these SNOs and IGOs in a nuanced and heterogeneous manner that acknowledges the differences between them. While a dominant strand of the World Bank educational agenda has certainly been the pursuit of 'reform agendas' of privatisation, deregulation and commercialisation of education (Levidow 2002, Bergeron 2008), the OECD could be said to have pursued a slightly less interventionist approach towards education, noticeably concentrating on the measurement and commensurability of educational systems in terms of their efficiency and high-skills nature. Moreover, the educational interests of an organisation focused on humanitarianism and security-related concerns such as the United Nations, for instance, may also privilege issues such as "educating global citizens committed to sustainable development; sustain and protect cultures and languages; gender equality; activist citizen[s]" (Spring 2009, p.81). The actions of all these organisations are therefore imbued with varying perspectives on what education is, and what education is for.

A key question to consider in the terms of our own discussion, then, is the extent to which these interests and agendas are replicated in the educational technology activities of the world's major IGOs and SNOs. In this sense, it is first important to recognise that the use of digital technology has long been a significant element of the educational activities of these organisations. Indeed, intergovernmental organisations such as the World Bank, OECD and United Nations have all been prominent advocates of educational technology since the 1980s and have played a substantial collective role in initiating and influencing the implementation of educational technology around the world. As Joel Spring (2009, p.48) describes in relation to the activities of the World Bank throughout the 2000s:

> Given the goal of preparation for the knowledge economy, the World Bank emphasises the classroom use of computers and resources from the internet. ICT allows the adaptation of globally available information to local learning situations ... It is important to highlight that a large percentage of the World Bank's education funds are used for the purchase of educational technology. Critics might complain that this channels large sums of money to be used for education to multinational producers of computers and educational software. On the other hand ICT is vital for education to enter the knowledge economy ... It is estimated that between 1997 and 2001 that [sic] 75 per cent of the World Bank-financed education projects included ICT,

education technology, and educational management information systems, along with courses being taught over the internet as part of distance learning.

What is perhaps most striking about Spring's lengthy description is the extent to which most of these aspects of the World Bank's educational technology programme have gone relatively unnoticed within academic analysis of educational technology. Despite the clearly extensive interests that an organisation such as the World Bank has had in educational technology, one would be hard-pressed to find acknowledgement (let alone critical analysis) of these efforts within the academic educational technology literature. As such, it is important that we take the time to examine the educational technology agendas of these SNOs and IGOs in further detail.

Mapping Supranational Involvement in Educational Technology: The Case of the United Nations

One of the most-involved 'public' international organisations in the field of educational technology is the United Nations (UN). As an organisation acting on behalf of every sovereign state in the world, the main concerns of the UN tend to be centred on major issues of international security and law, economic development, human rights and social progress. Yet within this substantial brief, the UN has long promoted the importance of educational technology. As Kofi Annan (then Secretary-General of the organisation) proclaimed in 2003, "while education unlocks the door to development, increasingly it is information technologies that can unlock the door to education" (cited in United Nations 2003). Beneath bold statements such as these, the UN has pursued a wide-ranging educational technology agenda over the past thirty years – from the direct sponsorship of discrete projects to more indirect efforts to influence the nature and form of educational technology use around the world.

Much of this work has taken place through the activities of a number of specialised UN agencies and programmes. At the beginning of the 2000s, for example, the UN's 'ICT Task Force' notably included education as a key component of its work, resulting in a series of forums and documents such as 'Harnessing the Potential of ICT for Education' and the running of the 'Global e-Schools and Communities Initiative'. Education also formed a prominent focus for the activities of the volunteer-led UN 'information technology service' (which oversaw educational technology projects in development contexts) and the UN's 'development programme' (which, for example, championed the use of 'open source' software in education).

Aside from specific activities of this kind, the main educational technology components of the UN's activities have been pursued through the organisation's educational agency – the United Nations Educational, Scientific and Cultural Organisation (UNESCO). UNESCO's educational technology activities have taken a number of forms, with its Bangkok office particularly active during the 2000s and into the 2010s in promoting educational technology across South and East Asia. This saw sustained efforts to offer 'tool-kits' and advice for school leaders and policy-makers, the production of policy publications alongside an extensive programme of measuring and monitoring technology use throughout the region. Similarly, UNESCO's Paris office pursued a number of educational technology programmes throughout the same time, not least through its 'communication and information' directorate. These included efforts to promote the use of open courseware in higher education, to encourage the development of national strategies for e-learning and distance learning, as well as supporting the development of model 'virtual university' provision. Perhaps most significant has been the work of UNESCO's Moscow-based 'Institute for Information Technologies in Education' (UN-IITE). This agency has been working since 1997 to influence the UN's general programme with regard to the potential of digital technology to contribute to educational quality and accessibility. As the UN-IITE mission statement suggests, much of this work is intended to reflect the 'humanistic' as well as economic concerns of the overall UN ethos: "ICT applications in education should help meet the challenges of knowledge societies, contribute to the reduction of the digital divide, including disparities in access to knowledge, and provide opportunities for attaining quality education and lifelong learning for all" (UNESCO 2010, p.7).

As this statement implies, the UN's work with digital technology in education tends to be informed by a number of wider non-technological concerns. These include, for example, ensuring the right for all individuals to access education, and supporting the 'modernisation' of education systems and establishment of 'inclusive' knowledge societies. All these issues, it could be argued, have underpinned the way that UN agencies have approached educational technology over the past thirty years. For example, the UN's recent emphasis on open source software, open courseware and 'open knowledge' networks could be said to be aimed at addressing emerging forms of social inclusion and knowledge production.

That said, the key focus of the UN educational technology agenda continues to be on the maintenance rather than disruption of formal educational systems. This can be seen in the recent 'UN ICT Competency Framework for Teachers' – an attempt to offer system-wide standards for educational technology use around the world and to provide a set of 'harmonised' standards for educational technology policy, curriculum, pedagogy and teacher professional development. While this framework is clearly intended to be of practical benefit to individual educators and institutions, its wider significance lies as a direct attempt on the part of the UN to shape national government educational technology agendas. Indeed, much of UNESCO's work takes a consultative, coercive and championing approach – as the agency puts it, seeking "to help governments and others responsible make informed decisions about selecting and implementing ICT support for education; and to broker and monitor new partnerships to make this happen" (UNESCO 2010, p.13).

The Educational Technology Agendas of other Supranational and Intergovernmental Organisations

Of course, the UN is just one of many SNOs and IGOs that act to influence the role of technology within education systems worldwide. While the UN's focus could be said to encompass issues of social and cultural development, the activities of other SNOs often reflect a more straightforward emphasis on economic competitiveness. Unsurprisingly, a contrasting approach to the UN is that of the World Bank, whose work tends to frame educational technology in more explicit terms of market-led economic development. This is not to say, however, that the scope of the World Bank's educational technology agenda is any less diverse than that of the UN. Over the past twenty years the World Bank educational technology portfolio has involved projects to equip schools with computer laboratories in countries as diverse as Armenia to Bhutan, through to supporting systematic technology-based reform of educational systems in countries such as Jordan, Turkey and Russia.

A similar diversity of action can be found in the educational technology work of the European Union (EU). The EU's promotion of educational technology has been evident across its long-running 'lifelong learning programme', encompassing a number of different programmes that boast an educational technology focus. These range from initiatives encouraging online support of learning outside formal educational institutions, bridging inequalities in individuals' access to information and communication technologies (the so-called 'digital divide') and improving technology skills in the workplace. One high-profile recent EU project was the 'eTwinning' initiative – a cross-Europe programme that aimed to use online resources and services to "promote European school cooperation, collaborative learning and project-based pedagogy". Aside from specific interventions such as these, the EU continues to seek to influence educational technology policymaking across its member states. In particular, the EU's European Schoolnet body has acted as a forum for the thirty or so national official agencies within Europe that are concerned with schools technology – from the Estonian Tiger Leap Foundation to the Turkish General Directorate of Educational Technologies. As befits the wider remit of the EU, all of these efforts reflect an agenda of 'harmonisation' – i.e. the reduction of individual and institutional differences between countries.

Educational technology has also been a significant aspect of the educational work of the OECD. Alongside the production of policy briefings and reports, the OECD has played a significant part in enrolling digital technology into the global 'competition' of education – not least through positional tools such as the 'PISA world education indicators' which provide performance comparison measures and global educational indicators between countries. While OECD's interest in educational technology during the 2000s concentrated primarily on policymaking and research on new forms of technology-rich educational provision for what it termed 'New Millennium Learners', in the early 2010s, this focus shifted to exploring the role of digital technologies in the comparative performance of education systems. The organisation's recent 'Teaching and Learning International Survey' project, for example, had an explicit focus on the role of digital technology on school and teacher effectiveness. As such, the recent activities of the OECD have tended to frame digital technology as part of the wider 'change management' of education systems.

Understanding the Significance of SNOs and IGOs in Educational Technology

While all these organisations have clear interests in promoting the use of digital technology in education systems, it could be argued that much of the work described above fulfils a primarily symbolic rather than practical purpose. Certainly, educational technology is a highly visible and tangible means of allowing otherwise remote international organisations and agencies to be 'seen to do something' about the social and economic conditions of the countries and regions that they are concerned with. Yet in pursuing these actions, SNOs and IGOs such as the UN, OECD and World Bank also are seeking to influence the global discourses and debates that frame educational technology provision and practice. While individually of limited practical outcome, these actions can nevertheless be said to have a significant cumulative influence on 'education politics' and policymaking – for instance, creating policy expectations of the role of technology in new curricular arrangements, or creating interest and awareness of common 'issues'. These motivations of advocacy and agenda-setting are certainly clear in the on-going efforts of SNOs and IGOs to create and sustain the 'imperative' for technology use throughout education systems. As Rizvi and Lingard (2010, p.79) observe: "organisations such as the OECD, the EU, APEC, UNESCO and the World Bank have become major sites for the organisation of knowledge about education, and have created a cajoling discourse of 'imperatives of the global economy' for education".

As such, most of these organisations' educational technology actions are based noticeably around non-coercive 'softer' forms of power rather than any direct 'hard' influence. Moreover, any actual effect of these organisations' interventions in educational technology could be said to depend very much on the economic and political situation of the countries where the work takes place. Through a combination of "relentless global marketing ... often backed by substantial financial clout" (Green 2003, p.86) organisations such as the World Bank and OECD are able to exert a noticeable influence on educational technology arrangements in some economically weaker countries and regions. Yet in more secure and wealthy countries, the provision of education (particularly the provision of compulsory schooling) tends to remain primarily a matter of national sovereignty. As Andy Green (2003, p.86) observed with regard to the influence of the European Union, "education still remains officially a matter of national competence, which few member states are willing to cede".

As such, many of the educational technology activities described above constitute attempts on the part of these international organisations to advance their agendas through voluntary rather than regulatory means. In this sense, many of these organisations' educational technology initiatives and programmes are perhaps best understood as attempts to establish standardised and harmonised 'ground-rules' and ways of 'doing' educational technology within nation states and their education systems. Thus, it could be argued that these organisations' activities are underpinned by a speculative expectation of the increased use of digital technology within educational systems around the world contributing "to a global uniformity of educational policies and practices" (Spring 2009, p.206).

The Role of Educational Technology in the Activities of Transnational and Multinational Corporations

Of course, these SNOs and IGOs are able rarely to orchestrate change of their own accord. Indeed, one of the key roles of SNOs and IGOs within the global politics of educational technology is in stimulating, supporting and guiding the actions of other actors. An organisation such as the OECD, for example, spends a great deal of time co-ordinating the actions of other interested parties such as national and regional governments, NGOs, academic researchers and educational administrators. These actors are all brought together through OECD-sponsored meetings, forums, publications and reports, research projects and other collaborative activities and dissemination events. Thus while working ostensibly on behalf of national governments, organisations such as the OECD play a particularly significant role in making and sustaining connections between public and private interests – in particular the major corporate interests in the global economy and the global IT marketplace. It is, therefore, appropriate that we turn our attention to the educational technology activities of these corporate actors in their own right.

Although usually overlooked in academic discussions of educational technology, it is important to recognise the influence of commercial and private actors. If nothing else, the design, production and sale of digital technology hardware and software to education is almost wholly dependent on commercial interests, most notably the many transnational and multinational IT companies responsible for supplying computer hardware, software, connectivity and 'content'. Private interests also sell a range of technology-based services to educators and educational institutions – such as IT training, technical support, systems management and other advisory services. The for-profit sector also plays a key role in the continued promotion of the notion of 'educational technology' in order to sustain demand for educational use of digital technologies. In all these instances, the nature, form and governance of digital technology use in education are being influenced by the involvement of commercial firms and other private sector interests.

Of course, in purely financial terms the significance of private sector involvement in the global educational market for technology is clear. For instance the worldwide e-learning industry was estimated in 2011 to be worth over US$160 billion. Similarly the 'instructional materials' market in the US alone was estimated to be worth around $8 billion (see Simba 2010). Yet the growing commercial involvement in educational technology is also indicative of wider shifts in the provision and governance of education – chiming with a growing influence that private interests are able to exert over educational arrangements within countries. Aside from immediate matters of profitability, the increased presence of commercial organisations in educational technology represents a potential substantial shift in authority from public to private interests. Thus in developing a better understanding of the global nature of educational technology we need to consider the full breadth of transnational and multinational corporate involvement – from the direct supplying of resources, to the more subtle assumption of responsibility for the organisation and governance of technology use in education.

Mapping Commercial Involvement in Educational Technology: The Case of Microsoft

The full extent of corporate involvement in educational technology is evident if we consider the education portfolios of some of the major IT corporations around the world. Microsoft, for example, remains the world's largest software company with nearly 90,000 employees and almost 700,000 'partner' organisations in over 100 countries. Despite the scope of its core commercial commitments, over the past twenty years Microsoft has assumed a central role in influencing global educational technology use above and beyond the direct selling of its products. Indeed, this is a company that has assumed a significant level of responsibility for educational technology leadership, governance and support around the world. As the company announces in its promotional literature, "we are investing our resources – people, partnerships, services, philanthropy and products – to stimulate positive change in education". One of Microsoft's key aims in doing this is to support the wide-scale use of digital technology throughout the world's education systems – as the company puts it, seeking to "increase adoption of innovative learning solutions through scale".

As these statements imply, Microsoft has an extensive and well-established portfolio of educational activities. The company has long operated large-scale educational programmes that are concerned with increasing individuals' access to and use of computers. These include the Unlimited Potential Community Technology Skills Programme which supports NGOs to set up and run over 40,000 community technology centres in more than 100 countries to deliver the Microsoft Digital Literacy Curriculum. The recent US-focused 'Elevate America' initiative similarly provided foundational skills to over 2 million unemployed workers. Other interventions are directed specifically at educational technology arrangements in less wealthy counties. In particular, the company's philanthropy programme (Microsoft Unlimited Potential) is focused explicitly on "help[ing] bring social and economic opportunity to the estimated 5 billion people who are not yet realizing the benefits of technology". These activities involve supporting a variety of educational NGOs around the world to sustain school-based and community-based computer use – with Microsoft therefore responsible for financing projects ranging from the Bangladesh Friendship Education Society to Education for an Open Society Romania.

Aside from these 'stand-alone' efforts to supply resources and train individuals, Microsoft has also developed ambitious on-going educational technology programmes aimed at stimulating the long-term technology-based change of education systems. For example, the company sustains a series of Dynamics Academic Alliances around the world where networks of higher education teaching staff in over 1,600 academic institutions are given access to classroom software, technical support from product experts, and bespoke product training. Similar networks are operated for college and high school teachers across 45 different countries. In the same manner, Microsoft's IT Academic programme provides accreditation to strategically selected schools to deliver training to other neighbouring schools. These intervention and support activities are complemented by a substantial programme of scientific and social research into education and technology. Through their 'external research' programme Microsoft pursues its own original research and collaborative relationships with universities, alongside series of seminars, fellowships and direct funding of projects in the area of education research. Recent areas of interest have included the funding of a Classroom of the Future initiative, an Institute for Personal Robots in Education as well as research programmes on topics ranging from 'games curricula' to 'tablet and pen-centric computing'.

Perhaps the most extensive example of the central positioning of education within Microsoft's corporate activities is the company's Partners in Learning network. Since its launch in 2003, this $500 million programme has involved over 121 million students and nearly 6 million educators in over 100 countries. Partners in Learning activities take many guises – offering professional training for teachers, online networking opportunities and the supply of curriculum resources, free tools and learning programmes. Partners in Learning has also allowed Microsoft to work closely with educators, schools, school districts, state departments of education and other organisations to create projects that can serve as models for the future. One notable instance of this was the company's partnership with the School District of Philadelphia to plan and build a 750-student high school based around principles of 'innovation and technology'. The ambitiously named 'School of the Future' opened in 2006 and despite its fractious initial years of operation was soon being offered by Microsoft to 'serve as a model of twenty-first-century learning' for other educational authorities to replicate elsewhere. This involvement in the broad reform of education systems was furthered in 2011 when Partners in Learning was given responsibility for operating the US government's nationwide teacher recruitment programme.

The Educational Technology Activities of Other Companies

While impressive, Microsoft's portfolio of educational technology activities is replicated (to a lesser or greater extent) by many major IT firms and corporations around the world. For example, having recently usurped Microsoft as the world's most profitable IT firm, Apple Inc. is involved in a similar range of educational activities. For example, Apple has long supported communities of teachers to work together and share resources. Over the past twenty years, these efforts have included the running of the Apple Learning Interchange and latterly the iTunes U programme – described as an 'educational content repository' where over 800 universities (including Stanford, Yale, MIT and Oxford) distribute their education 'content' publicly through the company's iTunes Store. Apple also runs extensive education training and research programmes, and since the 1980s has been involved in the subsidised provision of computer laboratories and other computing resources to educational institutions around the world. Similar to Microsoft, Apple has actively been involved in the promotion of school redesign – funding the establishment of their own 'School of the Future' public high school in 1990 in partnership with the New York City Department of Education. Somewhat ironically given Bill Gates' business background, the New York School of the Future has since gained financial support from, amongst others, the Bill and Melinda Gates Foundation.

Aside from the high-profile efforts of Apple and Microsoft, perhaps the most prominent commercial actors in educational technology are large-scale software and hardware producers such as Cisco, HP, Dell and Intel. The scope of these activities is illustrated through Cisco's programme of educational activities. Although less prominent than Microsoft or Apple in the minds of most technology users, Cisco remains one of the world's largest technology corporations with its interests concentrated on computer networking and hardware. Like its higher-profile competitors, Cisco also has developed an extensive involvement in technology-based educational reform. As the company's promotional material boasts, "Cisco is committed … [to] help reform and renew education throughout the world". As the company's 'Commitment to global education in the twenty-first century' statement goes on to contend: "We believe that the same technologies that created the internet and the information revolution have the power to transform education for the twenty-first century and lay the foundation for a better future for countless young people".

Underpinning this rhetoric is Cisco's involvement in a range of educational ventures around the world. Many of these efforts are focused on the redesign of education systems – a philosophy detailed in the company's production of an Education 3.0 roadmap. These discussions are supported by the hosting of online forums to support and stimulate 'the latest thinking' in educational leadership, alongside a range of practical interventions. For example, Cisco's 'Twenty-first Century Schools Initiative' has used a combination of hands-on expertise from the company's Education Fellows and funding for the rebuilding, re-equipping, retraining and redesigning of strategically selected schools. This saw the company involved, for example, in the rebuilding of schools affected by the 2005 hurricanes in the Gulf Coast region of the US. On a worldwide level, Cisco fund and support a Cisco Networking Academy designed to provide online training, testing and accreditation for individuals wishing to train as IT professionals regardless of geographic or socio-economic circumstance. Since 1997, this online initiative has included more than 2.7 million aspiring IT professionals in over 165 countries.

Understanding the Significance of the Private Sector in Educational Technology

All these examples illustrate the extensive and diverse nature of private and commercial activity in various forms of educational technology provision and practice. In many ways, then, the educational technology programmes of companies such as Cisco, Microsoft and Apple should be seen as approaching (and in some cases exceeding) the educational technology programmes of national governments. As such, the activities of these companies and their commercial competitors are key to the sustenance of many instances of educational technology use around the world. Often these commercial interests operate alongside each other, as evident in Michelle Selinger's (2009) recounting of a Kenyan scheme where schools were provided with laptops by British Airways, subsidised internet access from Microsoft and wireless access points paid for by Cisco. As this example suggests, technology is an area of educational provision where there is ample room for different commercial interests to get involved in whatever ways and for whatever reasons they see fit. Crucially, this has seen the increased involvement of commercial interests with no direct background in either technology or education. Considerable consternation was caused in 2009, for example, by the involvement of the McDonald's restaurant chain in funding state-endorsed online mathematics tuition for Australian school students.

Indeed, as with the non-profit activities of SNOs and IGOs described earlier, the intentions and effects of these commercial agendas are varied. On one hand, involvement with educational technology is clearly of symbolic value to the companies concerned – being seen 'to be doing something' above and beyond selling products and pursuing profits. The positioning of many of these activities within 'corporate social responsibility' and 'community programmes' reflects the desire of many companies to project a distinct philanthropic air to their support of educational technology use. In this sense, educational technology provides a ready means for what Stephen Ball terms the "import of American-style corporate philanthropy and the use of 'positional investments' by business organisations and the 'acting out' of corporate social responsibility" (Ball 2007, p.122). As just described, these positional investments take a variety of forms – from the 'donation' of computer equipment to local schools, to the commercially sponsored re-equipping and re-training of whole education systems.

Of course, it would be overly simplistic to attribute the actions of firms solely to motivations of altruism and philanthropy. It should be remembered that the procurement of educational technology represents a lucrative market within which IT industry actors operate. In making sense of these 'philanthropic' activities we should remain mindful of the overriding interest that these commercial organisations have in the selling and supplying of digital resources to educational institutions around the world. As Tim Unwin observes, this motivation could certainly be said to drive commercial involvement in the educational sectors of countries where domestic markets for digital technology are still emerging:

> The ICT sector has been a key agent in the processes of globalisation, and has likewise benefitted greatly in terms of expanded markets and reduced labour costs. It is therefore very much in the interests of private capital to see an expanded take-up of ICTs across the world. In the richest countries, increasing market saturation of mobile phones and computers means that companies involved in their production have to innovate ever more creatively in order to continue to expand their revenues. An alternative, though, is for them to seek to expand their markets more extensively in countries where the take-up of their technologies has so far been limited. Hence, global ICT corporations have a real interest in encouraging governments and international organisations to facilitate their penetration into such markets, and one way in which they do this is by engaging actively in programmes that propound the benefits of their technologies.
>
> *(Unwin 2009b, p. 161)*

As Unwin implies, if anything, the main commercial gains to be made from the involvement of major IT firms in educational technology are indirect and long term. Rather than resulting in immediate and substantial profits, most firm's educational technology activities could be said to be based around the establishment of 'brand awareness' and loyalty amongst future customers, as well as lending them the kudos of being visibly involved in apparently 'socially responsible' activities. These long-term motivations were illustrated, for example, in Google's justification for its development of online services for education institutions during the 2000s in terms of developing the brand-loyalty of young users 'for life' (Paton 2007, p.11). Similarly, as Jodi Dean observed with regard to the trend during the 1990s for the corporate donation of IT equipment to educational institutions, "computer companies' donations of computers to schools [...] are clearly implicated in the production of new users, consumers, and markets" (Dean 2002, p.143).

Of course, this is not to argue that the involvement of the private sector in supporting and sustaining the use of technology across educational contexts is a wholly cynical development. Indeed, such actions could be welcomed as bringing valuable industrial expertise and professionalism to bear on an area of education where the established educational community lacks expertise and experience. As Michelle Selinger (2009, p.240) reasons:

> For some this may look like the commodification and takeover of education by global corporations, whereas others see it as an opportunity to put relevant curricula into schools that provide students with some of the twenty-first century skills not currently being provided by the formal education system. In many cases the international private sector working with the local private sector has also led to capacity development and growth of local companies, and creating employment opportunities.

It should be noted, however, that Selinger writes from the position of working as an educational director for Cisco. As has been illustrated above, there are many other commentators who would disagree with her benevolent reading of the involvement of private interests in the global governance of educational technology. While suspicions of private interests getting involved in the educational technology marketplace purely for the motivation of chasing the "possibility of super profits" (Dean 2002, p.3) may be overly simplistic, the apparently non-commercial educational activities of major IT companies are clearly guided by an element of self-interest as well as 'social responsibility' and altruism. At best, then, we can concur with Daniel Menchik's (2004, p.197) conclusion that "the line that separates benevolent, authentic concern for student learning enrichment from self-interested entrepreneurship [is] difficult to ascertain".

Making Sense of the Involvement of International Organisations in Educational Technology

While these various for-profit and non-profit international organisations may differ in their specific agendas and approaches, they certainly exert a powerful influence on the ways that educational technology is implemented and engaged with around the world. Of course, it can be argued that the involvement of these international and multinational actors is a welcome element in the support of educational technology growth around the world. As Bergeron (2008, p.352) reasons, it perhaps makes little sense to deny the need for additional investment in any aspect of education provision and practice "when education remains so woefully underfunded in many locations". Nevertheless, it is important for us to retain a critical distance when considering the aims, interests and agendas that underlie the seemingly benign actions of these public and private international organisations. It is perhaps most important to recognise that these organisations are not acting independently of one another. Instead, in fully understanding the influence of these organisations on the nature of educational technology around the world we need to acknowledge the considerable interplay and interchange amongst these groups in terms of ideas, values, agendas and even personnel.

As such, the main influence and importance of these international organisations should not be seen in isolated or mutually exclusive terms. Instead, in making sense of how these different organisations shape educational technology, we need to recognise the inter-organisational dynamics and collaborative activities between different groups. Key here is understanding how the activities of these supranational agencies, intergovernmental organisations and multinational corporations work in combination to shape the nature and form of what is encountered as 'educational technology' around the world. We, therefore, need to recognise how these organisations add to the circulation of ideas and concepts that sharpen understandings and steer expectations of what educational technology is, and what educational technology is for. As such, it is useful to see the activities and influences of all these different interests as often mutually reinforcing and co-complementary, despite the clear differences that exist in terms of long-term motivations or ultimate aims.

A prominent example of the combined nature of these interests is the notion of 'twenty-first-century skills' – an increasingly pervasive feature of educational technology discourses and debates around the world throughout the 2000s and 2010s. At one level, the notion of 'twenty-first-century skills' is a straightforward and increasingly uncontested element of current educational thinking. As such, 'twenty-first-century skills' is now an accepted description of the required skill-sets, competencies, pedagogies, curricular and assessment reforms and systemic arrangements that are seen to underpin education reform over the 2010s and 2020s – quite simply a blueprint for education in a digital age. While descriptions of these 'twenty-first-century skills' may vary, the underlying imperatives remain the same – i.e. changing the structures, processes and practices of schools, teachers and students along more high-tech, networked and 'innovative' lines. While these descriptions may appear plausible, the questions of how and why the idea of 'twenty-first-century skills' came to be promoted with the success that it has, provides an interesting insight into the influence of all the actors and interests outlined in this chapter so far.

First, it is worth considering the many ways in which the idea of 'twenty-first-century skills' was developed and promoted over the 2000s. Here it would seem that the rise of the notion of 'twenty-first-century skills' was co-ordinated in no small part through the efforts of a number of supranational organisations involved in formulating frameworks, raising issues and agenda-setting. Key here was UNESCO's ICT Competency Framework for Teachers with its explicit focus on 'twenty-first-century skills'. Also of significance was the OECD New Millennium Learners programme with its positioning of so-called twenty-first-century competencies (defined as "the skills and competencies that a knowledge economy requires") within the educational agenda for the PISA comparative educational indicators. Alongside these developments, were the efforts of multinational technology corporations in facilitating research and development efforts to outline and promote the 'principles' of twenty-first-century skills. One such initiative was the 'Apple Classrooms of Tomorrow – Today' programme (ACOT²), run during the 2000s with its aim of "changing the conversation about teaching, technology and learning". Notably, the first phase of the ACOT[2] study identified six design principles for the twenty-first-century high school, including the reorientation of curriculum and content, assessment and the social/emotional environment of skills around the notion of 'twenty-first-century skills and outcomes'. Similar agendas were subsequently pursued through Microsoft's Innovative Teaching and Learning global research programme with its focus on 'twenty-first-century learning outcomes' and 'innovative teaching practices' characterised by student-centred pedagogy, knowledge building, problem-solving and innovation, skilled communication, collaboration, self-regulation, and use of technology for learning.

While each of these initiatives was significant in their own right, the influence of these efforts should be understood as occurring in a cumulative and iterative manner. Take, for example, the ways in which the internationally-articulated notion of 'twenty-first-century skills' has been operationalised in a country such as the US through the efforts of other intermediary organisations to promote, advocate and lobby these ideas and values in policy and practitioner circles. In the US, a major presence in this respect has been the 'Partnership for twenty-first-century skills' – a nationwide advocacy organisation that in its own words works to "help inform other major education conversations". The Partnership for twenty-first-century skills was formed in 2002 under the guidance of Ken Kay (CEO and co-founder of e-Luminate education consulting firm) and Diny Golder-Dardis on behalf of JES & Co (a publicly funded educational R&D programme in the US responsible for online learning systems and online content management). Through the initial support of the US Department of Education, commercial partners such as AOL Time Warner, Apple, Cisco, Dell and Microsoft, as well as public organisations such as the National Education Association, the partnership has established itself as a powerful self-styled 'advocacy organisation' for promoting the concept of 'twenty-first-century knowledge and skills'. Much of the partnership's public profile has been built around popularising the notion of 'the four Cs': i.e. critical thinking and problem solving; communication; collaboration; and creativity and innovation.

Of immediate interest here is the involvement of many of the international organisations highlighted throughout this chapter. In effect, Microsoft, Apple and other organisations are underwriting local support for agendas that they themselves were implicit in initiating at a global level. As such the 'Partnership for twenty-first-century skills' represents a powerful consortium of international interests: covering hardware companies (Microsoft, Apple, Intel, Dell, Cisco, HP); software companies (Adobe, Blackboard); educational publishers (Pearson, McGraw-Hill); edutainment producers (Lego, Disney); and various public and private groups (such as American Association of School Librarians, National Academy Foundation). More esoteric partners include Cable in the Classroom – a group promoting the interests of the cable television industry in providing educational content to schools; Knowledge-Works – a foundation dedicated to transforming US school education along learner-centred lines; and Education Networks of America – a private company providing 'managed internet services' to public school corporations. Despite its diverse constitution, this interest group has worked successfully to raise the profile of the issue of twenty-first-century skills within the US education system. The partnership has produced frameworks and resources, hosted National Summits for education leaders and policymakers, and even influenced state education policy. The partnership played a key role, for example, in supporting West Virginia to change the content of its state-wide assessment programmes and 'professional development expectations' to include the teaching and assessment of twenty-first-century skills in the classroom. The partnership also supported the US Conference of Mayors to pass a policy resolution supporting an educational framework for 'twenty-first-century readiness'.

Thus the fact that 'twenty-first-century skills' is now a component of assessment in West Virginian schools is due to a complex circuit of interests and events that originated far beyond local educational officials in Charleston or even federal officials in Washington, DC. Indeed, all of these examples show how the efforts of SNOs, TNCs, MNCs and IGOs interact with other private and public actors at national and local levels to produce a range of models, frameworks and evidence for what 'educational technology' is and what it is used for. These international organisations, therefore, play an extensive but largely obscured role in setting agendas and influencing 'the tone of the conversation' around educational technology. While working to construct cases for change, these organisations also work to provide the means to achieve that change – thus taking responsibility for defining problems *and* defining their solutions. The success of these actions is subtle but significant. Take, for example, the vocabulary that reflects recent shifts in the dominant discourses that surround popular, professional and policy discussions of education and technology – not least terms such as 'innovation', 'personalisation', 'enhancement' and 'redesign'.

Given this complex of activity, it is worth reminding ourselves of the reasons and rationales underpinning all these efforts. Of course, on the one hand, there is a desire to instigate a 'technological culture' into education systems and to ensure the continuation of markets for educational technology products. However, these efforts are also driven by wider efforts to pursue neo-liberal agendas of making the connection between technology use and the human capital interests of the knowledge economies and the continuation of the global economic competition outlined in Chapter 1. It is clear from the example above, how the 'twenty-first-century skills' agenda maps closely onto what are assumed to be the required skill-sets of the knowledge economy. Indeed, it could be argued that the focus of the 'twenty-first-century skills' concept was not simply to get more digital devices placed into schools, but to support the transformation of economy and society. As one of the intellectual architects of the 'twenty-first-century skills' agenda described it, "knowledge creation, technology, technological innovativeness and knowledge sharing can contribute to the transformation of the education system and to sustained economic growth and social development" (Kozma 2005, p.142).

Conclusions

As the case of the 'twenty-first-century skills' agenda highlights, the activities of international organisations play an important, if often low-profile, role in influencing the tone of national and regional policy agendas as well as the nature of actual practice 'on the ground'. Although the involvement of international actors can be seen as a necessary (or even welcome) component of the politics and provision of education technology, it is notable how their agendas and actions tend to coalesce around sets of common values and assumptions. Indeed, many of the actions that have been discussed in this chapter work to position educational technology as a central component of the neo-liberal framing of 'education' and – it follows – the promotion of corporatised and marketised restructurings of a technology-rich world system along market lines. Of course, in making these arguments, there is a danger of over-stating or exaggerating the influence of these international interests on educational use of digital technologies. As was noted earlier, these organisations are seeking largely to exert various forms of 'soft' power within the global politics of education and technology. As such, we need to remember that the efforts of all the international organisations outlined in this chapter are not necessarily expected to result in the direct change of educational technology *per se* – but rather to influence the general climate and context of educational technology provision and practice. As Rizvi and Lingard (2010, p.38) put it, these organisations are therefore concerned primarily with "influencing, cajoling and directing" national governments – or in the words of Stephen Ball (1998, p.124), suggesting and sponsoring particular policy 'solutions' to identified educational 'problems'.

One key point of significance to take forward into the next chapter, therefore, is the often unspoken linkages between the international and the national levels of influence on education and technology. The connections between the actions of these transnational and supranational interests and the actions of national governments are clearly complex. In terms of the significance of supranational agencies and intergovernmental organisations, for example, one hitherto "deceptively obvious point" is that many of these bodies (such as OECD, UNESCO and the EU) are the deliberate creation of national governments who have ceded a degree of their national sovereignty or autonomy in order to pursue the national interest more effectively (Dale and Robertson 2002, p.15). Similarly, the ultimate interests of multinational IT corporations such as Microsoft, Cisco and Apple could be said to be focused more on local markets than on the actions of national governments themselves. At best, then, the agendas and interests outlined in this chapter can only be expected to influence what goes on at the level of national government "by means of the trickle-down effect" (Dale and Robertson 2002, p.15). With this thought in mind, it is worth thinking further about the role of the nation state in the shaping of educational technology. In fact, given the extensive influence of all the international interests reviewed in this chapter, what role is there for the nation state at all?

4

EDUCATION, TECHNOLOGY AND NATIONAL POLICYMAKING

Introduction

While many commentators continue to predict the 'death' of the nation state, it would be unwise to overlook the influence of national governments on educational technology. As Andy Green (2003, p.86) observes, "governments still seek to manage their national systems – indeed, in some ways, more actively than before ... they know that education remains one area where they still have some control". This chapter therefore considers the influence of national policymaking and policy institutions on the educational technology arrangements of different countries. In particular we examine the political economy of national educational technology governance and explore the inter-relationships between educational technology policymaking and the economic, social and cultural fortunes of individual nations.

This approach implies the development of a historical perspective on the formation of educational technology policymaking. As such we need to look back to the emergence of national information technology policies during the 1980s, when governments and politicians in industrialised countries were keen to capitalise on the kudos of being seen to 'do something' about new forms of microelectronics and computer technology. The use of digital technology in educational settings then gained a heightened policy prominence during the mid-1990s with the mainstream emergence of the internet (see Ham and Cha 2009). From that time onwards, digital technology and 'new media' have attracted the sustained attention of public policymakers in developed and developing countries alike. This chapter considers what part such policymaking activity has played in shaping the use of technology in education around the world – not least in terms of setting an agenda for what 'educational technology' is and what values are associated with it.

Educational Technology Policymaking as a Global Trend

Although considered rarely in the academic study of educational technology, state governance has an obvious influence on contemporary education arrangements. At a basic level, education policies are an official representation of the courses of action taken by governments and other agencies of the state with respect to their obligations to deliver and regulate education provision. State policies therefore set out an official 'bottom line' on a wide range of educational issues – from the nature of what education institutions are legally obliged to provide to their students, to the amounts and types of funding that are directed towards different components of an education system. Education technology policy can therefore be seen as a formalisation of state intent to guide the implementation of digital technologies throughout national education systems. As Peeraer and Tran (2009, p.1) describe, "strategic policies can provide a rationale, a set of goals, and a vision for how education systems might be with the introduction of ICT".

It is therefore understandable that the integration of digital technology into education systems has been a growing feature of state education policymaking over the past three decades. From initial efforts in the UK, Sweden and Canada at the start of the 1980s, the past thirty years have witnessed a steady expansion of educational technology policymaking around the world. During the 1980s these policies revolved largely around the provision of computers in classrooms and the development of 'computer literacy' amongst students and teachers. Policymaking during the 1990s and 2000s then commonly took the form of nationwide programmes of teacher training and support for indigenous IT industries – introduced by national governments keen to ensure that the circumstances existed for the effective educational use of internet-based digital technologies.

Now as the 2010s progress, educational technology can be said to constitute a major policy concern across all nations, regardless of a country's global prominence or relative economic wealth. Whereas state policymaking during the 1980s and 1990s was confined mainly to (over)developed countries in North America, northern Europe and the 'tiger economies' of East Asia, the 2000s saw educational technology emerge as a 'global field' of educational policy (see Lingard *et al.* 2005). Now most countries in the world – regardless of political, economic or social circumstance – boast substantial educational technology strategies. For example, educational technology has become a common element of the efforts of African nations to progress to 'middle income' status – from the Ethiopian 'ICT in Education Implementation Strategy' to the Rwandan government's extensive twenty-year information and communication plan (Rubagiza *et al.* 2011). This trend is replicated across the northern and southern hemispheres – from the Jordanian 'National Goals for Schooling in the Twenty-First Century' to the Brazilian 'Proinfo Integrado' programme (see Qablan *et al.* 2009, Fidalgo-Neto *et al.* 2009). The worldwide scale of this policy activity during the 2000s prompted one review to conclude that "the unchecked fear of missing the fast ICT train to global prominence has resulted in [a] global chase after e-learning" (Zhao *et al.* 2006, p.673).

Some commentators have noted a distinct homogeneity across much of this policymaking activity, with the educational technology policy agendas of many countries appearing to conform to an 'unusually common' set of characteristics regardless of otherwise varied national contexts (Zhao *et al.* 2006). Indeed, while the educational technology policies of Jordan, Ethiopia, Brazil and Rwanda are not *wholly* indistinguishable from each other, there has certainly been a strong 'family resemblance' between state policies the world over. For instance, most countries' initial forms of educational technology policymaking shared a common focus on introducing computer equipment and internet connectivity into classrooms and establishing system-wide programmes of teacher training and development. These initial efforts tended to be followed by policies seeking to address issues of pedagogic practice and thereby stimulate 'bottom-up' demand for technology-based learning and teaching amongst teachers, parents and school administrators. In all these forms, most of the educational technology initiatives that emerged since the 1980s shared the characteristics of being well funded, focused on increasing the availability of digital technologies in schools and targeted carefully at a limited set of measurable outcomes. More often than not, they also involved the amendment of school curricula to require teaching and learning through technology, as well as the introduction of sets of measures to ensure that teachers had the knowledge and skills to make use of digital technologies in their classrooms. As such, there would seem to be a number of common 'operational components' underpinning most countries' educational technology policies – i.e. pedagogical and curricular change, content development, technical support and relatively high levels of funding for technical resources (Kozma 2008).

National Histories of Educational Technology Policymaking

In one sense, then, it is tempting to account for individual national policy programmes as simply part of a wider harmonised 'global policy convergence' towards technology and education (see Jenson *et al.* 2007). Following this line of argument, any specific educational technology policy could be seen as replicating a wider prevailing "international circulations of ideas" about technology and education reform, rather than marking a particularly national response (Halpin and Troyna 1995). Yet from a comparative perspective, the development of different national educational technology policies must be understood as historical, and thereby rooted in very different social contexts. As Rizvi and Lingard (2010, p.15) note, all "policies exist in context: they have a prior history, linked to earlier policies, particular individuals and agencies". We therefore need to consider the development of these different national educational technology policies and strategies from a more detached, critical and certainly more historical standpoint. As Robin Mansell (2004, p.102) suggests, this involves fostering an "understanding of pressures towards the commodification of [educational technology] and its consequences for the way in which power is distributed through the material conditions" of individual nations. The next sections of this chapter offer analyses of five different examples of the seemingly global turn towards educational technology. So what can be learnt from the policy histories of countries such as the UK, US, Japan, Chile and Singapore?

Educational Technology Policymaking in the UK

The UK has one of the longest records of state involvement in educational technology, with sustained government interest starting from the beginning of the 1980s. One of the most significant elements of early government activity was the 1981 Micros in Schools scheme, which saw the UK government subsidising 50 per cent of the cost of one microcomputer to every computerless school in the country. Although restricting schools' choice of machine to one of two British-made machines, over 4,000 secondary schools had ordered microcomputers by 1982 and over 27,000 primary schools by 1984. This impetus was further reinforced by the concurrent Microelectronics in Education Programme with its dual brief to promote the use of microcomputers in schools and to develop the teaching of IT as a subject of study. This burgeoning state interest in schools' use of technology continued into the mid-1980s with the formation of a National Council for Educational Technology and the continued funding of school IT equipment purchases through the Software in Schools and Modems in Schools programmes, as well as the subsequent New Technology for Better Schools programme. Then, at the end of the 1980s, came a commitment to place "basic IT skills at the heart" of the new National Curriculum (Dearing 1993, p.28). Politically, at least, the notion of 'educational' computing had certainly been affirmed in UK schools by the start of the 1990s (see Selwyn 2002).

A second wave of interest from policymakers came with the New Labour administration between 1997 and 2010, with its sustained agenda of policymaking focusing on the now rebranded area of 'information and communications technology' (ICT). Most notably the UK schools sector was subject to three distinct phases of policymaking: the 1998 to 2002 National Grid for Learning initiative which focused on establishing internet connectivity and a nationwide teacher-training programme; the 2002 to 2005 ICT in Schools drive and associated Curriculum Online and e-learning credit schemes; and the 2005 to 2010 Harnessing Technology agenda underpinned by a sector-wide e-learning strategy. This succession of well-resourced flagship agendas was complemented by a succession of smaller discrete programmes and schemes – such as the provision of laptop computers to head-teachers, the subsidised provision of broadband internet connections to low-income families, and the establishment of various regulatory bodies, advisory bodies and 'watchdogs'. Thus in terms of policy and practice, the 2000s saw schools technology once again transformed into a significant educational concern, involving the deployment of an estimated £5 billion of state funding during this time towards schools digital technology use.

Educational Technology Policymaking in the US

The United States also boasts a long history of educational technology policy activity. After a series of relatively modest initiatives during the 1980s, the first concerted educational technology policy efforts coincided with the launch of the Clinton/Gore administration's 'US National Information Infrastructure' (NII) initiative during the early 1990s. The broad aim of this initiative was to create a nationwide information and communications network connecting homes, businesses and public institutions to the so-called 'information superhighway'. Although the Federal government took responsibility for promoting the NII and creating the market conditions for private providers to flourish, the development and implementation of the NII was left largely to the private sector. In educational terms, the promise of an internet connection to every classroom in every school was a central tenet of the official promotion of this ambitious policy drive. These efforts were bolstered by the launch in 1996 of the country's first 'National Education Technology Plan' under the title of 'Getting America's students ready for the twenty-first century'. In order to facilitate these plans, the Federal Government issued a Technology Literacy Challenge that made available $2 billion of funding to provide every classroom with internet access and 'modern multimedia computers', technology-related training and support for all teachers and the establishment of a network of 'effective on-line learning resources'.

This interest in educational technology continued throughout the Clinton administration. The 1998 E-Rate initiative provided a further $2.25 billion per annum to the Universal Services Fund, effectively offering means-tested discounts for schools to purchase internal and external network connections. In practice, the connection of US schools to the internet varied from state to state with many business-led voluntary Net-Days taking the place of any centralised approach. A second National Education Technology Plan was released towards the end of the Clinton administration with the title of 'E-learning: putting a world-class education at the fingertips of all children'. This impetus continued (albeit at more modest levels) through the George W. Bush administrations between 2001 and 2008, primarily via the inclusion of a requirement within the 'No Child Left Behind' Act that all students should become technology literate by the end of the eighth grade. The Bush administration also oversaw the introduction of a third National Education Technology Plan in 2004 with the exhortative title 'Toward a new golden age in American Education – how the internet, the law and today's students are revolutionizing expectations'.

The Democrat administration of Barack Obama then oversaw the introduction of an extensive fourth National Education Technology Plan in 2010 – titled 'Transforming American education: learning powered by technology'. This outlined five areas of development: using digital technology to support 'engaging and empowering learning experiences'; technology-based assessment and data collection; ensuring 'teachers' access to data, content, resources, expertise and learning'; making technological infrastructure 'available for learning when and where learners and educators need it'; and the 'redesign of education processes and structures to take advantage' of technology-supported productivity. Alongside a continued commitment to fund the procurement of technology and teacher training, the Obama plan proved to be the impetus for a number of ambitious data-related programmes – not least providing 'open' access to educational resources through a Federal government-run Learning Registry, and sharing educational data on students and institutions through a 'National Education Data Model'.

Educational Technology Policymaking in Japan

While technology education (*gijutsu ka*) had been a required school subject since the end of the 1950s, the Japanese government was relatively slow to introduce computer technology into its formal education policy arrangements. In the late 1980s, the government introduced a computer literacy component into lower secondary school curriculum (entitled 'Fundamentals of Information') while also requiring the use of computers in upper-secondary school science and mathematics classes (see Murata and Stern 1993). During the latter half of the 1990s, the Japanese government then moved to establish a 'Japanese Information Infrastructure' (JII), keen to reaffirm its international technological reputation. The construction of the technological infrastructure alone was estimated to cost ¥100 trillion with targets of educational and health institutions being connected to the internet by 2000 and all homes by 2010 (Latzer 1995).

Although most of the JII plans were financed by the private sector, the health and education elements of network services were government led. This saw the introduction in 1999 of the 'IT in Education Project' with its original intention of having all primary and secondary schools connected to the internet by 2003 – a date that was later moved forward by a combination of additional government funding and private sector commitments to offer discounted rates to schools. In educational terms, then, the main focus of the JII drive was on meeting the perceived needs of an 'information-orientated society', with a practical emphasis placed on developing information literacy and encouraging the efficient use of information (see McLaughlin 1999). A revised IT based curriculum was introduced to all schools in 2002, with newly qualified teachers required to gain qualifications in information systems and information retrieval from the internet.

In 2003 an extensive 'e-Japan Strategy' was then introduced, featuring a number of new education-related targets and goals – not least the promise of high-speed internet connections to be established in classrooms in all public schools alongside the achievement of a student–computer ratio of 5.4 by 2005. Despite these targets only being partially met, a subsequent raft of digital technology-based plans was introduced as part of the Japanese government's 2009 'School New Deal Plan'. This proposed the introduction of electronic whiteboards into all schools, laptops provided to teachers, alongside the establishment of school local area networks and a reduction in student–computer ratios to 3.6. These technology-based elements of the School New Deal Plan were expected to exceed ¥200 billion.

Educational Technology Policymaking in Chile

While often considered a relatively peripheral nation in terms of its geographical location and economic power, Chile is nevertheless recognised as a leading nation in terms of educational technology policy. This stems in part from Chile's early educational technology pilot programmes – not least the country's 'Improvement of Educational Quality Program' that included an ambitious 'educational informatics' programme at the start of the 1990s. This sought to establish a computer communications network linking schools with selected universities and other educational institutions. These initial efforts led to the subsequent 'Enlaces' national educational technology initiative (translating as 'connections' or 'linkages'). The Enlaces programme was launched in 1992 with an initial goal of connecting 100 schools via networked computing within five years. The provision of computer equipment was soon extended to the majority of schools in 1994, with the programme now covering over 98 per cent of Chile's 11,000 publicly supported primary and secondary schools, and reaching 92 per cent of the student population (Hinostroza *et al.* 2011). As Sánchez and Salinas (2008, p.1622) conclude, "the Enlaces network has been considered one of the most systematic, successful and sustainable programs in the region in order to cope with the special geography and culture of the country, including rural, urban, indigenous, and community education".

Alongside the provision of computer equipment and internet connectivity, Enlaces has also promoted the development of educational digital resources, extensive programmes of in-service teacher training and support for technology-based pedagogical teaching methodologies. Under the programme, each school has been provided with computers (usually with the aim of establishing computer laboratories and local networks), basic teacher training and the support of a network of twenty-four universities. Enlaces is part of wider efforts to establish the digital transformation of Chilean society, with the government espousing broad and exhortative aims such as establishing 'a nation prepared for the future' and 'an economy integrated into the world'. Indeed, education featured in seven of the thirty-four initiatives within the 2004 'Chilean Digital Agenda', including targets of establishing fully equipped and internet connected schools and the integration of digital technology use into primary and secondary school curricula. Other goals outside school reforms included the 'National Digital Literacy Campaign' which promised digital literacy for half a million Chileans supported by a national system of certification of digital technology skills.

Enlaces has therefore been lauded for its longevity and continually evolving ambitions. The 2007 Chilean 'Technology Plan for Quality Education' programme worked towards the aim of achieving a student–computer ratio of 10:1, with over three-quarters of students in the public school system having access to computer technologies and internet, and over three-quarters of teachers having received training in digital technology use. Schools have been required to develop individual 'educational use of technology plans' committing them to technology use throughout most learning, teaching and management activities. A particular emphasis in light of the county's geographical and demographic diversity has been to ensure broadband and connectivity for rural schools – therefore aiming to ensure "access to the same resources of information and cultural interchange, regardless of social or geographical location" (Álvarez 2006, p.391). Over the first fifteen years of its operation Enlaces attracted funding levels in excess of US$200 million (Sánchez and Salinas 2008), with the programme continuing into the 2010s as an overarching framework for digital technology use in Chilean education.

Educational Technology Policymaking in Singapore

A final contrasting example is the small island city-state of Singapore which has also pursued a sustained and substantial educational technology drive over the past thirty years. The Singaporean government has long touted itself as overseeing the development of a world-leading information society, with the country's authorities pursuing what Mark Warschauer (2001, p.305) described as "one of the most far-reaching attempts to infuse information technology in society". These centralised political efforts have been embodied in three successive 'National ICT Master-plans' – part of an extensive series of wider carefully managed top-down techno-logical reforms. Originating with its first National Information Technology plan in 1987, Singapore followed a centralised 'IT2000 Vision' throughout the 1990s which was designed to establish the country as an 'intelligent island'. This was based initially around the integration of digital technology into eleven major sectors of society, ranging from construction and real estate to education and healthcare. Throughout the IT2000 and subsequent 'Singapore One' policy agendas, education was positioned as a major area in the creation of an advanced national information infrastructure. In educational terms, S$2 billion was committed to achieving the connection of every school to the internet, leading in 1998 to Singapore being the first nation to provide all of its primary and secondary schools with at least one internet connection.

From these beginnings, Singapore has consistently pursued the integration of digital technology in its educational system through the implementation of three 'Masterplan' policy agendas from 1997 to 2014. The first 'Masterplan for ICT in Education' committed S$2 billion of investment between 1997 and 2002, setting detailed targets for the equipping of schools with computers and internet connections, based on eventual targets of one computer for every two students and over a quarter of the school curriculum to be technologically-based. Further investments of S$600 million a year were made to maintain and replace hardware, develop new software, and provide for the continuous training of teachers. A second S$470 million Masterplan then maintained this momentum between 2003 and 2008, setting baseline technology standards for all schools, establishing technology-orientation assessment and accreditation schemes, as well as continuing state investment in hardware and software. This phase also saw the Singaporean government collaborating with the private sector to establish six technology-rich 'FutureSchools@Singapore' primary and secondary schools. A third S$840 million Masterplan (2009–14) has extended these efforts by concentrating, in the Singaporean government's words, on 'strengthening the integration of ICT into curriculum, assessment and pedagogy' and using digital technology to develop 'competencies for the twenty-first century'.

Unpacking the Motivations behind National Educational Technology Policymaking

The significance of all these policy programmes extends clearly beyond their varying financial scope and technological ambition. Indeed, at first glance it could be concluded that these different approaches to infusing national education systems with digital technology follow an essentially deterministic expectation of technological change leading to substantial educational improvement. Yet upon further inspection, it is difficult to argue convincingly that national policymakers have developed such policies and initiatives solely with 'educational' outcomes in mind. Instead, it could be observed that these are all policies intended to address a number of economic, social and cultural issues within each country. As such, all these different examples of educational technology policymaking could also be seen as ideological forms whose internal contradictions and 'fuzziness' serve to mask a range of wider non-educational agendas they have been used to propagate within their specific national contexts.

One significant aspect of the policy programmes just described is their role in shaping wider understandings and expectations of education – with nation states using these education policies to play an important legitimising and normalising role as discursive devices. The discursive role of policy refers to the meanings, intentions, values and beliefs that lie behind these formalised expressions of state intent. State policies can therefore be seen as symbolic systems of values, acting as a means of representing, accounting for and legitimating particular political decisions. In this discursive sense, then, the educational technology policies of the five countries described above could be seen as having been formulated not only to achieve material effects but also to manufacture support for those effects (see Ball 1998). With these distinctions in mind, it is therefore useful to reconsider the ways in which digital technology use has been imagined and 'written into' these state educational technology policies over the past thirty years, paying particular attention to the ideological values and implications that these policies set out to convey.

In this spirit, there are a number of themes and motivations that could be seen to underpin the educational technology policies of the UK, US, Japan, Chile and Singapore – not least the ways in which the educational implementation of digital technology appears to have been driven consistently by a well-worn set of mandates pertaining to deal with economic success in the globalised 'knowledge economy'. Indeed Zhao *et al.* (2006) pointed out 'tremendous' and 'remarkable' similarities between the policy agendas of developed and developing countries during the 1990s and 2000s – contending that most countries' national educational technology policy programmes portrayed a close relationship between the increased use of technology in educational institutions and later success in global economic markets. This had resulted in what these authors described as "a techno-centric, utopian and economic driven mind-set" amongst policymakers the world over (Zhao *et al.* 2006, p.674).

Linkages between education technology and global economic concerns are certainly evident throughout the recent history of educational technology policymaking in the UK, US, Japan, Chile and Singapore. For instance, it is noticeable how investment in education and technology was used during the 1990s as a major prop in the theatre of economic conflict between nations – especially in countries such as the US and UK. This was apparent in these countries' attempts to enhance national competitiveness by creating education systems seen fit to support and drive successful knowledge economies. Indeed, the framing of educational technology in terms of economic competition was laid out explicitly in official political pronouncements of the combination of education and technology being "the best economic policy we have" (Tony Blair, cited in DfEE 1998, p.9), and as a crucial element in 'winning' the twenty-first century (Bill Clinton, cited in Information Infrastructure Task Force 1993). In the eyes of these policymakers and others like them, the economic rather than pedagogic significance of educational technology could be said to have driven and shaped its implementation in the classroom.

It is, therefore, tempting to critique these educational technology policies as little more than speculative attempts by nation states to improve local educational conditions while also hoping to bolster their economic fortunes. Indeed, state technology policies such as these have tended to attract criticism from policy analysts for their "narrow definitions" and "simple-minded goals" predicated mainly upon a global form of economic success (Jensen and Lauritsen 2005, p.353). Yet the notion of these educational policies being driven solely by common aspirations of economic success is perhaps an over-simplification of more complex sets of struggles and negotiations that have shaped all of the national policy histories outlined in this chapter. As such, an economically determinist reading of educational technology policymaking could be said to run the risk of over-simplifying many subtle but significant divergences in the policymaking efforts of different nation states.

It is useful, therefore, to view the apparently global economic basis for educational technology policymaking as obscuring a more complex political economy of nation building. As we saw in Chapter 2, a political economy perspective focuses attention on the relationship between education, economy and society in different national contexts, and therefore challenges the extent to which globalisation is leading to a convergence in national approaches to these issues. An emphasis on the political economy of nation building, therefore, introduces questions of how educational technology policies are related to broader issues concerning the attempts of nation states to develop different models of contemporary society that ensure continued economic growth and social stability. The political economy of the educational technology strategies outlined in this chapter can therefore be explored in greater detail through a reconsideration of the stated aims of the programmes in each country. Indeed, the content of key policy documents produced over the last three decades the UK, US, Japan, Chile and Singapore can be reinterpreted in terms of a number of closely inter-related dimensions. These include issues relating to: the economics of education; the economy of education; education and the economy; citizenship building; and, finally, the construction of national identity. All these dimensions are now considered in further detail.

Educational Technology and the Economic Concerns of Nation States

Most cases of educational technology policy are certainly driven to some extent by the complex relationship between state, economy, industry and other economic stakeholders. As such, educational technology policies can be seen to satisfy at least three specific economic and political criteria (see Ball 2007). These can be described as the economics of education (i.e. the notion of technology contributing to the efficient logistics of educational provision); the economy and education (i.e. the notion of technology contributing to the profitability and commoditisation of education); and education and the economy (i.e. the notion of technology contributing to countries' economic competitiveness and efficiency of labour and knowledge production).

On one hand, many of the national policies outlined earlier can be understood as seeking to address the practical issue of the economics of education – i.e. the provision of education that is cost-effective and efficient. Indeed, the discourse of establishing technology-based provision and practices across the educational systems of the UK, US, Japan, Chile and Singapore has tended to be expressed in three different ways, namely: using digital technology to improve educational opportunities; using digital technology to improve educational standards; and, in a more radical form, using digital technology to remould or transform systems of education. Indeed, the UK policy drives of the late 1990s and 2000s were often positioned around the aims of 'modernising the classroom' (DfEE 1998) and 'driving up standards in schools' (David Blunkett in DfEE 1998). Over a decade later, the Chilean government was also describing digital technologies as "provid[ing] fundamental management tools on all levels of an educational system, from classrooms to ministries" (Chilean Ministry of Education 2011). The fourth US Educational Technology Plan similarly placed deliberate emphasis on using technology to "increase productivity", to "improv[ing] the education system at all levels" and the promise of achieving "revolutionary transformation rather than evolutionary tinkering"

(US Department of Education 2010). Indeed, the linkages between technology use and educational efficiency are exemplified in the following statement from the Obama administration's plan:

> To achieve our goal of transforming American education, we must rethink basic assumptions and redesign our education system. We must apply technology to implement personalised learning and ensure that students are making appropriate progress through our K-16 system so they graduate. These and other initiatives require investment, but tight economic times and basic fiscal responsibility demand that we get more out of each dollar we spend. We must leverage technology to plan, manage, monitor, and report spending to provide decision-makers with a reliable, accurate, and complete view of the financial performance of our education system at all levels. Such visibility is essential to meeting our goals for educational attainment within the budgets we can afford.
>
> *(US Department of Education 2010, p.x)*

These motivations notwithstanding, some instances of state interest in technology-based education are also centred on straightforward motivations of contemporary economic production. Indeed, the hope of using digital technology as a means of increasing the 'sale' of a nation's education products within domestic (and on occasion international) marketplaces is certainly evident in a few of the policy drives outlined above. As the UK government asserted at the launch of its planned 'e-University' initiative:

> Virtual networks eradicate the distance between the student and the provider, thus opening up a genuinely global learning market. Learning provision can be customised for individual need and delivered to specification, extending the boundaries of choice and flexibility beyond the confines of the seminar room or lecture hall. And learning is subject to new economies: once the investment in research and development of learning material has been made, the learning programme can be delivered at minimal marginal cost to an infinite number of people.
>
> *(Blunkett 2000)*

Instances such as these therefore see educational technology being used to reflect the dynamics of global capitalism and the intensification of the economic function of knowledge and learning. Interestingly, some of the rhetoric from the US government has stressed the use of digital technology to pursue redistributive rather than purely profit-making ends. In 1998, for example, President Clinton endorsed the expansion of technology-based education with a view to "guarantee universal, excellent education for every child on our planet". Similarly, the fourth Educational Technology Plan stressed the need to promote US-produced educational content into the non-profit 'open' economy of social media, arguing that: "information created or commissioned by the Government for educational use by teachers or students and made available online should clearly demarcate the public's right to use, modify, and distribute the information" (Federal Open Government Directive 2009, p.8).

These ambitions to use digital technology as a means of enhancing the distribution of education is often accompanied by a concurrent concern with supporting the economic function of a country's indigenous IT industry. For example, the 'infant industry' argument was certainly prominent in UK, US and Japanese efforts in the 1980s to introduce digital technology into educational settings. Here educational technology was presented as a means of stimulating the indigenous IT industry and technological research and development. Aside from offering a ready marketplace for local IT products, educational institutions were seen as a benign testing ground for the development of indigenous IT industries free from the more unforgiving realities of the open marketplace and critical consumers. As the UK government argued in 1980, "schools should be provided with small and low-cost micro-computers and software systems. To give a boost to our own hardware industry, they should be asked to design and supply these quickly" ('National Strategy for IT' 1980 – cited in Baker 1993, p.476).

Various aspects of the economics of educational technology notwithstanding, a further prominent theme that runs throughout all of the five nations' policy histories can be said to be one of comparative economic advantage. Within this discourse, educational technology policies have been presented typically as addressing two economic criteria. First, they represent a concerted attempt to change the economic 'mind-set' of future workers towards a technologically based global competition. This articulates with global economic concerns of national competitiveness, the up-skilling of workforces and performative logic of the labour market. As can be seen in the stated intentions of the US and Singaporean policy drives across the 1990s and 2000s:

> if we help all of our children to become technologically literate, we will give a generation of young people the skills they need to enter this new knowledge- and information-driven economy.
>
> *(US Department of Education 1996)*

> to equip [students] with the critical competencies and dispositions to succeed in a knowledge economy.
>
> *(Singapore Ministry of Education 2008)*

A further economic justification for investment in digital technology across education systems relates to the frequently stated need to up-grade the skills base of cohorts of new workers entering into national labour forces. This has often been articulated in terms of the notion of 'employability' and the increased importance attached to 'key' or 'core' skills, which include a working knowledge of digital technology. Such rhetoric can be seen as part of a larger discursive construction of the new 'model' workers considered necessary to meet the demands of the global knowledge economy. In this respect many governments have been explicit in their focus on the new 'high' skills requirements of the global economy. Technology-orientated education systems are thereby seen as supporting the development of the 'workforce flexibility' needed to counter the threat of a global labour market: "For students, using these real-world tools creates learning opportunities that allow them to grapple with real-world problems – opportunities that prepare them to be more productive members of a globally competitive workforce" (US Department of Education 2010, p.vii).

Over time, such justifications have developed around themes of using technology-based education as a way of addressing governments' perceived needs for future workforces with creative, innovative, critical, and active intellectual skills. Echoing the 'twenty-first-century skills' agenda outlined in Chapter 3, the policy agendas of Singapore, Chile and the US all reflect a set of similar intentions for technology-enhanced forms of flexible learning:

> We are looking deeper at how ICT enables our students to develop important twenty-first century competencies that are essential for their future. More time will be devoted in the curriculum to develop skills like self-directed and collaborative learning over the next five years.
>
> *(Grace Fu, Senior Minister of State, Singapore Ministry of Education 2010)*

> An important role of ICT inside a school is that of providing a new framework that can foster a revision and an improvement of teaching and learning practices to create more effective learning environments and improve life-long learning skills among students ... new learning strategies in which students can be more actively involved in learning, as opposed to being simply passive information receivers. Collaborative, project-based and self-paced learning are just a few alternatives largely documented and particularly appropriate to use when ICT are present.
>
> *(Chilean Ministry of Education 2011)*

> Whether the domain is English language, arts, mathematics, sciences, social studies, history, art, or music, twenty-first century competencies and expertise such as critical thinking, complex problem solving, collaboration, and multimedia communication should be woven into all content areas. These competencies are necessary to become expert learners, which we all must be if we are to adapt to our rapidly changing world over the course of our lives, and that involves developing deep understanding within specific content areas and making the connections between them.
>
> *(US Educational Technology Plan 2010, p.vi)*

Educational Technology and the Societal Concerns of Nation States

As all these examples suggest, the association between education technology and economic issues would seem to run deep across the policy agendas of all five nations. In many ways, then, educational technology is a prominent symbol of economic competitiveness between established and aspirant knowledge-driven economies. Yet these linkages notwithstanding, the complex social reality of educational technology should not be reduced solely to economic factors. Instead, we need to also consider the role of education technology in terms of the (re)formation of nation states. It is therefore worth reflecting on how the various education technology initiatives of the UK, US, Japan, Chile and Singapore also appear to fulfil similar functions with regard to the role of national education systems in the formation of nations as 'information societies'. In this sense, we need to explore the totemic use of education technology by nation states as a high-profile means of being seen to actually 'do something' about the reconstruction of society in the information age.

In this respect, a key societal aspect of the policy histories of the UK, US, Japan, Chile and Singapore has been the positioning of educational technology as a means of addressing issues of citizenship. For example, the Japanese and Singaporean educational technology policy agendas reflect a distinct recurrent desire to "equip children with the skills, attitudes and knowledge to participate in the modern nation state, including its bureaucracies, its morals and its ideological foundation" (Lim and Hedberg 2009, p.170). This has certainly been expressed in these countries' emphases on encouraging 'appropriate', 'responsible' and 'wise' use of technology amongst their student populations. In Singapore, for example, the third Masterplan included the provision of "cyber-wellness programmes in schools to encourage the responsible use of ICT among students" (Grace Fu – Ministry of Education, 2010). Conversely, in Japan, great emphasis was placed during the 2000s on "teaching children how to use wisely the new media" (e-Japan Strategy 2003).

In contrast to this promotion of a collective sense of technology-related citizenship, much attention has been paid in countries such as the US and UK to the role of educational technology in pre-empting potential problems of the emerging 'information society' for the individual citizen. In many countries – especially during the 1990s and 2000s – educational technology was positioned as a key aspect in state efforts to address issues of 'opportunity' especially for lower socio-economic groups and other marginalised communities. US and UK policy programmes over the last three decades, for example, have reflected long-standing concerns over using education as a means of countering the creation of 'digital divides' and new forms of digital exclusion. Early US policies spoke of the desire to "provide resources for those communities facing the greatest challenges" (US Department of Education 1996). As UK politicians argued nearly fifteen years later, the educational use of digital technology "is a powerful weapon in the fight against poverty"

(Iain Duncan Smith, cited in Manifesto for a Networked Britain 2010, p.62). These issues have also featured in the Chilean government's emphasis on extending the Enlaces initiative to the rural regions inhabited by the country's 'first people' populations. Similar sentiments could also be said to be reflected in the Singaporean concern with "offer[ing] a digital future for everyone" (Singapore Ministry of Education 2006).

Indeed, as Qi (2005, p.36) observes, in many East-Asian countries

> the innovation of the internet and on-line distance learning carry a special responsibility to bridge the existing gaps and discrepancies between lower-income and rich households, rural and urban areas, elder and younger generations, females and males, low and high educational levels.

One pertinent example of this was the Japanese emphasis during the 1990s on the ameliorative effects of new technology on individual citizens – not least in terms of righting existing 'wrongs' associated with previous stages of technological and industrial development. For example, Japanese government interest in creating an 'intellectually creative society' during the 1990s made much of developing a comprehensive information and communications infrastructure in order to reform the socio-economic system and 'improve people's lives'. The individual and social implications of the Japanese Information Infrastructure programme were therefore promoted in a diversity of social contexts, such as dealing with an ageing population (both in terms of health support and encouraging increased participation in society), rectifying over-concentration in urban areas, addressing the environmental concerns from an industrial structure based on the massive consumption of resources, and, perhaps most ambitiously, creating a 'comfortable lifestyle' for the country's citizens (Telecommunications Council 1994).

Following on from these points, the explicit goal of nation building has also been evident at different times throughout these policy agendas, albeit in ways that differ noticeably from country to country. One such notion is the recurring use of educational technology to support a sense of globalist nation building. As the Japanese government reasoned, "Japan's objectives are ... to achieve the free circulation of information at home and abroad in order to strongly promote the transparency of Japanese society and to build a Japan that is open to the world" (Telecommunications Council 1994, p.1). In some cases, therefore, educational technology has been linked to the promotion of values that reflect an idealised sense of national cultural diversity and cosmopolitanism – as with the case of the Chilean government's deliberate emphasis on extending the Enlaces initiative from the country's urban centres to the rural regions inhabited by the indigenous Mapuche people. Wider reconciliatory concerns were also evident during the 2000s in the US alignment of educational technology with the development of global citizenship and geopolitical stability in the wake of the post-9/11 'war on terror'. As the US government reasoned:

The context of global interdependence is especially important for this generation of students because only individuals and nations working together will solve many of today's challenges. The leadership of the United States in the world depends on educating a generation of young people who are capable of navigating an interdependent world and collaborating across borders and cultures to address today's great problems.

(US Department of Education 2010)

The Convergent and Divergent Nature of Educational Technology Policymaking

It should be clear from these brief descriptions that state educational technology policymaking has long fed into and reflected a range of national political concerns. Educational technology has therefore offered a consistent means for nation states to bring economic and societal issues to bear on the structural processes of contemporary educational provision and practice. As such, it is understandable that educational technology policymaking often appears to fulfil a function of supporting the 'extra-economic embedding' of capitalism as an economic system. As Dale (2005, p.121) describes, capitalism is reliant on the educational systems of the countries in which it operates to provide the necessary conditions of its continued expansion – i.e. addressing the 'core problems' of "supporting accumulation, ensuring societal cohesion and legitimation, that permanently confront capitalist states".

Seen in this light, then, all of the education technology policies reviewed in this chapter are perhaps best understood as symbolic interventions on the part of various types of capitalist state – offering a persuasive yet non-committal means for the governments of the UK, US, Japan, Chile and Singapore to maintain legitimacy as economic states and act as a high-profile means of keeping 'on message' with a number of broad political themes. These observations are certainly not restricted to the five countries highlighted in this chapter. As Robin Shields (2011, p.93) concludes with regard to the national educational technology efforts of successive governments in the far less economically powerful state of Nepal:

> While government policies on education consistently stress the need for ICT, there is an inconsistency and incoherence in their rationales for doing so. Instead of an authentic, self-identified justification, ideas such as economic competitiveness, 'computer literacy' and social equity are borrowed from the continually changing global discourse on ICT and development. These terms and concepts endow the national education system with a certain legitimacy and respectability, showing that it is progressive and modern while simultaneously avoiding the need for a national strategy on ICT in education that can stand up to close scrutiny.

This is not to argue that the educational technology policies of the UK, US, Japan, Chile, Singapore or Nepal are intended to fulfil no practical purpose at all. Yet it would seem that any intended outcomes are broader and less immediate than may first appear to be the case. For example, state interest in educational technology plays an emblematic role in terms of addressing wider ambitions towards the 'transformation' of countries' public sector organisations in ways that can support globally competitive economies. Many of the educational technology policies highlighted in this chapter certainly appear to support the logics of economic globalisation "which privilege choice, competition, performance management and individual responsibility and risk management" (Apple 2010, pp.1–2). In this sense, educational technology policymaking from the 1980s onwards can be seen in many countries as reflecting the economically focused nature of public sector policymaking during the last twenty years. As Stephen Ball (2007, p.188) argues:

> Generally speaking, within this new episteme, education is increasingly, indeed perhaps almost exclusively, spoken of within policy in terms of its economic value and its contribution to international market competitiveness. Even policies which are concerned to achieve greater social inclusion are edited, modified and co-opted by the requirements of economic participation and the labour markets and the values, principles and relations of trade/exchange ... Education is increasingly subject to the normative assumptions and prescriptions of economism ... Within policy this economism is articulated and enacted very generally in the joining up of [education] to the project of competitiveness and to the demands of globalisation and very specifically through the curriculum of enterprise and entrepreneurship.

Set against this background, digital technologies would seem to be a prominent instance of the recent tendency of educational policymakers to seize upon shared 'magical solutions' to the 'generic problems' that education policymaking is seen to face (Ball 1998). In many respects, then, digital technologies could be seen as conforming to the notion of globalisation as 'knowledge wars' – i.e. nations moving beyond the stage of 'bloody' armed conflict and, instead, competing "for ideas, skills and knowledge that contribute to economic advantage by 'out-smarting' economic rivals" (Brown et al. 2008, p.133). Yet it would perhaps be overstating the case to argue for digital technology as a straightforward instance of an increased shaping of education by concerns of economic competition and conflict. Instead, there are also distinct differences between the educational technology policy agendas of countries such as the UK, US, Japan, Chile and Singapore that are best understood in terms of the political economy of the countries under investigation. The policy drives of the US and UK, for example, reflect a clear interest in supporting the development of educational technology marketplaces within their borders, as well as supporting the distribution and sale of American and British educational provision in other countries. Policymaking in the US has also, on occasion, reflected an internationalist sense of using technology to support the distribution of American education and American values to developing contexts. In contrast, the educational technology policies of a country such as Japan could be said to reflect a more insular and ameliorative approach to the modernisation of the national education system – an approach also apparent in Chile's concerns with developing educational technology use through the country's different regions.

With these thoughts in mind, it is useful to draw upon the well-established distinction between neo-liberal and developmental approaches to national policy formation with their various privileging of individual and collective interests, alongside public and private forms of organisation. From this perspective, then, much of the policymaking pursued by the US and UK governments reflects an apparent desire to set educational technology up as a 'quasi-market place', with the state exerting an element of control over the formation of various policies, ensuring their successful establishment in the hope that momentum will 'trickle down' into the other market-driven sectors. This is apparent in the emphasis placed by the US and UK governments over the past thirty years on stimulating demand for digital technology 'beyond the four walls' of the school into domestic and wider community settings. In this sense, educational technology acts as a government constructed flagship for privately constructed networks throughout the rest of society. Indeed, in many ways, policy efforts such as the US National Information Infrastructure during the 1990s offer close examples of an ideal-typical model of neo-liberalism – reflecting a general wariness of centralised approaches to policymaking in American culture. Nevertheless, even here, education assumed a heightened importance, with the Federal government paying particular attention to the connection of US schools to the internet. Of course, perceived government involvement and concern over the educational aspects of the increased use of technology in society has obvious political advantages. For many governments, pledging to 'wire up' public school systems continues to carry far more electoral significance than promising to ensure the connection of the commercial sector to the internet.

In this way, education has proved to be a highly visible arena for neo-liberal governments seeking involvement in the increased use of digital technology throughout society. Conversely, in the case of more developmental states, governments appear far more prepared to be seen as a central catalyst for technology-based change, with educational technology policy implementation firmly "driven by the state acting in accordance with a predetermined set of objectives" (Moore 1998, p.154). This model typifies the approach taken by the likes of Singapore and Japan, who have leant towards highly centralised 'visions' with strong state leadership and direction. Manuel Castells (1996) has argued that a state is developmental when its main source of legitimacy is its ability to deliver consistently high rates of economic growth and modernisation of the economy both domestically and in relation to the international economy. This presupposes a societal approach to which "in East Asia took the form of the affirmation of national identity, and national culture, building or rebuilding the nation as a force in the world, in this case by means of economic competitiveness and socio-economic improvement" (Castells 1996, p.182). Thus it is perhaps to be expected that developmental governments have taken 'a proactive central role' in an area of national change such as educational technology (Teo and Lim 1998, p.122).

These distinctions are certainly apparent in the educational technology policy histories discussed in this chapter. For example, while differing somewhat in the degree of private involvement that has been encouraged over the past thirty years, the Japanese strategy continues to imply a strong belief in a 'hands on' approach to building information societies. As Latzer (1995, p.527) reasons, "the political/ administrative system, with strong central power in the hands of the ministry at the local and national level, and an unusually close relationship between the civil service and industry support this approach". Given this approach, the Japanese education system has tended to be treated as one element of a wider state coordinated strategy towards society-wide use of digital technology. Yet as for all ideal-typical models, this broad view runs the risk of obscuring important differences in empirical realities, such as the clear working differences in the educational and economic policies pursued by Japanese and Singaporean governments. Moreover, countries such as Chile cannot be said to have adopted either an avowedly neo-liberal or developmental model, given the importance attached to the politics of co-determination (see Streeck 1992). Indeed, had we extended our focus beyond the five national examples discussed in this chapter, then the number of ideal-typical models would undoubtedly increase. As such, it is best to conclude that despite the apparent commonalities between nations, there is clearly no common global approach to educational technology policymaking.

Conclusions

This chapter has considered a number of ways in which technology-based education is presented by national governments as a 'generic' solution to common policy 'problems' arising from the knowledge economy, information age and other recent global shifts. At first glance, then, it is tempting to see these policy expressions of educational technology as forming a 'global hyper-narrative' (Stronach 2010) – i.e. a shared discursive means that nation states turn to in an attempt to 'normalise' the economic and societal changes associated with globalisation. Yet while all educational policies and practices are undoubtedly internationalised to some degree, it would be a mistake to see educational technology policymaking as simply reflecting what Joel Spring (2009, p.119) terms a common 'global educational culture'. Indeed, despite the apparent similarities of these national educational technology programmes, what has taken place 'on the ground' has proven to be a very different and more diverse matter. At best, these shared discourses and common proclamations could be seen simply as part of the global language of 'education' that "enable[s] politicians the world over to talk nonsense" (Stronach 2010, p.1).

Nonsense or not, it certainly makes sense to conclude that the national strategies outlined in this chapter are not direct attempts to alter educational practice *per se*. Instead, following Jensen and Lauritsen's (2005, p.365) reasoning, all these state technology policies appear to work "rather like a relay between certain administrative and political practices and a diversity of local initiatives". Thus it is perhaps to be expected that education policies such as the Japanese 'New Deal for Schools' or the various US Educational Technology Plans will not have homogeneous and predictable 'effects'. While these policies may well have led to a number of intended consequences, they are also associated with a range of unintended and unexpected consequences. Such outcomes are often only apparent when the policies have entered local educational settings and have been enacted upon by managers, administrators, teachers and students. From this perspective, we need to remain mindful of the capacity of state policies to *produce* as well as address problems – especially in the medium and long term as "the second, third or fourth generation of effects produced by previous policy actions and instruments" begin to reveal themselves (Considine 2005, p.21). Indeed, the unintended consequences of education technology policymaking tend to be cumulative and certainly not under control of state authorities.

Thus despite the commonalities between the policy efforts of the UK, US, Japan, Chile, Singapore and others, it would be a mistake to see the implementation and use of digital technology in educational settings around the world as simply the product of national interpretations of global economic agendas. In making sense of education in a digital world, we also need to consider the influence and effects of local contexts in giving specific form and content to the otherwise generalised notions of educational technology as expressed through education policies. As with any area of educational intervention, the practices and processes of educational technology must also be made local, as general ideas and discourses are given 'specific form' and 'specific content' (Jenson and Santos 2000). So while the comparative education approach may well encourage an interest in "the similarities across national settings" (Samoff 2007, p.49), we need to remain mindful of the many differences and discontinuities that persist within national borders when it comes to educational technology use. It is, therefore, time to move our attention towards the importance of "local politics and culture and tradition and the processes of interpretation and struggle involved in translating these generic solutions into practical policies and institutional practices" (Ball 2006, p.76). The next chapter will now go on to explore the localised realities of education and technology.

5

LOCAL VARIATIONS IN EDUCATIONAL TECHNOLOGY PROVISION AND PRACTICE

Introduction

The past two chapters have depicted educational technology as a rather standardised 'top-down' affair. The totalising policy discourses of national governments and the grand gestures of international organisations certainly convey a confident sense of what educational technology should be. Yet it is important to remember that all of the activities, agendas, programmes and policies described in Chapters 3 and 4 bear little resemblance to the rather 'messier' realities of digital technology use in 'real-life' educational settings. The persuasive discourses of 'twenty-first-century skills' and 'intelligent islands' should be seen as idealistic rather than realistic depictions of educational technology – informed by politically driven desires and produced to promote particular sets of values. As David Nye (2007, p.35) reflects, such policies and programmes "are in essence little narratives about the future. They are not [necessarily] full-scale narratives of utopia, but they are usually presented as stories about a better world to come".

All of the agendas, strategies and visions reviewed up to this point in the book provide only a partial reading of educational technology use around the world. It would be unwise to ascribe any particular 'effect' or 'impact' to these programmes and policies – especially in terms of how digital technologies are actually used 'on the ground' by individuals and institutions whose interests and experiences may be far removed from the interests and experiences of national policymakers or inter-national organisations. As was argued in Chapter 4, education technology policies are in many ways not intended to result in significant realignments of education provision or practice *per se*. Indeed, it could be reasoned that many education policy drives are little more than symbolic interventions on the part of governments – a means for states to maintain legitimacy in terms of their governance of national education systems or their influence over national economic fortunes. Thus all of the policy programmes and initiatives reviewed in Chapter 4 are perhaps best understood as a way for governments to appear 'on message' with a number of key political concerns – not least global economic concerns of national competitiveness, the up-skilling of workforces, the dynamics of global capitalism and the intensification of the economic function of knowledge. What these policies and initiatives are not able to do, however, is tell us how and why digital technologies are *actually* being used in educational settings in any particular country or locality.

In one sense, then, educational technology policies and the educational technology actions of international organisations present a rather homogenised and partial account of educational technology use around the world. All of the policies reviewed in Chapter 4, for example, relay well-worn mantras of a computer for every student, technology-rich curricula, highly trained teacher workforces, thriving indigenous IT industries, and re-skilled workforces. We now need to move beyond these 'global models' of educational technology and, instead, pay attention to what is taking place at the local level of analysis. In this sense, we need to consider how the 'global flows' of educational policymaking and supranational activity end up being 'vernacularised' in the contexts of specific countries and societies as they meet local cultures and politics (Rizvi and Lingard 2010). Thus in order to develop a more rounded understanding of how and why educational technologies are used (and not used) in the diverse ways that they are around the world, we now need to consider the complex interactions between the global and the local.

At this point, we can return to the issues outlined in Chapter 2 as arising from the comparative education tradition – in particular the 'culturalist' tradition of comparative education that seeks to examine "the way global policies are interpreted, adapted and changed at the local level" (Spring 2009, p.117). This approach raises a number of questions that can be of use in understanding the local recontextualisations of educational technology policies and the actions of organisations such as the UN, OECD and Microsoft. For example, how do local actors borrow and adapt concepts and practices from the national and global flows of educational ideas about technology? How are these concepts of 'educational technology' subject to local distinctiveness and resilience, or even what Gabriel and Sturdy (2002) term a 'politicisation of local identity'? How are digital technologies framed in terms of local social, political, economic and cultural imperatives?

These questions certainly chime with the socio-technical tradition of viewing digital technologies as shaped continually by the social contexts in which they are implemented and used. From the social shaping perspective, it is simply not good enough to assume, for example, that any specific educational technology will have an essentially similar influence on classrooms and learners in London as it would in Lima or Lahore. Instead, social shaping warns against discounting the local influences that shape the nature and form of 'educational technology' in these very different contexts. As Cherian George (2005, p.914) reminds us, "communication technologies are not independent variables appearing from out the blue ... their forms and functions are shaped by the societies that absorb them, even as they influence those societies". As many other academic accounts of general media and technology development have shown, these shaping features can include the influence of local cultures and contexts through to issues of language, religion and other structured forms of social relations. What significance, then, do these 'local' issues have for the development and implementation of *educational* media and technology? With these issues in mind, the remainder of this chapter is devoted to exploring the localised realities of digital technology use in education.

Evidence and Indicators of Differences in 'Educational Technology' between Countries

We first need to consider the extent and nature of differences in educational technology use between countries. Before we can draw any conclusions regarding why differences may exist, it makes sense to have a clear picture of the nature and extent of these differences. Here, then, we can turn to the succession of comparative indicators and measures of educational technology use that have been produced around the world during the past thirty years. A considerable number of international surveys and studies have been conducted throughout this time, produced by organisations as diverse as the 'Latin American Laboratory for the Assessment of Quality in Education' to the 'Southern and East Africa Consortium for Monitoring Educational Quality'. All these studies and indicators have sought to map the rise of digital technology use throughout educational systems and, in so doing, are a valuable means of highlighting the variations that exist between and within countries. Of course, these studies have tended to concentrate on similar sets of indicators – not least 'student to computer ratios', the percentage of schools with internet connectivity and various measures of actual usage of technology. Yet while the absolute numbers behind these analyses may have changed over the past three decades, the persistence of relative differences and variations suggest that educational technology is far from a globally converging phenomenon.

Perhaps the most sustained of these datasets has been the succession of measurements produced by the IEA (the International Association for the Evaluation of Educational Achievement). This international cooperative of government research agencies and national research institutions is best known for its comparative measure of school system outputs – the TIMSS (Trends in International Mathematics and Science) study. However, the organisation has also conducted studies of digital technology use in education over the past twenty-five years, from the 'CompEd' surveys in the 1980s and 1990s through to the 'SITES' projects during the 2000s and 2010s. The initial IEA 'Computers in Education' study collected data between 1989 and 1992 to produce a comparative picture of computer use in twenty-three countries and regions from India to British Columbia. These surveys sought to document the 'rapid changes' across all of the participating education systems in terms of access to computers at all levels of schooling. As the survey co-ordinators noted at the time, these "increases were the result of governmental programs, as well as support by local communities and the efforts of individual schools" (Pelgrum *et al.* 1993, n.p). That said, even during the early emergence of mainstream computer use in schools, some interesting national differences were apparent. For example, just why were differences in students' use of computers by gender apparent in all countries apart from in French-speaking systems and in Greece (see Pelgrum and Plomp 1993)?

The so-called 'SITES' study (i.e. the Second Information Technology in Education Study) ran throughout the 1997 to 2008 period, and focused on an extended sample of twenty-seven countries and regions. Although documenting the generally increasing levels of digital technology access and use in schools, here, too, the data highlighted a number of notable differences between countries. For example, student–computer ratios in lower secondary schools were reported to be as low as 9:1 in Canada and 12:1 in Denmark and Singapore, as opposed to ratios of 133:1 in Lithuania and 210:1 in Cyprus. The phases of the study which included observation and interview data also highlighted a "great deal of diversity and variation" with regard to teachers' and students' in-school uses of digital technology. Significantly, these differences were reported primarily at the country/system level rather than between 'clusters' of countries (Law *et al.* 2008). In other words, different countries in similar regions (e.g. the countries across 'northern Europe') would nevertheless display noticeably different patterns of technology use. One key finding emerging from these data was the lack of clear correlation between observed technology use in schools and the nature of national policy drives or the general conditions of national school systems. As the study concluded, "findings indicate that the extent of ICT use does not only depend on overall national level ICT policies and school level conditions" (Carstens and Pelgrum 2009, n.p).

The data from these IEA studies, therefore, provide useful insights into the changing (and non-changing) patterns of educational technology use throughout the 1980s, 1990s and 2000s, and have continued into the 2010s through online computer-based assessments of students' skills in the guise of the 'International Computer and Information Literacy Study'. Although based on admittedly 'broad brush' measures and indicators, and while limited to those countries whose governments were willing to finance their participation (hence the inconsistent inclusion of different national cases), these data nevertheless suggest a clear sense of national difference and variation. Similar patterns and trends are also evident in other programmes of comparative educational measurement. For example, the OECD's long-running PISA (Programme for International Student Assessment) study provides a valuable measure of educational technology use over time through its repeated surveys of secondary school students across the organisation's member countries. While illustrating generally rising levels of students' access to and familiarity with digital technology, the PISA data nevertheless highlight a number of differences between national cases (see OECD 2005, 2010). A number of interesting questions therefore arise from the PISA data. For example, why are the reported educational benefits of home computer use seemingly more pronounced in Canada, Germany, Spain, Finland, Japan and Croatia, yet less so in Belgium, Greece, Italy, Bulgaria and Serbia? Why do rural schools in countries such as Denmark, Italy and Korea have relatively more computers *per capita* than their city counterparts? Why is this trend reversed in Brazil and Poland? Why do students making frequent use of school computers appear to display lower levels of test attainment than non-frequent users in Finland, Japan, Korea, New Zealand and Spain? Why is this trend reversed in countries such as Canada, Iceland, Netherlands and Switzerland?

One of the key patterns that run throughout the PISA studies' measures are the clear differences that appear to persist between nations that could otherwise be considered to be comparative in most other senses. For example, PISA data show that while frequent use of a computer at home is correlated strongly to Austrian students' frequent use of school computers, this is not the case in neighbouring Germany. Similarly, countries such as Korea and Japan display almost opposite relationships between home and school use of digital technologies. Gender differences in student confidence are evident in many northern and central European countries, but not Japan, Korea and Jordan. The OECD's own analysis of the PISA data in terms of students' reported 'digital profiles' reveals a range of unexpected patterns. If these data are to be believed, why does Japan have the highest number of what OECD classifies as 'analogue' students, with nearly 80 per cent displaying a lack of interest in educational and leisure-related use of digital technologies? Conversely, why does Turkey have the highest levels of what OECD classifies as 'digi-zapper' students, with 17 per cent reported to be frequent leisure and educational users?

Without dwelling too long on the minutiae of any particular case, it would be fair to conclude from these surveys that "the range of what is pedagogically possible [with digital technology] in one region, or country, or school … can be very different from another" (Brown 2009, p.1147). Of course, the precise nature of these apparent differences at various points during the past thirty years is perhaps of less significance than their general persistence over time. Data such as these therefore clearly contradict the depictions of almost universal digital technology use that emerge from national policy strategies and many academic discussions. So why is it that many people are convinced so easily of the globalising nature of technology use in education, when much of the evidence points to clear local and regional disparities? More importantly, what factors underpin these differences, and how may they vary between countries and contexts? Given the varied findings of these surveys, there is clearly a need for us to develop better understandings of the localised nature of educational technology practices.

Possible Explanations for Differences in Educational Technology Use – Issues of Choice and Context

It is clear that the *actual* implementation and use of educational technology varies considerably (but not altogether consistently) around the world. So how then can these variations and differences be explained, especially in light of the broad policy agendas and (inter)national strategies outlined in Chapters 3 and 4, and the universal discourses that surround them? One popular explanation is that all these macro-level descriptions of educational technology undergo a process of 'translation' and 'enactment' in specific local settings. In this sense, it could be argued that many of the differing patterns and trends outlined in the PISA and SITES surveys are due to the selective 'adopting' and 'adapting' of educational policies and practices by local actors. In other words, it could be that aspects of an educational technology 'solution' are only being appropriated and enacted when there is sufficient correspondence between the interests of local actors and the dominant political ideologies promoting the reform (see Halpin and Troyna 1995). In this sense, local actors could be said to be selecting from multiple and competing models of 'educational technology' in their everyday practice. Thus while local actors may be using the same language and concepts as are being promoted at the international and national levels, in practice, any global model of change is altered to fit local circumstances (see Spring 2009). For example, as Ball *et al.* (2012) demonstrate, what national policymakers may mean by technology-based 'personalisation' and how this is then enacted within local school settings may be very different in nature and form. In short, what is initially said about educational technology may often not fully describe what is subsequently done with educational technology.

Of course, it would be a mistake to imagine this process of selection and reinterpretation as an unconstrained process of free choice. As Ball (1998) argues, words such as 'select' or 'choose' are perhaps not appropriate ways to describe the actions of either national or local actors – subject as all these interests are to the pressures of international economic markets, new managerialism, performativity and various forms of de-regulation. To assume that any organisation or individual is free to pick and 'choose' what path of action they take (and do not take) is to overlook the many structures that constrain the actions of even the most seemingly unconstrained of actors. As Ball (2006, p.75) continues, the enactment of any forms of national policymaking is therefore better understood as an on-going process of 'bricolage' – i.e.:

> a matter of borrowing and copying bits and pieces of ideas from elsewhere, drawing upon and amending locally tried and tested approaches, cannibalising theories, research, trends and fashions and not infrequently flailing around for anything at all that looks as though it might work. Most policies are ramshackle, compromise, hit and miss affairs, that are reworked, tinkered with, nuanced and inflected through complex processes of influence, text production, dissemination and, ultimately, re-creation in contexts of practice.

As this description implies, any enactment of a globalised education form (such as 'educational technology') at a local level is a convoluted and compromised business. In this sense, it is useful to reconsider the emphasis placed within the tradition of comparative education study on the significance of *context*. Here, then, we are referring back to the importance of what Grant (2000, p.310) terms "understanding the background conditions", or what Phillips and Ochs (2007, p.377) term the 'embeddedness' of educational approaches and provision in "the locally prevailing cultural and other conditions". In these terms, any apparent 'choice' of one form of educational technology over another needs to be understood as being contextually influenced rather than driven by individual choice. The important aspects of 'context' in this respect are varied – including the political history and political present of a country, its linguistic, cultural, religious heritage, as well as economic, demographic and geographical circumstances.

These contextual factors are therefore a potential influence on any instance of educational technology 'implementation' in any national or local setting. For example, all of the nations considered in this book so far vary considerably in terms of geography – from small island states to vast multi-state federations. They also vary considerably in terms of topography – from mountainous regions to remote low-lying plain lands. While matters of physical geography feature rarely in analyses of educational technology, it would be unwise to discount the bearing of these characteristics on basic technical issues such as network connectivity. As we shall explore further on in this chapter, the relative ease with which a country such as Singapore has been able to coordinate the mass implementation of digital technology across its education system is due in part to the constrained geography of the island state. Other instances of educational technology implementation have conversely been influenced by environmental issues such as climate change, weather patterns and natural disasters. For example, heavy storms in Inner Mongolia provided a major impediment to the Chinese government's planned use of satellite dishes and antennae through the 'Modern Distance Education Project for Rural Schools' initiative (Latchem and Jung 2010). Similarly, the socio-economic consequences of earthquakes in countries such as Chile, Haiti and Turkey have been obvious mitigating factors in the recent use of educational technology in these contexts. In short, it is often too easy to overlook the natural contexts within which educational technology interventions are placed.

In a similar manner, educational technology is also shaped significantly by variations in the man-made physical environment and infrastructure. In understanding fully the success of any education technology initiative, thought needs to be given to key underpinning material factors such as energy supplies, cabling and wiring, wireless and satellite coverage, environmental sustainability and so on. Although unremarkable and usually un-noticed, all these infrastructural factors are nevertheless critical to the success of any form of educational technology-based change. For example, the failure of many educational technology projects in sub-Saharan Africa has often been attributed – in part – to the "lack or weakness of connectivity, dilapidated infrastructure and power shortages" (Traore 2008, p.8). As Tim Unwin has also observed in an African context, "on more than one occasion, ambitious programmes have been developed to introduce computers into schools, only for it to be realised subsequently that the absence of electricity has meant that only a few such schools would actually be able to benefit. Indeed, much of the inequality in the distribution of the benefits of ICTs can be attributed to a spatially differentiated supply of basic infrastructure" (Unwin 2009c, p.92). In contrast to these African experiences, the relative success of rural educational television in China has been conversely attributed, at least in part, to preceding governmental programmes of rural electrification (ibid.).

Of course, the underpinning contexts of educational technology implementation are not all physical and material in nature. Factors such as countries' varied economic and natural resources, and changing socio-political arrangements are also of key importance. All of the countries considered in Chapter 4's overview of educational technology policy formation are significantly different in terms of their philosophy of governance, economic power, history of political unrest and involvement in internal and external conflicts, wars and other disturbances. Educational technology is therefore party to a range of these geo-political and geo-economic influences. As Perkins and Neumayer (2011) point out, contextual differences in trade openness, wealth and large capital investment have all had longstanding bearings on the uptake of communications technologies from the telegram to the internet. When considering the application of educational technology programmes in much of sub-Saharan Africa, for example, it is important to take account of these wider geo-political issues. Many African nations are negotiating large national debts that often serve to reduce the actual ability of states to intervene autonomously through social policy. In terms of political ideology, the lasting legacy of some countries' past and present leanings (be it Marxist-Leninist, fascistic, dictatorial or market capitalist) have a clear bearing on the nature of any public policy intervention. In addition, the unresolved nature of some countries' post-colonial transitions have led to on-going civil wars, genocides and tribal/racial divisions that understandably mitigate the context-free promises of educational technology.

Indeed, the educational technology policies outlined in Chapter 4 vary considerably in their political contexts – from the centralised system of Singapore to decentralised systems such as the US. Looking beyond the countries reviewed in Chapter 4, the whole-country education technology efforts in centralised small states such as Malta and Brunei Darussalam are clearly different from the efforts of many African nations where centralised government efforts tend to take root more readily in urban centres rather than rural peripheral regions. The ease of implementing educational change in a relatively dirigiste country such as Singapore will be different in comparison to a more laissez-faire democracy such as the UK. Indeed, the few comparative analyses of educational technology policymaking that have been conducted suggest that countries with more centralised systems are more likely to place an emphasis on developing digital technology use in schools – regardless of relative wealth or economic status (see Zhang 2007).

Possible Explanations for Differences in Educational Technology Use – Issues of Culture

It is clear from our discussions so far that regional, national and local variations in geography, physical and material resourcing alongside issues of geo-politics can all

have a significant influence on the implementation and use of educational technology. Yet in making sense of local variations in educational technology use, it is
important to also acknowledge the more nebulous issue of 'culture' as an additional
set of significant contextual influences. Here we are using 'culture' to denote the
shared understandings, assumptions, beliefs, values and ideas of any particular society
or group – be it in terms of local cultural values, traditional forms of knowledge or
ways of thinking. Thus as Alison Carr-Chellman (2005, p.17) observes, any form
of technology-based learning cannot be considered to be acultural, "but rather is
highly dependent on the culture and context in which the learning and learners
are embedded".

One of the most prominent cultural variations between countries is that of
language. Although estimates vary, there may be up to 5,000 languages and up to
200 writing systems in use around the world. It is no longer the case that English
(even the simplified versions of 'global English' that are used around the world) is
the only *lingua franca*, or that the Roman alphabet is the common standard writing
system. Any instance of educational technology is therefore set against the linguistic
pluralism of the contexts in which it is being implemented. In countries such as
India this can entail over twenty different spoken languages and dialects co-existing
within a few hundred miles of each other. Language is a practical and political issue
in many other countries, from Nigeria to Israel, and Canada to Belgium. This
situation is complicated further by the importance of dialects – such as the different
forms of English that can be found around the world such as Jamaican patois and
other forms of English-based creole. In all these cases, "language becomes a repre-
sentative proxy of culture, and thus asking any one culture to cede to others
[through technology use] is particularly problematic" (Carr-Chellman 2005, p.69).

Aside from the immediate matter of language, another important cultural influence relates to the dominant traditions of thought that underpin the historical
development of countries and regions. In a basic sense, these traditions and philosophies can be traced back to the various dominant 'world' civilisations – such as
the Sinic (Confucian-based), the Western, the Islamic and the Latin American
(cf. Huntington 2003). While it may appear anachronistic when seeking to explain
the use of contemporary digital technologies to hark back to the influence of these
civilisations, they constitute an important background to any educational technology analysis. For example, as Joel Spring (2009) argues, despite the dominant secu-
larist tendency in the vast majority of educational analysis and theory, we would do
well to consider the underpinning influence of spiritual and religious values on
contemporary educational technology use.

Indeed, it can be argued that clear differences are evident between the educational
philosophies and arrangements in Sinic, Japanese, Islamic, Buddhist and Hindu
cultures (see Zhao *et al.* 2011). One set of comparisons that is often made is that
between Eastern thought (i.e. deriving from holistic Asian philosophies) and Western
thought (i.e. deriving from Greek philosophy). As Latchem and Jung (2010) detail,
Western thought can be characterised along a number of lines – e.g. seeking

consistency, encouraging individualism and valuing autonomy, egalitarianism, competitiveness, self-reliance and directness. In contrast, Eastern thought can be characterised in a number of other ways – e.g. accepting contradiction, encouraging collectivism, valuing deference to older or authoritative persons and encouraging 'high context communication' where words are seen to be less important than context. While these precise differences between 'Eastern' and 'Western' traditions are contestable, it is clear that many of the dominant ways in which educational technology is positioned and discussed within academic, political and commercial circles is done through Western values and principles. For example, as Dillon *et al.* (2008) observe, many of the assumptions of 'sociocultural' learning that underpin dominant educational technology thinking are strongly Western constructs that are associated with settled and largely urban lifestyles. In an East-Asian nomadic context such as Outer Mongolia – where the majority of people are what Dillon describes as 'mobile pastoralists' – talk of learning 'environments' and 'context-dependent' learning are of perhaps of less meaning and relevance.

Such contradictions are prompting some educational technologists to begin to question the compatibility (or otherwise) of Western conceptions of technology and education with other traditions of thought and philosophy – not least the 'Confucian heritage education' that shapes much of the educational provision in East Asia. Indeed, it could be argued that the Eastern educational tradition is often at odds with many aspects of 'globalised' educational technology thought. As Richard Nisbett (2003) has reasoned, the Confucian emphasis on valuing group success and achievement and regarding the individual learner as a subordinate part of a larger independent collective could be seen to clash with many of the prevailing assumptions surrounding the individually-empowering potential of digital technologies in education. Similarly, the Confucian tendency to see education in terms of a "teacher-dominated and centrally organized pedagogical culture" (Zhang 2007, p.302) could be seen to clash with the notion of the technology-empowered individual learner. Thus in Confucian-led countries the use of digital technology in education may well be valued in different ways than is assumed by Western commentators. As Fang and Warschauer (2004, pp.314–15) observe with regard to Chinese forms of educational technology use:

> In China deep-rooted cultural norms and beliefs mandate that teachers control the classroom and deserve utmost student respect. The methods suggested by the [digital technology intervention] – which focused teachers' efforts on providing guidance, scaffolding, and feedback rather than lecturing – ran contrary to these cultural norms and beliefs. Teachers who engaged in student–centred learning risked disapproval from their students, who were used to other forms of learning, and from their peers, who view linguistic knowledge and lecturing ability as the cornerstones of good teaching.

Of course, culturally-based explanations are not restricted to the clashes between Eastern holistic thought and Western notions of technology-based learning. For instance, other authors have questioned how dominant Western notions of educational technology use correspond with the Islamic prioritising of the sacredness of the text and associated preference for 'teaching-to-the-text' and encouraging text memorisation. As Latchem and Jung (2010, p.15) reason, "in Arab countries, teacher-led, face-to-face instruction is considered quality education and ICT is primarily used for information transmission and passive learning". Thus it has been argued, for example, that the strong face-to-face, oral, kinship and respect traditions within Islamic understandings of education may mitigate against the relative success of autonomous forms of online learning. As Usun (2004, n.p) observes:

> Turkey's roots in an oral tradition, along with its emphasis on rote memorisation and the sacredness of text, make learning independently less suitable … The transition from teacher-centred education to individual-based learning, where students learn alone and support is minimal, creates many difficulties for Turkish distance education students.

To take another example, it has been conversely reasoned that the customary preference within Maori education for face-to-face (*kanohi-a-kanohi*) situations and the cultural recognition of the need for an intimate connection between teacher and learner leads to a potential preference for synchronous rather than asynchronous forms of online education (Anderson 2005). Accurate or not, arguments such as these certainly act to highlight the significance of differences in collective understandings and values.

We must, of course, be mindful of slipping into (over)generalisations and stereotypes when identifying the importance of these local cultural variations. It could be argued that the use of digital technologies for what Latchem and Jung identify as "information transmission and passive learning" is by no means a uniquely Islamic trait. Conversely, many forms of East Asian education are not bounded by rigidly Confucian, Taoist or Zen principles, and many instances of technology-related innovation do occur within these countries. Indeed, as Cameron Richards (2004, p.342) reasons, "abstract ideas about learner-centred pedagogy, life-long education and flexible learning are well known and even perhaps the theoretical orthodoxy today in many Asian contexts of education".

These caveats notwithstanding, it would seem sensible for any account of educational technology to give greater acknowledgement to contextual differences in cultural values and perspectives. This is perhaps also important with regard to any specific 'national ideologies' that could be said to stem from broader philosophical and spiritual traditions. As anthropologists such as Florence Kluckhohn have long observed, national understandings and norms can be seen to differ in terms of people's relationships to others – in particular the valuing of the individual as opposed to the collective and the autonomous as opposed to the authoritarian. In these terms, then, differences in the positioning and the privileging of the individual within national cultures underpin many local variations in educational technology use. Take, for instance, the differences between the collective social-welfare orientations of Scandinavian Lutheran societies as opposed to the individualistic market-led cultures of North America. Similarly, clear differences exist between the class-based systems of status and entitlement within the UK and French class system as well as the Indian caste system, as opposed to more ostensibly meritocratic systems. While subtle, these differences can be said to influence perceptions of educational technology. For instance, as Carr-Chellman (2005, p.149) observes with regard to the cultural 'fit' of online learning and American values:

> We, in America, love our independence. There is almost nothing that is more precious to us than the ability to determine our own individual destinies and to pursue with all vigor, potentially alone … Online learning is directly in line with this stereotypical American value.

Making Sense of the Localisations of Education and Technology

It should now be clear from these brief examples alone that the local implementation and enactment of educational technology is a complicated affair. Despite the best 'global' intentions of technology designers, learning scientists and pedagogical experts, a host of powerful 'local' factors will influence how similar educational technologies are received and used in different social contexts and circumstances. It is important to note here that these issues are not occasional interruptions of otherwise pervasive global trends. These are not peripheral factors that simply 'add colour' at the margins of generally universal forms of educational technology use. As such, these are not local peculiarities that can be countered by the addition of some tokenistic local adjustments in a manner akin to the 'glocalisation' of US fast-food menus throughout the world (where, for example, one can order a McFalafel burger in Egypt or a McHuevo burger in Uruguay). Instead, these are deep-rooted influences that impact upon any instance of education technology use, and therefore should underpin any understanding of how digital technologies are actually being used by different sets of groups of people in different social, cultural and political contexts. It is important, therefore, that we take time to consider fully how these issues of local context and local circumstance act to shape technology use in education.

Let us take, for example, 'virtual' and 'de-territorialised' forms of technology-based education. A growing number of recent studies have focused on how individuals in different national contexts and from different cultural backgrounds engage with ostensibly the same forms of online learning. In Selwyn's (2011) study of distance learners from around the world taking the same UK-provided degree courses, a range of 'local' contextual influences were found to underpin students' diverse experiences of what was assumed by the educational providers to be a global common experience. These influences included individuals in countries undergoing civil wars facing obvious restrictions in terms of the times that they could study due to curfews and military restrictions on travel between work and home. Individuals in some countries faced intermittent internet access and frequent electricity 'brownouts'. Other individuals' experiences were shaped by their 'translocal' life-styles – i.e. having to live significantly in more than one location and therefore often having to learn online while in transit around the world. Thus behind all these learners' experiences of technology-based learning were a range of contextual influences – from matters of (im)mobility and geo-politics through to variations in income and social class. As Andrew Brown (2009, p.1166) has also observed, "online courses in virtual settings are as much party to the play of pedagogic, social and cultural identities as any localized, located and demarcated face-to-face educational programme".

Clearly, then, at the level of the individual learner, even the most 'inter-nationalised' and 'virtual' instances of technology-based education provision are party to a host of local reinterpretations and cultural re-mediations. These issues are perhaps even more pronounced at the level of educational technology provision within national systems of education. It therefore makes sense to consider how the local shaping of education and technology is manifest in the offline physical contexts of national educational systems. This can be seen, for example, in two very different examples of educational technology implementation in Singapore and in Japan.

The Realities of Digital Technology Use with Singapore's School System

As outlined in Chapter 4, one of the most supposedly successful cases of system-wide educational technology implementation is that of Singapore. At first glance, Singapore is an exemplary example of nationwide educational technology reform, with the increased provision of digital technology coinciding with a resur-gence of Singaporean education. Indeed, Singapore is now considered to have one of the best public school systems in the world, with its students ranking regularly near the top of international test results in mathematics and science. Yet these suc-cesses notwithstanding the *actual* uses of digital technology in Singaporean schools are modest. Despite the high levels of technological resourcing and access, growing numbers of Singaporean commentators are beginning to acknowledge that the infusion of digital technology into the country's school system "has not really transformed traditional classroom practice" (Chai *et al.* 2009, p.125). As Toh and So (2011, p.349) conclude: "the use of technology in [Singaporean] education remains sporadic and disjointed. The promise that technology will bring deep-seated changes in the way that educators teach and students learn remains, disappointedly, elusive".

This disparity is best understood in the light of a number of local contextual issues – not least Singapore's distinctly 'authoritarian/communitarian' society. Singapore is best described as an 'electoral autocracy' or 'semi-democracy', with the country's leaders "exert[ing] a level of social and political control that is unique among wealthy nations" (Warschauer 2001, p.309). This notion of highly centralised and authoritarian control within Singapore is certainly apparent in the state governance of schools and schooling. Indeed, despite the Singaporean government's apparent desire to support the use of potentially 'disruptive' digital technologies, the nation's schools remain highly disciplined and regulated in all aspects of their conduct – from issues of student appearance and dress, to matters of time keeping and work ethic. In particular, Singaporean schooling could be said to be based around a teacher-centred sense of order and discipline that often precludes the more expansive forms of technology use associated with technology-based education. In comparison to Australian students, for example, Singaporean learners have been found to be less individualistic, less prone to take risks and more prone to be bureaucratic, to prefer hierarchy and respect for people of perceived higher status (Munro-Smith 2002). While Singapore may be less tied to traditional cultures and philosophies than some of its East Asian neighbours, a notable 'collectivist culture' persists that mitigates against the more social aspects of technology-based learning (Munro-Smith 2002). As Mark Warschauer (2001, p.308) continues, "the traditional teacher-centred classroom in Singapore is not necessarily compatible with the kinds of project-oriented group work that exploit the value of information technology and that Singapore's leaders are now promoting".

Perhaps the major local stumbling block to the expansive use of digital technology is Singapore's emphasis on external systems of examination, assessment and testing. Unlike American-influenced systems in the region (in particular that of South Korea and Taiwan) the post-colonial education system in Singapore retains a strong legacy of the British system of schooling and its emphasis on 'high-stakes' testing. Lim Cher Ping's (2007) case study of Singapore's high-technology-using schools, for example, concluded that digital technology use was clearly compromised by a distinctly Singaporean emphasis on exaggeratedly instructional relationships between teachers and learners, as well as an overt emphasis on eventual success in high-stakes examinations. As Lim concluded:

> the over-emphasis on results in schools may put pressure on teachers to conduct more remedial and drill-and-practice classes, as well as discuss more exam-type questions. They may follow the transmission model of teaching when using ICT to meet the objective of achieving good examination grades.
> *(Lim 2007, p.112)*

Other commentators have also criticised the restrictive nature of the top-down model of digital technology policymaking that has in practice been pursued in Singapore. Ng (2010, p.177) points towards "the inadequacies of a linear Newtonian model of [technology] implementation" – arguing that the successive 'Masterplans for ICT in Education' were limited by a tight coupling between fixed government and school structures. This has perhaps been most noticeable in terms of the official sanctioning of internet-based content in schools, with the Singaporean government maintaining close control over what can and what cannot be accessed online in terms of internet censorship across all sectors of society. More subtle is the governmental direction of the language used in technology-based teaching and learning. Aside from studying five or six periods of Chinese a week, all secondary school lessons are required to be taught in standard forms of English (Chai *et al.* 2009). Government and educational authorities are therefore keen to promote technology-based learning in standard English – thus ignoring content in the English-based form of 'Singlish' creole that is spoken and written colloquially by nearly all Singaporean adults, young people and children. In all these ways, what Singaporean teachers and students do with digital technology inside their classrooms is qualitatively and quantitatively different from what they are likely to be doing outside school. All these issues can therefore be seen to contribute to a situation where digital technology is used within schools in a restrained and 'artificial' manner. Whereas the official policies have undoubtedly facilitated the central presence of technology within Singaporean education, the local politics of technology use and non-use remain more complex and certainly more compromised.

Why Robot? The Case of Educational Robotics in Japan

A more esoteric example of the local shaping of education and technology can be found in the on-going efforts in Japan (and to a lesser extent South Korea and Taiwan) to develop roboticised teachers and teaching assistants. Indeed, the past twenty years have seen a growing interest amongst Japanese technologists in the design and implementation of 'real' humanoid robots that coexist and interact with human beings in the home and in the workplace. Over half of the world's industrial robots can now be found in Japan, and while currently prevalent mainly in heavily urbanised areas it is predicted that each Japanese household will be home to at least one robot by the end of the 2010s – the domestic side of what some commentators see as an impending 'robotic moment' in humanity (see Turkle 2011). Alongside the popular categories of 'entertainment' and 'compa-nionship', many of the 60 or so currently available types of household robots have been designed specifically to function as 'human sector' service employees – i.e. fulfilling functions in nursing, child-care, cleaning, security and surveillance. As such, the notion of the 'teaching robot' is an obvious combination of many of these functions.

Early efforts such as the 'IROBI' robotic teaching assistants were relatively rudimentary – little more than machines with monitors in their midriffs that stu-dents could interact with. Yet the 2000s saw the development of more deliberately 'humanised' teacher robots, typified by the 'Saya' robot. Originally designed as a receptionist robot, the teacher version of Saya was designed to resemble a female primary teacher – with fully prosthetic rubberised face and hands, skirt suit, brown hair and facial make-up. Saya's face was programmed to express basic emotions such as happiness, sadness, surprise, fear, disgust and anger. The robot was trialled successfully with ten- and eleven-year-old students, taking class registers, monitoring students' behaviour and issuing behavioural orders (such as 'be quiet') when appropriate.

At first glance the official justifications for robots such as Saya appear to replicate that of any other educational technology. Roboticists at the Tokyo University of Science promoted Saya as 'just a tool', giving children "the opportunity to come into contact with new technology" and providing teachers for remote rural areas where "there are few teachers out there that can teach these lessons" (Kobayashi 2009). Again, as with most educational technologies, a sizable body of empirical and anecdotal evidence has been produced to support the belief that teaching robots are 'effective' classroom tools. As Li *et al.* (2009, p.479) reported:

> In Japan two robots visited a children's elementary school for two weeks, with the purpose of teaching English to children. This experiment showed that, with the robot, children's recall of new words improved, and that there was a positive correlation between the frequencies of interacting with the robot and learning performance.

Much is therefore being made within Japanese educational technology circles of the educational potential of these new technologies (see also Carey and Markoff 2010, You *et al.* 2006). As the chief scientist behind the Saya robot recounted proudly, "children even start crying when they are scolded" (Kobayashi 2009). Yet despite these apparent successes, the enthusiasm for robotic and holographic 'teachers' remains a largely Japanese phenomenon – therefore raising a number of questions regarding the factors and issues that lie behind the Japanese acceptance of robot teachers.

As the US anthropologist Jennifer Robertson (2010) reasons, a number of social, economic, political and cultural issues can be seen to underpin the 'robotic turn' within Japanese society. First, from a global economic perspective, Japanese industry and government have focused strategically on robotics as the next 'new' technology to re-establish Japan as the world's leading high-technology producing economy. As Robertson (2010, p.8) reasons, "Japanese robots are forecast to be in this century's global marketplace what Japanese automobiles where in the last century". However, the Japanese enthusiasm for robotic teachers stems far beyond economic competitiveness. In particular, Japanese society is beset by a combination of demographic problems – not least a rising shortage of labour, a rapidly ageing population and a declining birth-rate. For Robertson, then, the notion of the *female* robot teacher is an important aspect of the Japanese development of roboticised technologies as a technological fix to these societal issues. As she explains, there is a growing movement within male sectors of Japanese society against the trend of Japanese women aged in their twenties and thirties refusing to marry and preferring instead to pursue careers and continue living with their parents (the so-called *parasaito shinguru* – 'parasite single' as Yamada [1999] terms them). Infusing traditionally feminised professions (such as teaching, nursing, receptionists) with robot workers thereby goes some way to countering this trend.

It is also important to acknowledge a range of cultural aspects to the Japanese acceptance of these technologies in the classroom. As Robertson argues, humanoid robots are regarded by some Japanese people as preferable to foreign labourers – negating the sociocultural anxieties and difficulties associated with working with and living alongside non-Japanese people. This links particularly with the issues of *honne* and *tatamae* (face and truth) where one is expected to present a good face regardless of discomfort or dislike for another. Perhaps even more subtly than implicit ethnocentrism, it can be argued that the dominant belief systems of Japanese culture are also arranged in such a way that supports the acceptance of robots as "benign, benevolent *living* entities" (Robertson 2010, p.12). The Shinto belief system, for example, contains a number of complex animistic beliefs about life and death – not least the notion that vital energies and forces (*kami*) are present in all aspects of the world, be they animate and non-animate, living and non-living. The notion of *basho* – a key element of modern Japanese philosophy – also places less emphasis on a definite subject/object distinction than is the case in Western thought. Thus in contrast to the logic of Western rationality, this way of thinking allows for contingency, co-creation and shared spaces of emergent relationships between humans and artificial systems.

The Japanese enthusiasm for roboticised teachers may be an extreme case, yet it illustrates the need to position technological change within the influences of local context. Admittedly, in the case of Saya, IROBI and their successors throughout the 2010s, these local contextual issues are wide-ranging – from global and local economic concerns, demographic shifts, cultural understandings and what Robertson (2010, p.28) describes as "quite unprogressive notions of gender dynamics and the sexual division of labour, along with discriminatory attitudes towards non-Japanese migrant workers". The robotic teacher is therefore not simply a neutral 'tool' or a 'piece of cool kit' that is likely to spread in popularity the world over. This particularly Japanese instance of educational technology is the result of a specific combination of cultural, social, economic and political issues that is unlikely to be reflected in many other contexts.

Conclusions

This chapter has focused on the importance of local context, circumstance and culture in shaping what are often presented as global forms of educational technology. Of course, highlighting the importance of culture and context in shaping educational technology use, carries an attendant risk of presenting overly holistic, exaggerated or exoticised accounts of local settings. In focusing on the case of educational robotics in Japan, for example, care must be taken not to descend into a digitally reversed form of imaginative Orientalism, where the post-industrial East is venerated as somehow being more technologically attuned and inclined than the industrial West. Indeed, it has been argued that Western (especially North American) commentators have long held a misplaced fascination for the apparently roboticised nature of social relations within Japanese society and Japanese classrooms (see Cummings 1989). In considering these examples of local forms of educational technology provision and practice, it is important to resist replicating unfounded national generalisations and cultural mythologising (see Takayama 2011).

Thus, while adding to the richness of our understanding of educational technology, all the analyses of 'local' factors presented in the chapter should be seen as generalised and not without their problems. As Macfadyen (2011, p.280) reasons, any functionalist 'national culture' approach to education technology – such as descriptions of the Confucian or Taoist tradition – will inevitably over-simplify the "multiple and dynamic conditions influencing the field of cultural practices in human societies". In raising the need to be aware of the influence of these issues, we should remain mindful of the dynamic nature of any individuals' circumstances and their scope for individual agency within local contexts. Rather than attribute technology (non)use solely to issues relating to 'national culture' or dominant religion or philosophy, we need to consider the specific and situational conditions and social forces that bring such groupings into being, and with which they continue to interact (Macfadyen 2011). In this sense, it would be unwise to presume a cultural homogeneity and denial of plural perspective within any local setting or grouping. The overriding argument that should emerge from this chapter is simply that matters of local context need to be *added* to any account of education and technology. As Andrew Brown (2009, p.1147) reasons:

> The point here is that, again, the form of realization of this digital technology in practice relates to the context in which it is embedded. As the technology moves from place to place, its meaning changes. The technology itself is both re-contextualized and re-contextualizing.

In this sense, we must add the issues and factors raised in this chapter to the multi-layered picture of education and technology that is emerging as this book progresses. The global forms and trends outlined in Chapters 3 and 4 still stand, and care should be taken when considering the points made in this chapter to avoid becoming "immured to the ghetto of the local" (Chakravartty and Sarikakis 2006, p.171). As we develop the depth and breadth of our discussion throughout forthcoming chapters in this book, it is important to remember that a balance is required in any analysis. At best, then, we should take up Joel Spring's (2009, p.143) conclusion that:

> the findings of culturalists do not negate the existence of this superstructure, but they do bring into question their actual impact on local policies ...

> [Policy] borrowing does not mean that national and local communities will implement an exact replica of these policies and practices. Changes are made to meet the conditions and desires of local communities.

One key point that has emerged from this chapter and is certainly worth taking forward into the remainder of our discussion is the idea that many forms of educational technology as used in regions such as the Middle East, South and East Asia and sub-Saharan Africa perhaps represent a grafting of Western values into non-Western contexts. Could it be that most dominant forms of educational technology constitute a digital form of the 'Eurocentricism' of education provision and practice – thereby doing little more than reinforcing the linguistic codes, cultural assumptions and models of what constitute 'desirable' knowledge particular to a Western perspective? Certainly, it could be concluded that most of the forms of educational technology discussed up until this point in the book do not appear to particularly "respect indigenous knowledge present in any given context and tend to view Western solutions as superior regardless of the systematic implications of those solutions in different cultures" (Carr-Chellman 2005, p.8).

This charge of an implicit cultural imperialism in educational technology is a serious and wide-ranging one, and certainly merits more detailed consideration. At best, these issues are usually only acknowledged briefly in the educational technology literature – and even when highlighted are usually quickly moved on from. Indeed, the implications of most of the issues raised in this chapter could be considered as simply too disruptive to be taken up within the field of educational technology. As Alison Carr-Chellman (2005, p.9) reflects:

> How can American professors, instructional designers, and web educators realistically be expected to anticipate the cultural needs and contextual sensitivities necessary to create a course deliverable worldwide? Or will we focus instead on creating completely homogenised courses that will not offend anyone from Kazakhstan to California? Can education *be* homogenised? ... Isn't learning necessarily contextualised in our own cultures and contexts?

Clearly we cannot afford to take such an evasive position on the significance of context and culture. These are certainly matters that educational technologists should be obliged to engage with – however uncomfortable this may make them feel. With such thoughts in mind, it is now time to move our attention away from the forms of educational technology found in rich (over)industrialised contexts and, instead, consider the forms of educational technology that can be found in the majority of the world's less-wealthy countries. We shall now go on to consider the role of educational technology in what is often termed 'international development'.

6

THE ROLE OF EDUCATIONAL TECHNOLOGY IN INTERNATIONAL DEVELOPMENT

Introduction

Our discussions so far have tended to concentrate on educational technology in the context of relatively wealthy nations and regions. Of course, this provides only a partial analysis of the 'global' phenomenon of digital technology in education. We have not yet given sufficient attention to the experiences of those who live outside the (over)developed and (post)industrialised nations that tend to be feature less in academic analyses of educational technology. With this in mind, the next two chapters look towards the experiences of countries, regions and communities that constitute the 'grey areas' and 'black holes' of the digital world (Warschauer 2004). These are the parts of the world that are least connected to the information society – from the shantytowns of Karachi to the villages of Eastern and Southern Africa. In particular, this chapter concentrates on the nature and form of educational technology in low-income 'developing' nations.

Before the chapter continues, it is necessary to acknowledge the limitations of using labels such as 'development' and 'developing' – not least the implication of delayed progress towards a more advanced level of being a 'developed' nation. Using these labels runs the risk of oversimplifying the economic, political and cultural situations of a diversity of countries and societies, as well as erroneously relegating nations to the status of subordinate 'other'. In practice, the term 'developing nation' encompasses a range of different forms – from 'newly industrialised countries' such as India and South Africa, to so-called 'failed states' such as Yemen and Somalia. Many developing countries should be more accurately classified as 'middle powers' with moderate economic capacity and political power. Moreover, levels of development vary *within* as well as *between* countries, especially between urban centres and rural 'peripheries'. Countries can be relatively developed in some aspects, but less developed in others. Cuba, for example, has highly developed education and health systems, despite being relatively disadvantaged in other areas of society. Conversely, relatively wealthy countries such as Saudi Arabia and Qatar are relatively undeveloped in areas such as democratic freedom and plurality.

Any form of labelling therefore encounters a host of complex issues that cannot be resolved in the space of these few pages alone. Indeed, there is probably no wholly satisfactory means of delineating countries in terms of their relative economic, political and societal development. Even the most carefully worded distinction between nations will incur some element of inaccuracy and reductionism. Take, for instance, the differences often drawn between the 'global South' and the 'global North', the 'industrialising' south and 'industrialised' west; the 'Occident' and 'Orient'; or the now unfashionable 'First World' and 'Third World'. Thus the rest of this chapter will make guarded reference to 'low-income' and 'developing' nations – while acknowledging these to be flawed terms intended only to reflect the unequal share of global wealth that persists between these countries (Nordtveit 2010). With these semantic caveats now established, the remainder of the chapter will go on to examine the nature of educational technology 'elsewhere' – i.e. beyond the privileged (over)developed settings that previous chapters have so far mostly considered.

The Role of Technology in International Development

As we saw in Chapter 4, educational technology is a prominent policy issue for most nations, regardless of economic or societal circumstance. Indeed, the governments of many low-income countries have introduced sophisticated national strategies and policy-programmes that purport to address the need to introduce technology into their education systems. Yet as was also argued in Chapter 4, these policy-programmes have proved for the most part to be symbolic and aspirational rather than substantive and transformative. This is due, in part, to the indirect patterns of governance between national governments and local educational arrangements. In terms of actual change 'on the ground' the integration of digital technologies into the education systems of many low-income nations is often not driven primarily by national government policy but entwined with long-established 'international development' efforts on the part of state, market *and* international actors. In this sense, the role of educational technology in low-income nations must be set against the historical context of international development and aid within these countries. As ever, educational technology is a globally connected affair – even in the most globally peripheral contexts.

Notions of 'international development', 'developmental intervention' and 'international aid' have been prominent features of international relations between low-income countries and 'the rest-of-the-world' since the end of the Second World War. In official terms, development is often defined simply as the elimination of poverty through economic growth and good governance. As this description implies, a key concern here is the issue of social inclusion – i.e. the assistance of individuals, families and communities to engage and participate fully in society. The field of international development therefore seeks to focus on the equitable redistribution of economic resources, and the reduction of inequalities in employment, education, housing, health, recreation, culture and civic activity. In this manner, the application of educational technology within the field of international development is often framed in straightforward terms of the efforts of organisations outside low-income countries to use digital technologies to reduce poverty and increase individuals' life-chances.

These broad-brush descriptions do little to convey the complexity of international development and international aid. In particular it is important to recognise that the goals of international development are driven by political agendas beyond assisting those individuals who could be considered to be 'in need'. As Tim Unwin contends:

> [there is] an increasingly hegemonic approach by international donors and financial institutions about how best to support development in the poor countries of the world, based fundamentally on devising mechanisms to ensure economic growth through the creation of liberal democratic political systems.
>
> *(Unwin 2009a, p.14)*

As such, international development should be seen as an inherently directive as well as redistributive act on the part of an 'international community' seeking to reorganise the economic, political and societal arrangements of low-income nations (Mosse 2005). As Susan Robertson and colleagues have detailed, the nature of these change agendas has shifted continuously throughout different phases of development activity since the 1980s (Robertson *et al.* 2007). For instance, international development efforts during the 1980s under the so-called 'Washington Consensus' saw a set of policy prescriptions and 'structural adjustments' aimed at bringing low-income countries into the increasingly globalised form of financial markets that had emerged since the 1950s. During the 1990s, this emphasis shifted towards a notion of 'adjustment with a human face' – especially the pursuit of 'good governance' where countries were supported to supposedly develop their own policy processes. Then following the September 2001 terrorist attacks in the US, a distinct merging of concerns over developmental aid and concerns over global security took place (Robertson *et al.* 2007). Throughout all these phases, international development can be said to have been a politically and ideologically driven field of activity – coming to define the social reality *and* the social problems of life in many societies. As Arturo Escobar (2000, p.11) concludes, development is "a pervasive cultural discourse with profound consequences for the production of social reality in the so-called Third World".

Understanding the role of digital technology in 'developmental' terms therefore involves more than celebrating the use of technology as a neutral tool to address the problems of low-income countries. This is an important distinction to make, as the notion of the 'technical fix' has long pervaded the field of international development. Indeed, it could be argued that the field of international development has grown up historically around a mind-set of recasting social, political and economic problems into neutral scientific terms with neutral scientific solutions (Escobar 1995). In this sense, it is easy to see how digital technology has assumed a central and usually unchallenged role within contemporary international development efforts – not least in the area of educational development. Yet as has been discussed from the first chapter of this book onwards, it is a mistake to see educational technology as a neutral tool through which economic, political and societal fortunes can be improved. If we are to make full sense of the role of educational technology within low-income contexts, we therefore need first to unpack the assumptions underlying the role of technology in international development.

Here, it is important to remember that 'pre-digital' technologies have long played an important role in international development efforts. Many international development contexts during the twentieth century included a focus on 'appropriate' and 'sustainable' technology – i.e. the support of technology use that was felt to meet local needs and capabilities, but had a minimal impact on environments and societies. Appropriate technologies are seen to offer a transitional stage of technological development, promising a means of 'shifting' countries towards fully modern technology use (Hazeltine and Bull 1999). One of the advantages of this 'intermediate' approach is that tools and technologies are more effective than existing traditional methods, but cheaper and easier for local populations to purchase than the most technically-sophisticated technologies that could be provided. Appropriate technologies also have an advantage of remaining close enough to traditional methods as to be produced and sustained through locally available materials and knowledge – remaining sensitive to local issues of resources, environment, knowledge and customs.

One of the earliest – and most enduring – examples of appropriate technology was Mahatma Gandhi's championing of the charkha (spinning wheel) within rural Indian communities. For Gandhi, the charkha was a technically efficient means of production that was also capable of supporting the increased economic participation of the general peasant population (Rybczynski 1980). More subtly, it was also a powerful symbol of self-reliance and freedom from colonial rule – eventually being depicted at the centre of the national flag of the independent Indian nation. As this now iconic example illustrates, the use of technology in international development has long been infused with political intent as well as practical benefit. As Anthony Akubue (2000, n.p.) observes, "appropriate technology cannot be seen simply as some identifiable technical device; rather, it is an approach to community development consisting of a body of knowledge, techniques, and an underlying philosophy".

Of course, these principles and processes of appropriate technology sit in stark contrast to the more recent 'digital turn' taken by many international development programmes and initiatives. Here, the transitional ethos has been replaced by a prevailing faith in 'leapfrogging' – i.e. the implementation of advanced technologies that can support accelerated rates of economic development and social progress. Technological leapfrogging can be described in uncritical terms as "the imple-mentation of a new and up-to-date technology in an application area in which at least the previous version of that technology has not been deployed" (Davison *et al.*, 2000, p.2). A much-celebrated example of technology-based leapfrogging during the 2000s was that of Cambodia – one of the first countries where mobile phone users outnumbered fixed-line telephone users. As Latchem and Jung (2010) describe, huge parts of the Cambodian population were judged to have progressed into using mobile digital telecommunications having made little or no previous use of telecommunications technology at all. Thus in the eyes of many commentators, the otherwise non-industrialised country of Cambodia demonstrated an ability to advance to the status of a post-industrial 'information society' without having to endure the stages of 'smoke-stack' industrialism that blighted much of the Western world throughout the nineteenth and twentieth centuries.

While appropriate and intermediate technology initiatives continue to play a role in some international development efforts, much more attention is now directed towards the use of digital technologies as advanced solutions to development pro-blems – not least in the area of education and educational development. These efforts have coalesced over the past ten years into the field of 'information and communications for development' – or 'ICT4D' as it has come to be known. ICT4D certainly represents a more aggressive and ambitious approach to technology-based development than its predecessors, the appropriate and intermediate technology movements. Here an emphasis is placed on using digital technologies to achieve system-wide economic, social and political growth, as well as supporting the increased participation and empowerment of individuals and local communities who otherwise face conditions of 'poverty' and 'marginalisation' (see Colle and Roman 2003). In these terms, ICT4D is built around an explicit assumption of a direct linkage between the use of digital technologies and economic growth and 'enterprise', as well as liberal democracy and enhanced 'governance'. ICT4D efforts are therefore based around distinctly Euro-American notions of development – usually centred on goals of "progress and growth towards a greater good, be this economic, social or political" (Unwin 2009a, p.9). Thus, while ICT4D interven-tions are concerned ostensibly with using digital technologies to help poor and marginalised people and communities make a difference to their lives, they nevertheless operate within a decidedly business-oriented basic framework. As Chakravartty and Sarikakis (2006, p.54) observe:

> [an] emphasis on 'business models', the involvement of private industry with the corrective presence of civil society organizations and the assumed neutrality of communications technologies are some of the key features of this new global policy framework.

It is important that any analysis of the role of digital technology in educational development remains mindful of these different values and agendas that underpin the use of digital technology to achieve social change and international development. We shall return to these ideological dimensions of technology and development later on in the chapter. For the time being, we should now move on to consider the specific contribution of digital technology to education-based development.

The Rise of Education and Digital Technology in International Development

Alongside areas such as healthcare, agriculture and housing, education constitutes a central element of international development work. At one level, the educational issues faced by those living in low-income countries are centred on fundamental matters of ensuring access to learning and teaching. As David Hollow (2009) observed, even as Africa entered the second decade of the twenty-first century, more than 20 million children in the continent had missed out on receiving *any* form of schooling at any time during their childhood. Moreover, the quality of learning for those who had received some form of schooling was often compromised by large class sizes, poor quality teaching and lack of resources. From this perspective, many of the educational concerns of international development continue to be straightforward – i.e. ensuring that all individuals receive a 'basic' level of education. This issue was a key element of the United Nations 'Millennium Development Goals' that were set in 2000 – making explicit the promise of achieving universal primary education by 2015. In the light of this ambition, providing children and young people with access to good quality education was established as a priority for global and regional development efforts throughout the 2000s and into the 2010s.

While the goal of universal primary education continues to provide a dominant frame of reference, education is also seen as a key aspect of other areas of development work – such as efforts to improve adult employment, health awareness, community cohesion and environmental sustainability. All of these areas illustrate the breadth of what is known as 'education for development' – i.e. the use of education to promote development and prosperity, to improve quality of life for individuals and societies, and to help remove 'unfreedoms' for individuals to satisfy their basic needs (Daniel 2002). All these concerns of ensuring equitable access to education, and promoting education for development have therefore formed key aspects of the ICT4D field. Indeed, digital technology has come to be seen as a ready means of overcoming entrenched educational inequalities across low-income nations. As Michelle Selinger (2009, p.206) reasons:

ICTs can indeed hold the key to a step change towards improvement in the world's education systems. ICT is certainly not a panacea for education, but it is a powerful tool that when implemented appropriately can catalyse and accelerate education reform and development.

Powerful rhetoric of this sort has been used over the past twenty years or so to justify a large number of initiatives that seek to utilise the potential of digital technologies to enhance education provision in developing countries and regions. In practice, the scale and scope of these efforts vary considerably. On one hand are hugely ambitious large-scale programmes that aim to use digital technology to offer mass forms of basic distance education – such as the 'mega-schools' and 'mega-universities' outlined in Chapter 1 (see Daniel 2010). Similarly, there has been a recent growth of region-wide 'm-learning' solutions based on the rise of mobile telephony and satellite-based internet connectivity. On a far more localised and low-tech basis, however, are small-scale projects seeking to provide 'solar powered schools' and motorbike-mounted 'mobile internet access' points to local communities.

The field of 'educational ICT4D' therefore covers a diverse range of activities – from the placement of a few computers in a single community building to the provision of continent-wide virtual education programmes. Yet despite variations in size and scale, all of these educational ICT4D efforts raise similar sets of issues. Perhaps most significantly, any attempt to use digital technologies in educational development involves a diversity of stakeholders – from non-governmental organi-sations and charities to national government and private sector organisations. All of these stakeholders are responsible for directing substantial resources towards vast numbers of technology-based education programmes and initiatives. In order to understand better this diversity of technology-based educational development activity, we should now go on to consider further the specific nature of some of these actors and the programmes and initiatives that they are responsible for.

Educational Technology as Part of Government Aid

For the past thirty years, educational technology has been a prominent part of the international aid work carried out by the governments of developed nations – both in their own right and through intergovernmental organisations. Of course, educa-tion has been a key focus for governmental aid efforts since the end of Second World War. Even in the aftermath of the global financial crisis of the late 2000s, the UK government's 'Department for International Development' (DFID) was com-mitted to spending at least £1 billion annually on education aid in sub-Saharan Africa and Asia. Similarly, nearly one-fifth of Australia's 'Official Development Assistance' budget at this time was devoted to education – with around AUS$750 million directed towards increasing the quality of primary, vocational and technical education in the Pacific region. Education was also established as one of the core elements of the African Union's 'New Partnership for Africa's Development' (NEPAD) economic development programme. Perhaps most substantially, the

US government's 'USAID' programme has long been focused on education – directing over US$925 million to basic education in forty-three countries in 2010, and an additional US$200 million to higher education (USAID 2011). Tellingly, as with all US aid, these monies are used to enable local and national recipients to work in partnership with American 'interests' such as universities and colleges, private firms, foundations and other bilateral and multilateral donors.

These forms of governmental aid programmes and funding play a significant role in setting the educational agendas in recipient countries. As Bjorn Nordtveit (2010, p.326) notes, most low-income countries "do not have the economic possibility to finance education by their own resources and are therefore to a large extent dependent on international discourses". As described above, the discursive framing of much of the overseas aid work that has taken place during the 2000s and 2010s has been framed by the UN's 'Millennium Development Goals' – especially the stated need to ensure universal primary education, gender equality, assisting progression to higher education, and improving the quality and quantity of technical and vocational education. Within all of these priorities, it can be noted how educational technology has become a significant component of international aid efforts over the past twenty years or so regardless of country or context.

For example, from the 1990s onwards USAID developed a growing portfolio of technology-related initiatives. Under its stated aim of "help[ing] more children and teachers use education technology for improved learning", USAID developed and ran a 'Global Learning Portal' programme during the 2000s to support teachers around the world to access shared teaching materials and other educational resources. Under its US$15 million 'Digital Opportunity through Technology and Communication Partnerships' project (otherwise known as the 'DOT-COM' programme), USAID has also supported local recipients of aid funding in the broadly defined area of 'learning systems' to work with US educational organisations and corporations such as Sun, IBM, Intel and ThinkQuest. Similar educational technology-related programmes and projects feature in the international aid profiles of most other developed 'donor' countries. The UK government, for example, also has an established record of focusing on technology in education through its Department for International Development – not least through its 'Imfundo' initiative during the 2000s that saw the implementation of various technology-based education programmes throughout sub-Saharan Africa.

These efforts notwithstanding, perhaps some of the most significant recent efforts in this area have come through the NEPAD 'e-Schools' initiative. This ambitious Africa-wide programme was launched at the Africa Summit of the 2003 World Economic Forum, seeking to extend internet connectivity and technology-related teacher training to around 600,000 high schools over a ten-year period. Since then, the initiative has been implemented in seventeen African nations with a stated aim of "impart[ing] ICT skills to young Africans in primary and secondary schools as well as harness[ing] ICT technology to improve, enrich and expand education in African countries". In practice, the programme started with an initial 'demonstration phase' where eighty schools in fifteen countries were equipped with computers and printers, local networks, audio/visual equipment, and internet connectivity. Soon after national governments were encouraged to adopt and adapt a prescribed 'e-Schools Business Plan' as a broad policy framework that would allow them to implement the initiative in their country's schools. This business plan was also intended to provide a basis for the later development of individual national educational technology policies and plans. The NEPAD programme also provided participating countries with a framework for teacher training and professional development, as well as attempting to establish a satellite network offering broadband connectivity to the many rural areas where the high schools are located.

The e-Schools programme has certainly supported the adoption and integration of educational technology into national school systems at a rate of change that individual governments may not have been able to achieve in isolation. Yet initiatives such as these have also shaped the nature and form of educational technology in these countries in other ways that would otherwise not have occurred. For example, a key element of the e-Schools initiative has been the establishment of partnerships between a variety of for-profit and not-for-profit organisations. In practice, the programme has been delivered by five consortia led by large IT corporations such as Microsoft, Cisco, HP, AMD and Oracle. These partnerships involve more than fifty private sector companies and other organisations such as the Commonwealth of Learning and African Development Bank. As such, programmes such as NEPAD have been successful in bringing a considerable amount of public and private expertise to bear on the educational activities of individual countries. For instance, the guiding 'e-schools business plan' that governments have been encouraged to use as a policy template was developed by the international auditor and accountancy firm Ernst & Young. The activities therefore have significant implications for the governance of educational technology in each participating nation – not least the heightened role of commercial interests in public policymaking.

Educational Technology as Part of Corporate Philanthropy

As the example of the NEPAD e-Schools programme suggests, educational ICT4D is not the sole preserve of national governments. The integration of digital technology into the educational systems of low-income countries forms a major element of the philanthropy programmes of most – if not all – multinational IT corporations. Of course, philanthropic activities by private and commercial interests have long been a feature of education. As Anheier and Daly (2004, p.159) describe, "the voluntary use of private assets (finance, real estate, know-how and skills) for the benefit of specific public causes" can be traced back to the early twentieth-century 'scientific philanthropy' pursued by the likes of Carnegie and Rockefeller. At one level, then, the intentions that underlie such philanthropic activity – now as then – are based around straightforward motivations of altruism and concern with the public good.

Yet, far from being unilateral gifts, the philanthropic activities of commercial and corporate interests clearly involve more than a straightforward desire to receive the non-economic reward of what Andreoni (1989) describes as a 'warm glow'. As Ball (2008) and others have noted, corporate philanthropy in education is a key means of gaining policy influence, raising the public profile and standing of a company, and gaining public and/or political legitimacy. All of these benefits can be associated with the philanthropic activities of commercial and corporate actors in developing countries and regions – nowhere more so than in the area of educational technology where a wide range of multinational IT industry interests have developed extensive programmes of intervention.

The scope of this involvement is illustrated through the example of Cisco. Educational ICT4D forms an integral part of Cisco's boldly worded 'Commitment to Global Education in the Twenty-First Century' – not least its aim to "help reform and renew education throughout the world". One key element of this was the company's involvement in a series of 'Global Education Initiatives' during the 2000s delivered under the banner of 'Enabling education reform through technology'. The stated focus of this work was that of 'capacity building' through sustained programmes of teacher training, increasing student skills and working with local IT industry partners to establish technology use in local schools. These efforts started in 2003 with Cisco leading the three-year 'Jordan Education Initiative'. This was a public-private partnership that involved forty-five different partners ranging from Microsoft, Intel, Computer Associates and Hewlett-Packard, alongside departments from the Jordanian government and local charities and community groups. The focus of this programme was on developing practical ways to support the effective use of digital technology in Jordanian schools, as well as building the capacity of the local technology industry. Alongside the equipping of schools with digital technology, perhaps the most significant outcome of this work was the creation of a 'sustainable model of education reform' that was designed intentionally to be adapted and 'rolled out' in other countries – as it subsequently was in the later 'Egyptian Education Initiative' and 'Rajasthan Education Initiative'.

This sustained approach to supporting educational technology use in countries around the world is evident throughout Cisco's recent work in developing countries. For example, the company has invested $1.5 million to support the non-profit 'Teachers Without Borders' programme which was set up to enhance 'the quality and dignity' of the global teaching workforce. One of Cisco's main roles here was to support the development and delivery of online teaching training programmes and certification. The company was responsible not only for assisting with the technical aspects of the programme, but also for convening expert conferences on teaching and pedagogy, and developing local centres and networks of teachers and resources. Less visibly, Cisco continues to fund and support the activities of various 'Cisco Fellows' – individual educational experts that work across the world to lead and inspire consortia of partners and other stakeholders in technology-based educational improvements and reforms.

Cisco is certainly not the only IT-industry actor that is pursuing such activities and interventions. Indeed, most similarly sized companies display a comparable involvement in educational technology use in low-income countries. As the case of Cisco suggests, these commercial activities certainly match – if not exceed – the remit of many national ministries of education. While some of these efforts are based around profit-led motivations of developing future markets for technology products, there is also a clear extension of the role of these corporations' remits to assume an expert educational role as well as an expert technology role. This blurring of interests can also be seen in the efforts of IT corporations to fund social welfare-orientated projects. For example, as well as being involved in the donation of refurbished computers to non-profit organisations in developing countries, Dell has offered US$8 million direct funding through its 'Youth Connect' programme to charities, voluntary groups and community organisations working on educational projects with deprived populations of children and young people in India, South Africa, China, Morocco, Mexico, Brazil. As such, the role of technology firms in philanthropic work in low-income contexts is clearly a multifaceted area – motivated as much by the longer-term benefits of building stable national participants in the global 'knowledge economy', as they are by the shorter-term benefits of increased sales in 'emerging markets'.

Educational Technology as Part of Non-governmental and Non-profit Projects

Of course, despite the high-profile activities of multinational corporations, national governments and intergovernmental organisations, much educational ICT4D work is actually initiated and delivered through groups of smaller non-governmental organisations (NGOs) alongside other 'not-for-profit' and charitable organisations. As such, the highly-branded multinational efforts discussed so far should not overshadow the significance of these less well-funded interests in the promotion and provision of educational technology in developing countries. Indeed, the diversity of these 'other' actors involved in educational ICT4D is considerable – ranging from international agencies to local non-profit organisations, and also encompassing international and national NGOs, faith-based organisations, communities and civil society organisations. These groups, therefore, constitute a prominent feature of education provision and practice in developing nations – taking responsibility for channelling the funding that comes into countries from international aid organisations, as well as financing their own initiatives and projects. In Egypt alone, it was estimated that over 1,300 different non-profit organisations were involved in the country's education provision – making up nearly 10 per cent of all NGOs working in the country at the end of the 2000s (Amen 2008). As such, these organisations seek to complement the efforts of national governments, while on occasion also offering alternatives to state provision.

These groups are now involved heavily in educational technology projects and programmes. These have tended to take a number of different forms over the past twenty years – from providing basic technological access for those without, to supporting the community generated networks of learning. During the 1990s and into the 2000s, much of the NGO and charity efforts in the area of ICT4D attempted to tackle basic inequalities of access to digital technology and, it follows, to technology-based education. Initiatives of this kind continue to take a variety of guises – in particular the subsidised provision of access to computers for those without. For instance, a range of non-profit organisations such as the Belgian 'Close the Gap' and the US 'World Computer Exchange' charities, all work to supply developing countries with refurbished and recycled computers that have been donated from firms and individuals in developed nations – selling them to groups and individuals in low-income countries at prices that cover their expenses (see Streicher-Porte 2009). Many initiatives have also followed what is known as a 'telecottage' or 'telecentre' model, where community-based rooms and buildings are equipped with one or more internet-connected computer. Programmes from developed nations from the 1980s onwards have seen governments and charities sponsoring the public provision of computer and internet access in community-based sites such as shops, churches and even solar-powered shipping containers.

The aim of all these public resource initiatives has primarily been to provide flexible access to new technologies for those without such facilities at home or at work. While becoming less prevalent with the decline of the fixed 'desktop' computer, these approaches continue to be important components of NGO work in remote and rural regions (see Zhang 2008). Besides the setting up of community technology centres, sustained efforts have been made over the past thirty years by those working in the NGO sector to support the technical resourcing of educational institutions. As early as 1983, for example, non-profit programmes such as the Aga Khan Foundation financed Kenyan 'Computers in Education Project' and have worked to provide computers to schools, universities and other educational institutions (Wims and Lawler 2007). Thirty years after, much of the digital technology resourcing of primary and secondary schools remains the 'gift' of NGOs and charities.

While programmes of this type continue throughout developing contexts, one of the most celebrated technology provision programmes of the past twenty years has been the less formal and less institutionalised 'Hole-in-the-wall' initiative. This programme originated in the 1990s in a slum area of New Delhi and has since extended to over 500 sites and over 40,000 young people across India, Cambodia and Africa. As its name suggests, the premise of the project is simple. The monitor of an internet-connected computer is sunk into the external wall of a building in a local community. The monitor has no keyboard but is accompanied by specially designed joysticks and buttons to act as a mouse. Although a local volunteer is usually responsible for the maintenance of the computer, there are no teachers or technical support on hand. Instead, an ethos of 'minimally invasive education' is followed, where children and young people can access the computer at any time, and teach themselves how to use the computer on an individually paced basis.

The guiding ethos for the programme has been to locate digital technologies in what Arora (2010) characterises as 'out-of-the-way, out-of-the-mind locations' rather than in formal settings such as schools or universities.

Despite its unconventional approach, Hole-in-the-wall is considered one of the more successful educational ICT4D interventions of the past twenty years. While dependent on corporate backing from the likes of NIIT Limited and the World Bank sponsored International Finance Corporation, the Hole-in-the-wall programme retains a distinctly anti-authoritarian ethos. Indeed, the programme's credo of 'minimally-invasive education' is a non-institutionalised one, with children expected to engage with the technology "free of charge and free of any supervision" (Mitra 2010, n.p). The initiative has since been extended – with a recent incarnation attempting to use internet-based telephony to allow older community members in high-income countries to act as mentors and 'friendly but not knowledgeable' mediators to these young autonomous learners. As such the provision of such access and support is seen to underpin what the project team term a 'self-organised learning environment' – thus providing an alternative "for those denied formal schooling" in low-income countries, as well as "remind[ing] schools of their purpose and duty to the community" (Arora 2010).

While 'Hole-in-the-wall' and 'telecentre' projects continue to run, recent NGO and community initiatives have also sought to utilise the increased portability and personalisation of computer hardware (increasingly in the form of internet-embedded mobile telephones) as well as the rise of wireless connectivity. Now an emphasis tends to be put on providing internet connectivity and portable computerised devices to otherwise disconnected individuals in order to develop technology skills and, more importantly, support their learning. As Richard Heeks (2008, p.28) observes, these 'open network' projects usually seek to collect, share and disseminate "relevant local data content focused on livelihood-appropriate issues such as health, education, agriculture, and rights". These projects are often community-based, with individuals developing content and information off-line, and then using the internet, mobile phones and other communication technologies to share with other users. One of the advantages of this user-created content is seen to be its relevance and usefulness, with content being produced in a variety of national languages and local dialects, combining official information with indigenous knowledge. Examples of these projects abound – such as the Open Knowledge Network that ran during the 2000s in countries such as Kenya, Tanzania, Mali, Uganda, Senegal, Zimbabwe and Mozambique using mobile technology to support 'a human network, which collects, shares and disseminates local knowledge and is supported by flexible technical solutions'. Another, celebrated initiative was the Vidiyal mobile telephony programme in Southern India, where mobile telephones were used to support information exchange and self-education across a federation of over 200 women's self-help groups – mainly pursuing self-employed business activities around goat and sheep rearing (see Balasubramanian *et al*. 2010).

These latter projects reflect a growing trend within the field of educational ICT4D to encourage and support localised communities to make the most of so-called 'open source' products and processes to access and build their own learning tools (see Ngimwa and Wilson 2013). Much attention is now being paid by NGOs, charities and other community organisations to the use of local, 'bespoke' open source production and reproduction of learning content – thereby providing opportunities within low-income communities for "customising to fulfil specific educational needs and for the development of collaborative on-line learning communities" (Carmichael and Honour 2002, p.47). Popular instances of this open approach involve communities of local educators and technologists adopting principles of 'open education resources' and 'open courseware' to provide education to more disadvantaged learners – thus freeing up the 'intellectual property of learning' to low-income contexts where it otherwise could not be accessed readily (Willinsky 2009, p.xiii).

Assessing the Effectiveness of Educational ICT4D Interventions

All of the actors and interests discussed in this chapter – along with the supranational organisations discussed in Chapter 3 such as the UN, World Bank and IMF – are a significant part of global educational technology provision, practice and policy. As such, these forms of educational technology provision certainly demand sustained consideration and attention. Yet while academic commentators are often prepared to acknowledge the shortcomings of educational technology in developed industrialised regions of North America, Europe and East Asia, the forms of educational technology discussed in this chapter are less often the subject of a similarly rigorous critique. Instead, educational efforts in the field of ICT4D are often welcomed broadly and uncritically as an inherently 'good thing' regardless of their outcome. It could be argued that the 'good intentions' that such initiatives are seemingly built around leave these forms of educational technology almost beyond reproach in the minds of many commentators.

In particular, a noticeably acritical and confirmatory tone pervades many of the official studies and 'evaluations' that are conducted of educational ICT4D projects. While the claimed gains from many studies of educational ICT4D programmes and initiatives remain measured and reasonable, some evaluations adopt an impassioned and evangelical tone. For example, the Hole-in-the-wall initiative has attracted all manner of plaudits and transformative claims. Soon after the initial pilot stages, it was reported that the majority of children visiting the Hole-in-the-wall computers had been able to teach themselves basic operational skills of word-processing, drawing and internet searching. Moreover, the longer-term outcomes of what the project's director termed the 'self-activated learning' nature of the initiative were reported in even more breathless terms:

> Ten years later, a girl in rural Maharashtra is studying aeronautical engineering following her encounter with the computer in the wall. A village boy who

became a genetic engineer in one of India's premier laboratories found the subject by reading the *New Scientist* at his hole-in-the-wall. What else could children learn on their own, apart from the use of computers? In Hyderabad, groups of children showed significant improvements in English pronunciation, with just few hours of practice on their own. They used a computer and a speech-to-text programme that had been trained in a native English accent. In the tsunami-hit village of Kalikuppam in southern India, children with access to a hole-in-the-wall computer taught themselves basic biotechnology, reaching a test score of 30 per cent in just two months. They had started with a score of zero. If Tamil-speaking children could teach themselves biotechnology in English, on their own, how far can we go?

(Mitra 2010, p.5)

Of course, not all educational ICT4D initiatives are subject to quite these levels of promotion and 'spin'. Most people working within the field of ICT4D display a degree of awareness of the generally compromised nature of any technology-rich intervention in what are otherwise 'technology-poor' contexts (see Shohel and Kirkwood 2013). Amidst the generally positive evaluation literature it is sometimes acknowledged, for example, that digital technologies tend to be used to reinforce established forms of education and didactic learning rather than to disrupt existing pedagogic practices. Indeed, most people involved in ICT4D interventions acknowledge the on-going and incremental nature of their work. As Michelle Selinger – one of the expert group of 'Cisco Fellows' – concluded with regard to the recent NEPAD efforts throughout the 2000s:

while there have been some successes, salutary lessons have also been learnt, most notably that such initiatives take longer to deliver than expected, that there needs to be effective management and leadership, that many assumptions about ICT and education in Africa have been proved to be invalid.

(Selinger 2009, p.240)

Despite instances of such circumspection, the general consensus remains that educational ICT4D efforts are essentially successful and ultimately of clear benefit to the communities and individuals that are involved. Yet if one looks beyond the "good intentions and seemingly good projects" (Zembylas 2009, p.24), it could be concluded that this area of educational technology is in fact largely unsuccessful in achieving its core aims. Indeed although celebrated widely, all the initiatives covered in this chapter could be said to have had only a marginal bearing on the economic, political and social issues that they set out to address. Within most low-income countries and regions over the past thirty years, substantial inequalities in people's capacities and general levels of educational participation have persisted, and in many cases worsened. As Richard Heeks (2010) observes, even ICT4D projects that could be said to have had an 'impact' in particular communities and localities have rarely 'reached' beyond their specific contexts or 'survived' beyond the terms of their funding. As such technology-based educational development efforts can be accused of resulting in "an excess of cost over economic benefit" (Heeks 2010, p.635). As Tim Unwin (2009d, p.3) continues, "despite all the rhetoric of success, very few ICT4D activities, especially in Africa, have yet proved to be sustainable".

Although challenged rarely in academic or policy circles, educational ICT4D therefore needs to be understood in problematic rather than celebratory terms. Indeed, digital technology is clearly not a 'silver bullet' solution to issues of poverty, deprivation and disadvantage that beset many low-income countries. At best, it could be concluded that digital technology more often than not contributes to the maintenance of an inequitable *status quo*, rather than markedly disrupting patterns of inequality. Why, then, is this the case given the considerable transformative promises made on the part of digital technology and educational development? Perhaps more significantly, why is this relative 'failure' so rarely acknowledged and acted upon?

Accounting for the Relative 'Failure' of Digital Technology and Educational Development

One obvious tension in this area concerns the appropriateness and relevance of 'high-tech' digital initiatives in otherwise 'low-tech' and largely non-digital contexts. Even in basic terms of the appropriateness of the digital device being used, it could be argued that these initiatives are often at odds with the contexts they are situated within. For instance, with only 15 per cent of rural households in sub-Saharan Africa having access to electricity, basic operational issues of power are often of paramount importance. Another major challenge is the provision of low-cost and robust technological devices that are capable of working in under-resourced communities where fundamental necessities such as shelter, water and food are still sparse. Indeed, as Jenny Leach (2008, p.787) observed, it could be argued that "basic needs such as water and food should be the priorities for rural communities, not ICT". All these technical disparities highlight the 'opportunity-cost' of directing finite efforts and resources towards the provision of digital technologies at the expense of concentrating on more basic interventions. From this perspective, the fairly straightforward argument can be advanced that high-tech digital 'leapfrogging' agendas are perhaps an inappropriate and ultimately unhelpful approach to furthering the fortunes of low-income communities. As Michalinos Zembylas (2009, p.19) concludes, "focusing on the effects of ICT on development, considering its limited impact in addressing poverty and inequality in some parts of the world, distracts attention from efforts pressing basic needs that alleviate poverty and injustice".

Of course, it can be argued that denying people in poorer countries access to the most advanced digital technologies only serves to compound their relative inequality in a world where access to digital technology has come to be "a fundamental human right" (Fuchs and Horak 2008, p.11). Yet it could be countered that arguments of this sort vastly overestimate the importance of technology, while underestimating the social nature of inequality. Instead, it can be contended that reducing inequalities in power is not simply a technical matter of increasing technological capacity and technological access within disadvantaged nations. Instead, appropriate consideration needs to be given to what Doreen Massey referred to as issues of 'power-geometry':

> For different social groups and different individuals are placed in very distinct ways in relation to these flows and interconnections. The point concerns not merely the issue of who moves and who doesn't, although that is an important element of it; it is also about power in relation to the flows and the movement. Different social groups have distinct relationships to this anyway-differentiated mobility; some are more in charge of it than others; some initiate flows and movement; others don't; some are more on the receiving end of it than others; some are effectively imprisoned by it.
>
> *(Massey 1993, p.61)*

From this perspective ICT4D projects, programmes and initiatives are clearly located with complex sets of existing differentiated power relations and social structures, which can often mitigate *against* the empowerment of the 'disadvantaged' people that they seek to reach. In contrast to the global claims made for technological change, it should be remembered that these existing social relations are entrenched within local contexts, regardless of technological provision or digital connectivity. As Mark Warschauer (2004) points out, if one considers the existing social structures of a country such as India, then any enhancement of the agency of the rural poor through digital means can only occur alongside a more fundamental transformation of class, caste, ethnic and gender relations within which many poor people exist. To complicate matters further, these social structures vary from region to region. In hill-forest areas of India, for example, where almost entire communities suffer from poverty, class contradictions are minimal. In contrast, in the Indian plains a major cause of poverty is landlessness, with huge contradictions persisting between the landless-poor and land-holders. Similarly, religion and caste distinctions are more pronounced in some regions than others. All in all, in a context such as India, there is often no one clear 'need' that technology can be used to 'address', or one clear 'enhancement' that technology can 'provide' for all. Thus as Rizvi and Lingard (2010, p.157) observe, few educational technology interventions address

> the broader historical and political contexts that produce disadvantage in the first place, and none looks seriously at the conditions under which access is provided and might succeed ... These assume that access alone is enough to produce educational justice. In this way, they work with a very weak definition of justice.

If we reconsider the examples highlighted in this chapter, then it would appear that issues of unequal power relations and imbalanced social structures are a recurrent feature of educational ICT4D. This is especially the case with regard to the underlying 'official agendas' that are being pursued through such projects. As Tim Unwin (2009a, p.33) reminds us, any form of development work conveys a "profoundly moral agenda" of "what *should* be done and *how* we should do it". Thus, while not discounting the good intentions of many individuals working in the field, we should not overlook the moral agendas of the organisations and institutions that lie at the heart of the projects and interventions outlined in this chapter. As well as having the necessary economic power to develop and finance such schemes, these organisations also have the power to influence the nature of how the technology is used and the nature of what it is being used for. Here, then, a wide range of agendas, values and goals are being pursued by a large number of actors and interests. Indeed, one of the striking features of this chapter has been the complex of 'stakeholders' who are involved in the field of educational ICT4D – ranging from private sector organisations to donor agencies, governments of low-income countries, civil society organisations and other international bodies.

As many of the examples in this chapter suggest, the values and agendas of many of these groups are focused (whether directly or indirectly) on economic concerns. One implicit agenda within many educational ICT4D initiatives is the continued enrolment of countries and individual citizens into the 'global' neo-liberal knowledge economy. In particular, many of the initiatives described in this chapter have been built around an economically focused 'modernisation development' approach where digital technology is seen as a key means of economic "development spreading from the West to the rest of the world" (Zembylas 2009, p.19). In this sense, digital technologies such as the internet and mobile telephony are utilised as effective and efficient 'carriers' of cultural ideas to still-developing countries – "tools through which traditionally impoverished nations can acquire the content, if not the epistemologies, of Western technologists" (Ananny and Winters 2007, p.108). Here, then, it is assumed that a range of political and economic competencies – as well as more general cultural dispositions – can be demonstrated and disseminated through 'advanced' Western information and communication technologies.

In some instances, educational technology is used to advance free-market values and sensibilities. One particular motivation for commercial interests (and the governments to which these commercial interests are nominally attached) is the extension of markets for technologies and techniques that have reached a sufficient point of functional stability and affordability to make them ready for deployment in less-developed commercial territories and emerging markets. Thus, as in the case of Cambodian mobile telephony, it is assumed that the market-driven 'diffusion' of these technologies into low-income countries will allow individuals to broaden their choices and their activities – and thereby become more self-determined and self-empowered. From the point of view of private, commercial interests, the area of ICT4D presents what Richard Heeks (2008, p.26) describes as "opportunities for informatics professionals and offers new markets for ICT vendors".

While these interests are often concerned with the development of commercial 'for-profit' markets for digital technology, there is also a sense of encouraging the increased use of market principles that operate along community-driven 'not-for-profit' lines. Indeed, interventions such as the open knowledge networks and 'Hole-in-the-wall' constitute explicit attempts to promote a Western sensibility of what Yochai Benkler terms 'the wealth of networks' – i.e. a non-commercial wealth that is "distinguished by the 'non-propriety' and 'non-market' basis by which people are creating the means for others to collaborate and share in the production of software, research and scholarship, and learning materials" (Willinsky 2009, p.xiii). This promotion of a libertarian sensibility may not be related directly to profit-making, but is nevertheless a key aspect of the new knowledge economy and 'fast capitalism' that underpins it. As such there is clearly a vested interest amongst governments and corporations in extending and encouraging the adoption of these networked habits and 'ways of doing' in citizens around the world – regardless if an immediate profit is at stake or not.

Of course, these market-driven motivations of economic modernisation are not unique to educational or technology initiatives. As Nicolas King (2002, p.763) has argued, most aspects of the public health development strategies for low-income countries are similarly "closely associated with the needs of ... international commerce". Yet, this 'economicisation' of action does appear to be especially prevalent in the field of educational technology and development, regardless of whether public or private interests are involved. This is especially the case in the use of educational technology as a means through which to position low-income countries as full participants in the global economic order. Here, it could be argued that many of the educational ICT4D interventions delivered on behalf of intergovernmental organisations seek to present 'official' interventions and solutions – often concerned with building indigenous IT industry capacity and 'up-skilling' future workforces of developing countries with digitally oriented skills. Similarly, many governments of low-income countries clearly see educational ICT4D projects as a ready means of attracting foreign capital and multinational corporate interest into their countries. Indeed, it could be argued that for many poorer nation-states, the act of allowing large multinational corporations to work in (and on occasion effectively take control of) 'public sector' areas such as education marks an attempt to encourage further foreign investment in other areas of the national economy. These governments' apparent relinquishing of sovereign rights to determine their educational provision also acts as a signal to the wider economic and political community of a willingness to act as functioning 'players' on the world economic stage. In all these ways, educational technology is clearly not being driven by purely 'educational' motivations in the narrow sense of enhancing teaching or learning.

All these issues therefore raise questions concerning the compatibility of the self-interest of the organisations involved in educational ICT4D against the value and nature of the 'empowerment' that some of the most vulnerable and needy citizens in the world are being offered through digital technology use. As Masschelein and

Quaghebeur (2005) remind us, the forms of 'participation' and 'inclusion' that are promised through any political intervention are often based on official 'supply-side' needs and assumptions. For example, many of the initiatives outlined in this chapter purport to promote the increased and active involvement of people in activities and decisions that concern their lives. Yet often these official notions of 'participation' and involvement' can be seen as conforming to official expectations of what it is to learn productively or to gain skills related to the contemporary economic order. In other words, it could be argued that under many forms of educational ICT4D the individual 'participant' is not actively self-determining (and self-empowering) but submitting themselves to conform to official agendas of what it is to be a learner, a technology-user or a future functioning member and 'productive' participant in the knowledge economy. While understandable from an official point of view, it could well be that many of these 'socially inclusive' benefits are not especially desirable – or even that advantageous – for the individuals in the low-income contexts who are supposedly being 'developed' and advantaged. As such, ICT4D efforts in education could be seen as "divert[ing] attention from social and power structures that perpetuate many forms of inequality and social exclusion" (Zembylas 2009, p.18).

Conclusions

Criticising an area of educational technology that is more socially-focused and progressively-minded than most others may appear, at first glance, to be an unfair and disproportionate response. Yet educational ICT4D should not be spared critical analysis simply because of the seemingly 'good work' and 'good intentions' of many of those involved. The mis-application of digital technologies in the context of educational development cannot simply be excused as a case of 'anything is better than nothing'. Instead, ICT4D is a major element of educational technology use in 'a digital world', and deserves the scrutiny that has long been afforded to technology interventions in wealthier 'developed' countries. In pursuing a critical approach, this chapter has therefore highlighted a number of key themes that have also emerged during previous chapters of the book – not least issues of power and, in particular, the question of whose interests in which digital technologies are being developed and introduced.

One key issue to take from the discussions in this chapter are the unbalanced relationships between those being 'developed' and those responsible for the 'developing'. As Richard Heeks argues, the majority of these innovations can still be characterised as 'pro-poor' in their approach, i.e. where the innovation occurs "outside poor communities but on their behalf". Only a small number of innovations could be said to adopt a 'para-poor' approach that involves working within or alongside poor communities, adopting participative, user-engaged design processes. Finally, an even smaller number of ICT4D initiatives could be seen as 'per-poor' – namely innovations that occur within and by poor communities with little or no outside stimulus. While these latter approaches are beginning to be seen by some commentators as the most desirable and sustainable approaches to take in theory, in practice the vast majority of educational ICT4D projects remain resolutely 'pro-poor' in their approach and intent – therefore facing all of the "danger[s] of design versus reality gaps" that this engenders (Heeks 2008, p.29).

The persistence of the pro–poor approach in the area of educational ICT4D runs the risk of replicating the notion of the 'technical fix' that has recurred throughout many of the discussions in this book. In particular, the false promise of potential transformation on behalf of an incoming technology runs the risk of distracting attention away from the wider, deeper and more fundamental issues that underpin the provision of education in developing countries and contexts. We shall return to these issues in the final chapter – not least the suspicion that educational ICT4D solutions remain largely 'external' impositions onto low-income and marginalised people and communities. However, before we can expand this line of reasoning, the next chapter will consider one further initiative in the field of educational technology and development that is reckoned by many commentators to have the potential to transform the educational – and it follows societal – conditions of countries around the world. Chapter 7 therefore goes on to examine the much-celebrated 'One Laptop Per Child' initiative – one of the most significant educational technology programmes of the past thirty years. As well as constituting a prominent element of global educational technology, OLPC offers a rich and revealing case study of many of the critical issues and concerns that have emerged from our discussions so far. We will now go on to make critical sense of this hugely ambitious educational technology intervention. Is *this* the instance where the globalising potential of educational technology could be realised once and for all?

7

'ONE LAPTOP PER CHILD' – A CRITICAL ANALYSIS

Introduction

The past six chapters have highlighted a wide range of interests and influences that underpin the worldwide implementation of educational technology. In particular, a picture has emerged of educational technology being shaped by an array of factors at international, national *and* local levels. Rather than being a globalised and determining force, any form of 'educational technology' is itself dependent upon a number of social, cultural, political and economic interests. Of course, this is not to deny that educational technologies are associated with some significant changes in education around the world. Yet anyone wishing to understand fully the nature and outcomes of educational technologies use has to look far beyond the technical specifications and features of specific devices and gadgets. As has been reiterated throughout this book, educational technology has to be described and discussed as a set of socio-technical arrangements.

Focusing on the social aspects of educational technology inevitably raises questions of how, why and in whose interests these devices and artefacts are used. In this manner, we have seen so far how the use of digital technology in education – as with any aspect of society – is a profoundly political concern. The past six chapters have attempted to look beyond the harmonious portrayals of educational technology that can often be found in popular, political and academic discussions, and instead examine the areas of tension, contradiction and conflict that underlie any instance of digital technology use in education. As all our examples so far have demonstrated – from the most advanced Singaporean 'Future School' to the most basic Indian 'Hole-in-the-wall' – educational technology is perhaps best understood as an intense site of struggle. As we have seen over the past six chapters, these are struggles that take place across a number of fronts – from the allocation of resources and production of knowledge, to the maximising of profit and political gain. As such, most of the questions that surround education and technology are the fundamental questions of education and society – i.e. questions of what education *is*, and questions of what education should *be*. At this stage of our discussion it should be now clear that digital technologies are drawn inexorably into the global, national and local politics of education – for better and for worse.

In this penultimate chapter, our critical reading of educational technology is advanced further through a detailed examination of what many people consider to be the most significant global educational technology programme of recent times. The 'One Laptop Per Child' initiative (OLPC) is one of the most ambitious, most publicised and most lauded educational technology initiatives of the past thirty years. This is a programme that claims to address many of the ICT4D issues outlined in Chapter 6, yet at its heart has a universal agenda of promoting 'technology enhanced learning' across low-income and high-income contexts. Indeed, throughout the 2000s and into the 2010s, the goal of building and supplying a low-cost laptop computer for children and young people around the world has become a touchstone for progressively-minded technologists and educationalists alike. Many people's faith in OLPC as a transformatory example of educational technology persists to this day. The initiative therefore offers an excellent case study through which to refine many of the themes that have emerged so far from this book's analysis. The remainder of this chapter now goes on to examine the case of the OLPC initiative in detail – making sense of the rhetoric and the reality of one of the defining global educational technology programmes of recent times.

The Technological Allure of OLPC

Many people find it difficult when discussing the OLPC initiative to look beyond the 'laptop' device itself. Indeed, over the lifetime of the programme the technological artefacts at the centre of the 'One Laptop' initiative have inspired many different descriptions. In monetary terms, the initially proposed '$200 Laptop' soon became touted as the '$100 Laptop' as the cost of its production began to fall. During the early years of the initiative, commentators referred playfully to the 'Little Green Machine' and the 'Children's Computer' as word spread of the devices' striking appearance and simplicity. Yet while prompting a number of different labels, OLPC has remained based around a disarmingly straightforward concept – i.e. producing a low-cost, low-specification but highly durable personal computing device that can be handed over to children and young people around the world. As with many educational technology ventures, OLPC is often considered by its advocates to be an intuitive and common-sensical idea that transcends any future debate – what many people would describe as a technological 'no-brainer'. As Laurie Rowell (2007, n.p.) enthused a couple of years after the public launch of the programme:

> Here's an outrageous idea: what if every child in the world could have a free personal laptop? Put some e-books on it, make it web-capable, and add a

palette of media tools so children could work on creative projects. Wouldn't that be incredible?

While reassuring in its tone, the homespun enthusiasm that surrounds the project often serves to overshadow the precise nature and form of the OLPC initiative. From its inception, the programme has been built around a central belief in developing and distributing devices that are designed specifically to bring networked computing (and, it follows, networked learning) to populations of children and young people who are otherwise living in disadvantaged conditions. While spokespeople for OLPC have constantly reiterated the claim that theirs is *not* a technology project, the outstanding feature of the initiative has been the innovative and ever-changing technical specifications of its computerised devices. At present the $100 'laptop' is in its third incarnation – the so-called 'XO-3' device that was developed after the programme received a grant of over $5 million from the multinational IT manufacturer Marvell to develop a low-cost tablet device built around low-power silicon chips. The XO-3 followed on from the 'XO-2' – a flip-back, touch-screen 'hand-book' device which can open flat to provide a square display supportive of writing, typing and touch-sensitive input. Both these designs, in turn, followed on from the most iconic (and still predominant) OLPC device – the original 'XO' laptop. While subsequent designs may have differed in their appearance, the XO laptop continues to embody the design principles and philosophies of the OLPC programme. As such, the XO remains the flagship technology of the programme – especially in terms of the numbers of devices being used. Thus before going on to consider the OLPC programme in socio-technical terms, it is important to be clear first about exactly what the XO is as a technological device.

The XO certainly stood out in terms of its appearance when introduced into the 2000s' consumer electronics marketplace. Described at the time of its launch as "a striking little green machine" (Naughton 2005, p.6), the XO gives the impression of being a sleek but durable child's plastic toy. Housed in rounded toughened plastic casing with a moulded handle that resembled a lunch-box, the most immediate qualities of the original XO was its size and colour. This was a small lime-green and white device – weighing around 1.5 kilograms, and measuring little more than 22 centimetres square and 3 centimetres thick. When opened, a rubber-sealed keyboard, touch-pad and stylus were accompanied by a small pivoting display monitor. The idiosyncratic appearance of the computer was heightened by the inclusion of two extendible antenna 'ears', designed to provide network connectivity to the internet as well as to other XO users within a radius of one kilometre.

Much of the initial excitement over the XO came from technology programmers and 'hackers' who were drawn to this innovative technical design. Thanks largely to work from in-house developers and the Chinese Quanta computer company, the XO housed an impressive array of hardware features for a machine of its size and price – such as a microphone, camera, loudspeakers, 'game controller' buttons, USB and audio ports. Many of these technical features were intended to allow the XO to operate in inhospitable outdoor conditions. The laptop's keyboard, for instance, was rubber-sealed and designed to be resistant to dirt and moisture. The plastic casing included built-in shock absorbers that were claimed to have been drop-tested successfully from heights of up to fifteen feet. The display monitor was designed to offer low-power but high resolution displays that altered appearance according to lighting conditions. The XO's screen could appear either to be full colour, pale colour or monochrome – thereby ensuring a readable display in even the brightest of conditions. Perhaps the most eye-catching components were the options for powering the XO – including wind-up hand-crank mechanisms and 'yo-yo' pull-string power generators. These features, coupled with their non-toxic and fully recyclable design, were reckoned to make the XO computers "the most eco-green laptops that have ever been made." (Tabb 2008, pp.338–9).

Another technically appealing characteristic was the XO's innovative software design – in particular its reliance on open source software and open-architecture hardware principles. Early incarnations of the laptop ran exclusively on slimmed-down versions of the Linux operating system coupled with a newly designed software interface titled 'Sugar'. This interface was intended to move beyond the usual 'desktop' operating system design and provide users with an abstracted spatial navigation environment which supported navigation and collaboration via four levels of viewpoint labelled 'home', 'friends', 'neighbourhood and 'activity'. Later versions of the XO offered a 'dual boot' system that allowed the Microsoft Windows operating system and familiar 'Office' software to also be used.

In the years following its launch, the XO has been roundly praised for its appearance, aesthetics and overall quality of design. Indeed, most aspects of the OLPC programme have reflected a high level of attention to design and detail that is often not found in mainstream computer production. While the XO hardware was developed by teams of in-house designers and small independent companies, the innovative design of the Sugar interface software was outsourced to the international product design company Pentagram. OLPC therefore joined Pentagram's illustrious client list of Timex, Nike, United Airlines and Swatch as part of the company's commitment to carrying out *pro-bono* work for non-profit organisations. Even otherwise sceptical commentators were forced to concede the design qualities of the OLPC machines. As Linda Smith Tabb reported at the time of the laptop's deployment in US urban contexts, "the machines are truly revolutionary in design and almost every possible feature has been thoughtfully planned" (Tabb 2008, pp.338–9).

Aside from its high standards, the technical design of the XO is a particularly important aspect of understanding OLPC in socio-technical terms – especially with regard to the values and agendas that have shaped the project from its start. Indeed, in terms of technical design, everything that has been described so far was influenced strongly by ideological values and intent. One recurring aim of the design of the XO was to produce an engaging and playful device that would appeal especially to young users. For example, the inclusion of the mesh-network antennae 'ears' were intended to give the laptop an animalistic appearance akin to a rabbit (as well as giving it much-needed internet connectivity). Similarly, the design of the software interface was designed deliberately to embody a philosophy of child-centred learning – placing the individual user at the centre of a familiar environment that also promoted communal activity and collaboration. In all these ways, the XO devices were the result of a great deal of thought and attention. This was certainly not a profit-making 'off-the-shelf' means of increasing levels of educational technology use around the world.

Unpacking the Socio-technical Background of OLPC

On the face of it, then, OLPC could be seen as being an educational technology project almost beyond criticism – involving an innovative and thoughtfully-designed piece of technology with the laudable aim of allowing children and young people to learn regardless of social circumstance. Indeed, many people within the educational technology community have been generally supportive of the promise to "create educational opportunities for the world's poorest children" through the production of a "rugged, low-cost, low-power, connected laptop with content and software designed for collaborative, joyful, self-empowered learning" (OLPC 2010, n.p.). It is at this point, then, that we need to take a step back from the obvious allure of OLPC as a technological concept. What is there that should be said about OLPC beyond its good intentions and innovative design?

First, it is necessary to place the programme within a historical context. While undeniably ambitious, the OLPC was not the first initiative to seek to support low-cost computing for the masses (see Pal *et al.* 2009). Even within the commercial confines of the consumer electronics market, US computer manufacturers were developing 'low-cost, low-spec' computers throughout the 1980s – not least IBM's 1984 'PC Jr' model and subsequent competitor models such as the Tandy 1000. In terms of the development of low-cost computers for low-income countries, the Indian 'Simputer' project was another prominent forerunner of OLPC. This attempt to develop a 'Simple Inexpensive Multilingual Computer' also resulted in the non-profit production of low-cost, open source hand-held computers with touch sensitive screens. The Simputer was also accompanied by similar claims to the OLPC – as one commentator stated soon after its release, "this nondescript little computer may hold the key to bringing information technology to Third World countries" (Harvey 2002, n.p.).

The past fifteen years have also seen the production of a number of low-cost technological devices intended for sale in developing regions. These included the production of 'ultra-basic and ultra-cheap' computing devices based on Linux such as the Taiwanese ASUSTek computer and the Chinese Lemote laptop. Similarly, in terms of desktop computing, OLPC follows on from programmes such as Brazil's Linux-based Computador Popular (people's computer), the Chinese Rural PC, the 'SuperGenius' Bharat PC and the Apna PC – all relatively cheap devices aimed at extending access to computer technology to poor communities. These efforts reflect a long-held enthusiasm within the IT industry and professional technology community to establish 'one-to-one' computing around the world – marked by the founding of an international group of high-profile technologists titled 'G1:1' (in full, 'Globally, One Computer for One Person'). All of these precedents therefore raise a key point of interest – why has the OLPC initiative progressed so much further than these other ventures, and with what ultimate effect? Here, then, attention needs to be moved away from the technical aspects of OLPC devices and towards the nature of OLPC as a social and political project. As we shall see, the OLPC programme is as much a global political initiative as it is an educational technology initiative.

The Origins of OLPC

The team of academics and technology entrepreneurs behind the OLPC initiative came to the area of educational technology with considerable experience of similar ventures. The driving force behind the initiative from its start has been Nicholas Negroponte – a high-profile technologist and academic who was one of the founding members of MIT's prestigious MediaLab department. Along with MIT colleagues (and subsequent OLPC figureheads) such as Seymour Papert, Negroponte had been involved in an early computing project sponsored by the French government in 1982 (Le Centre Mondial pour l'Informatique et Ressource Humaine) which provided Apple II computers to Senegalese schools. Although relatively unsuccessful, the idea that children in developing regions of the world could benefit from the provision of computing resources was replicated in further projects during the 1990s and 2000s – in particular the involvement of MIT and Negroponte in the provision of internet-connected laptops to small groups of children in rural Cambodia, and the larger-scale distribution of laptops to seventh-grade students throughout the US state of Maine.

These early practical projects – and much of the intellectual work that occurred at MediaLab-sponsored conferences such as the 2B1 conference in 1997 – were considered to provide an adequate 'proof of concept' for this notion of one-to-one educational computing, prompting Negroponte's establishment of the non-profit organisation One Laptop Per Child Association Inc. After the official announcement of the organisation and its intentions in January 2005 at the World Economic Forum in Davos, Negroponte presented a working prototype of the Children's Machine 1 at the subsequent World Summit on the Information Society in Tunis. The choice of this high-profile audience for the launch of a still-to-be-finalised device resulted in considerable support being given to OLPC from across the international community, not least from the UN Secretary Kofi Annan. Negroponte was celebrated in the New York Times as "the Johnny Appleseed of the digital era" (Markoff 2005) and – despite appearing to break the prototype during the official launch – Kofi Annan himself welcomed the programme as opening up a 'new front' in the education of 'the world's children'.

In terms of actual production of the machines, the small-scale OLPC team worked hard during 2005 to gain formal support from other technology and media organisations – securing backing from the likes of Google, Nortel, News Corporation as well as hardware manufacturers such as AMD (Advanced Micro Devices), RedHat and Quanta. After a further announcement at the 2006 World Economic Forum, the UN Development Program offered its formal endorsement and promised to act as a distribution agent for countries unable to purchase the minimum requirement. The actual production of the newly titled 'XO' laptop then began in November 2007.

At this stage, the 'business plan' for the OLPC programme was a defiantly simple one. Each national government that wished to participate was expected to commit to the minimum bulk order of 1 million laptops. In turn, these governments would distribute the machines through their national educational networks to children and young people. In all cases, the distribution and implementation of the machines was to be conducted according to OLPC's five core principles, i.e.: "the kids keep the laptops, focus on early education, no-one gets left out, connection to the internet, and free to grow and adapt". Although a top-down model of state-directed distribution belied these bottom-up, open and individually centred sentiments, the OLPC leadership viewed it as a necessary means of generating the volumes of investment needed to develop the technology. As such, only China, Brazil, Egypt, Thailand, and South Africa were considered initially to be worthwhile participants in the initiative. At this point, the OLPC programme had clearly marked itself as a large-scale and politically-astute social technology project – aiming to forcibly disrupt unequal patterns of access to digital technology in some of the world's largest but most deprived countries.

Initial Progress and Change

In practice, the progression of the initiative throughout the latter half of the 2000s was not as straightforward as these initial intentions would suggest. First and foremost, the relatively rapid introduction of the XO into the global information technology marketplace of the 2000s provoked considerable criticism and resistance from other IT organisations – especially the XO's commercial competitors. This included Bill Gates' much-reported initial dismissal of the device in 2005. As Gates reasoned in a speech to a Microsoft Government Leaders' Forum, "if you are going to go have people share the computer … get a decent computer where you can actually read the text and you're not sitting there cranking the thing while you're trying to type". The XO's promise of low-cost internet connected computing therefore attracted a diversity of opposition within and outside the technology community – from the figureheads of worldwide technology corporations to individual developers and designers.

Perhaps the most significant challenge to OLPC to this time was the decision of Intel – then the world's leading producer of microchips – to produce its own low-cost, low-specification netbook computer for educational markets in developing countries. Titled the 'Classmate' PC, this laptop was designed to be sold to schools and students in low-income countries for between US$199 and US$299. Over a short period of time, Negroponte was forced to move from a position of defence (initially labelling Intel's intentions as 'predatory' and 'hurting the mission') to a position of consolidation – announcing a formal partnership between OLPC and Intel in 2007. However, this partnership was nullified after six months, with Negroponte demanding that production of the Classmate was discontinued before the two organisations could work together any further.

After this disjuncture, the Classmate programme continued with laptops being produced and sold to governments around the world in conjunction with the Taiwanese manufacturer Asus. Part of the attraction to government purchasers of the Classmate products was their inclusion of Microsoft Windows and Office software, in comparison to the OLPC initiative's preference for bespoke open-source systems. Indeed, Microsoft's introduction at this time of a $3 'Student Innovation' package of software to be sold in developing countries marked another direct challenge to the OLPC programme. Many commentators were then only partially surprised by Negroponte's subsequent decision in 2007 to offer a version of the XO laptop with the dual option of open-source software and Microsoft Windows and Office software. This decision prompted widespread dismay from many of the OLPC's supporters – including the resignation for a time of the organisation's 'President for Software and Content', Walter Bender. Nevertheless, it highlighted a clear willingness to compromise the OLPC philosophy and the ideals of those involved in the face of commercial market-based concerns.

Throughout this period, actual sales of the XO continued to fall short of the initiative's projected numbers – with many of the early deals that appeared to have been secured with national governments failing to be completed. Most notably, contracts with Libya for 1.2 million XO computers, Nigeria for 1 million units, and with Thailand for 1 million units all fell through. In an effort to counter this trend, further changes to the OLPC business model were then introduced – in particular the introduction of the 'Give 1, Get 1' (GIGI) scheme during the Christmas season of 2007. Here, North American consumers were allowed to purchase an XO computer for US$399, with this cost covering the donation of an additional laptop to specified programmes in low-income countries. As a further inducement, customers were able to have the donated computer considered as a tax-deductible charitable contribution. This subsidising of XO donations by the North American market saw nearly 84,000 donations being made. Tellingly, a second GIGI scheme the following Christmas through the on-line retailer Amazon saw only 12,500 laptops being sold. Nevertheless, this renewed momentum saw XO laptops distributed to countries such as Haiti, Afghanistan, Mongolia, Ethiopia and Vanuatu. This geographical spread of the XO continued with the sale of thousands of laptops to the New York City Department of Education, as well as the education departments of Chester County in Pennsylvania, and Birmingham, Alabama. At this point, the OLPC initiative was certainly increasing its global reach, although without necessarily achieving the levels of saturation that had been promised initially.

Recent Developments

The OLPC initiative has latterly found itself continuing to be one of the most substantial – and certainly most visible – global educational technology projects of recent times. The programme has continued to attract considerable amounts of support and publicity into the 2010s. The donation of XO computers were part of aid efforts in the aftermath of the 2010 Haiti earthquake, as well as being deployed into other high-profile humanitarian zones such as Iraq, Gaza and Afghanistan. In commercial terms, the concept of the XO is considered to have hastened the emergence of the low-cost 'net book' market in Western countries. Conversely, politicians have continued to laud the initiative as an example of innovative inter-national development – to the point of calls "for the OLPC program to be designated by the UN as a new Millennium Development Goal" (Tabb 2008, p.337).

In this respect, the OLPC could be judged to have been one of the most successful educational technology programme of recent times. The initiative has been imple-mented in a number of South American countries, with governments in sub-Saharan Africa also participating. This has seen the introduction of over 1 million machines into Peru and Uruguay, with smaller amounts in countries such as Ghana, Argentina, Colombia, Mexico and Rwanda. Coupled with the machines that have been introduced through loss-leading pilot programmes and the GIGI donations, this means that OLPC computers can be found in over thirty countries from Nicaragua to Nepal. The initiative has certainly prompted changes in the patterns of educational technology use in some of these countries. In Uruguay, for example, XO laptops have been at the heart of the Conectividad Educativa de Informática Básica para el Apredizaje en Línea (CEIBAL) initiative – reckoned to be the first national programme to achieve a one-to-one ratio of primary school pupils to computers.

That said, these levels of adoption have failed to match the initial expectations and claims of Negroponte and his team. As Yujuico and Gelb (2011, p.50) concluded,

> if the criterion for success was admiration for an innovative concept, the OLPC project would be an unqualified triumph ... however, if the criterion was achieving its sales goals, the project would have to be judged a failure, despite some recent glimmers of progress.

For many commentators within the technology community, one key failing of the initiative has been the stabilisation of the actual price-per-laptop at a level approaching US$200. Coupled with the added 'financial burden' of maintenance, technical support and other aspects of programme maintenance, then the OLPC devices clearly cost far more than the mooted price of US$100 (Streicher-Porte *et al.* 2009).

Yet despite these issues of price and penetration, OLPC remains a beacon project for many educational and technological commentators – seen to offer clear proof that digital technology *can* be an integral element of a transformative agenda in the field of international development. As de Bastion and Rolf (2008, p.31) conclude with regard to the continued rollout of the XO machines in sub-Saharan Africa:

> As an integral part of a robust overall strategy, it is indeed correct to give children in Ethiopia a laptop ... It may seem ironic to distribute emergency aid and computers at the same time, but it is one way of breaking the endless cycle of dependency. The true madness would be to underestimate the lasting value of the learning which ICT4D can additionally deliver.

Unpacking the Values of the OLPC Programme

As this brief overview of its progress suggests, OLPC is certainly not a straightforward technology production and distribution programme. Indeed, in terms of our theoretical focus on the 'social shaping' of technology outlined in Chapter 2, the OLPC initiative is better understood as being driven at all stages of its development by a complex set of interests, values and guiding agendas. As such, the idea of putting an XO laptop in the hands of every child in the world clearly has been – and continues to be – informed by a set of accompanying ideological interests and agendas. In this respect, OLPC is no different from all of the other examples of educational technology considered up until this point in the book.

The notion of educational technology as an ideologically driven process is not lost on those involved in the OLPC initiative. As Nicholas Negroponte has himself reasoned, "we're not building an empire, we're building a movement" (Negroponte, cited in Hamm and Smith 2008). Thus as Ananny and Winters (2007, p.107) continue:

> We suggest that this and other ICT4D projects be critiqued not only in terms of their technological feasibility, economic rationales or models of education but, more fundamentally, in terms of the ideologies they intend their users to enact. [Even] the OLPC's interface guidelines ... serve – intentionally or otherwise – as powerful signals to policy makers, cultural critics and local communities of the particular ideologies intended to be enacted by the XO's users.

In this manner, we now need to move beyond our initial descriptions of the OLPC as a set of artefacts (e.g. the XO devices and their software designs) and as a set of practices (e.g. the design decisions of OLPC, its partnering organisations and community of open-source developers). Instead, we now need to consider the OLPC initiative as embodying a set of values, and approach the XO laptops as "sites in which designers, users, policy-makers and evangelists of all stripes perform ideology – explicitly or otherwise" (Ananny and Winters 2007, p.117). From this perspective, a number of different ideological assumptions can be identified as having underpinned the OLPC implementation to date.

First is the assumption that the XO laptops offer a means of achieving significant social, economic, cultural and political change in developing regions and countries. Indeed, much of the popular appeal of the OLPC project stems from the grandiose 'noble dream' (Rowell 2007) that informs many of the initiative's actions and activities. Behind the impressive proclamations relating to "the idea that universal laptop computer use will revolutionise the world for the better" (Luyt 2008, n.p.), lies an aggressive modernisation agenda, similar to many of the educational ICT4D projects discussed in Chapter 6. Indeed, much of the impetus behind the OLPC initiative stems from a belief that enhanced access to technology can lead to a range of educational, health and life-related improvements. As Nicholas Negroponte has asserted:

> Laptops, as we know them, are a luxury. Education is not. At $100, this is about learning and exploration, not giving kids costly tools and toys. Almost anything, from healthcare to food to birth control, can be addressed well, if not best, through education. The deeper divides are unequivocally proportional to education. Peace will never happen as long as there is poverty. Poverty can only be eliminated through education.
>
> *(cited in Witchalls 2005, p.23)*

As this bold statement implies, many of these societal benefits are seen as achievable through the stimulation and support of technology-enhanced learning directly and indirectly. In this sense, it is also important to note that the XO laptop has been built around a very specific set of assumptions about education and learning. From its start, OLPC has been positioned deliberately around a set of social constructivist learning principles common to most MIT MediaLab projects. Here the initial involvement of the prominent MIT professor Seymour Papert in OLPC is an important factor in understanding the values underpinning the programme. Papert's well-known refinement of social constructivist learning theory into the notion of 'constructionism' during the 1970s and 1980s provides a clear underpinning principle for the technological and pedagogical design of the XO laptops. Through constructionism, Papert proposed that learning is most effective when individuals are engaged in socially rich informal learning environments where they can create computational objects and systems that act as concrete representations of their cognitive development. As such, constructivist principles have been explicitly 'built-in' to most aspects of the XO design – from the 'Sugar' interface to the anthropomorphic network antennae. Indeed, the early label of the Children's Machine 1 for the XO laptop deliberately referred back to Papert's 1996 book on constructionism and computers entitled *The Children's Machine*.

Allied to these beliefs in learner-centredness is a guiding value throughout OLPC of networked individualism and a belief in the self-determining power of the individual. Indeed, the constructionist ethos is built around an individualised notion of learning – with the individual learner responsible for co-ordinating and directing their own educational experiences. This philosophy is reflected, for example, in the positioning of the OLPC initiative around "a particular model of children as agents of change and networks as the mechanisms of change" (Ananny and Winters 2007, p.107). Politically, then, the OLPC initiative moves beyond supporting the increased engagement of individuals with learning, to wider issues of supporting individuals in taking complete control of the process of education. Thus, as Michael Klebl observes, the OLPC initiative does not seek to support change through the enhancement of education systems or education institutions – "instead of traditional methods for improving an educational system like building schools, spreading textbooks, reforming the curriculum or educating teachers, self-determination of the children themselves is at the midst of this educational reform, leveraged by a technical device" (Klebl 2008, p.280).

As was observed in Chapter 1, a belief in individualised self-empowerment runs throughout the field of educational technology, reflecting an implicit (and sometimes unconscious) 'romantic individualism' amongst many technologists that positions individual technology users as "inherently expressive and self-transforming" (Luyt 2008). Yet there is also a clear anti-institutional element to the OLPC philosophy that is less common to other educational technology projects and programmes. Despite relying on national school systems to facilitate the distribution of XO laptops to children and young people, there is a distinct anti-school sentiment to the OLPC project. As Laurie Rowell (2007, n.p) reported at the time of production of the first incarnation of the XO laptop:

> Walter Bender has been clear in saying that education could benefit from a paradigm that allows more critical evaluation from people at all levels, and he's frank in suggesting that the traditional school hierarchy is a barrier to quality improvement. In his words, the education community, because of the way school and (perhaps more significantly) school systems are structured typically top-down, tends to suppress the spread of best practice as it is developed bottom-up in the classroom.

While concerned with wider social issues such as the deinstitutionalisation of education, a further set of philosophies that have underpinned the OLPC initiative since its inception are more explicitly technologically driven – what Andrew Brown (2009, p.1152) has labelled "the fetishising of technology, and the pursuit of access as a social project in and of itself". These values were perhaps best expressed by one of the early slogans adopted by the community of programmers responsible for the initial development of the XO – stating succinctly that: "Not every child in the world has a laptop. This is a bug. We're fixing it" (cited in Klebl 2008, p.280). As this melding of programming logic and social welfare suggests, the OLPC initiative has gained considerable momentum from its positioning as a collective effort on behalf of the technology community to develop technically sophisticated and exciting machines. This is noticeably the case in the high-profile alignment of the XO devices with open-source principles. Of course, the notion that the XO hardware and software is 'open' to user reconfiguration and improvement chimes with the constructionist and constructivist learning theories outlined previously. Yet the open source label has also been valuable in giving the XO a technologically 'cool' cache that some critics argue has gone some way to obscuring – or even overcoming – any criticism of the devices' clear technical limitations. As Brown (2009, p.1168) concludes, "though it is claimed that this is an education not a technology project, the development of the laptop, rather than the principles of its use, have been to the fore".

Of course, this 'core' philosophy of following open-source principles belies the OLPC programme's almost ruthless commercial and political pragmatism when it has come to achieving its aims. As described above, the history of the OLPC initiative has been characterised by an ability to broker deals and partnerships with previously conflicting interests and organisations. This can be seen in successive arrangements with commercially hostile organisations such as Intel and Microsoft, as well as the maintenance of partnerships with supranational and intergovernmental organisations such as the World Bank and UN, alongside corporate partners such as Google, Amazon, Citigroup and EBay. As such, a clear philosophy of political adaptability and pragmatism runs throughout many of the OLPC team's actions. As Nicholas Negroponte reasoned when defending the decision to offer a dual open source/Microsoft product, "it's like Greenpeace cutting a deal with Exxon. You're sleeping with the enemy, but you do it" (cited in Hamm and Smith 2008).

OLPC – Towards a Critical Perspective

The scale of these ambitions – and the aggressive and often self-important manner in which they have been pursued over the past ten years – has understandably begun to attract a burgeoning critical commentary. Yet it is telling that popular discussion of OLPC has, for the most part, taken place in an empirical vacuum. Despite some hagiographic 'evaluation' and 'assessment' studies, there has been little tangible evidence of sustained effectiveness and outcomes. The few independent studies that have been conducted of XO implementation have raised doubts of any substantial changes taking place *in situ*. As the authors of one evaluation of the OLPC implementation in South America concluded:

> Our interviews and observations in Paraguay suggest that XO use there is stratified, with a minority of youth making use of the XOs in creative and cognitively challenging ways, and a majority using them only for simpler forms of games and entertainment. We also found that the children who are already most privileged socially and economically tend to make use of the XOs most creatively. Thus, independent XO use by children might exacerbate divides rather than overcome them.
>
> *(Warschauer and Ames 2010, p.44)*

This lack of empirical 'evidence' stems, in part, from the OLPC programme's dismissive stance against the need for evaluations and pilot studies to be conducted. As Nicholas Negroponte reasoned in a 2009 speech entitled 'Lessons Learned and Future Challenges':

> I'd like you to imagine that I told you 'I have a technology that is going to change the quality of life'. And then I tell you, 'Really the right thing to do is to set up a pilot project to test my technology. And then the second thing to do is, once the pilot has been running for some period of time, is to go and measure very carefully the benefits of that technology'. And then I am to tell you what we are going to do is very scientifically evaluate this technology, with control groups – giving it to some, giving it to others. This all is very reasonable until I tell you the technology is electricity, and you say 'Wait, you don't have to do that'. But you don't have to do that with laptops and learning either. The fact that somebody in the room would say the impact is unclear is to me amazing – unbelievably amazing.

It could be argued that Negroponte's bullishness reflects an imperviousness to criticism that leaders of large-scale global projects undoubtedly require to succeed. Indeed, a strong conviction and sense of righteousness pervades much of the commentary that surrounds OLPC. Yet as even its most ardent supporters acknowledge, the enormity of the project has left the OLPC programme falling short of its much publicised ambitions. For example, while the initial stated target of the Australian OLPC programme was the provision of 400,000 laptops to children in remote regions, the actual delivery achieved since January 2008 has been closer to 5,000 machines. Through instances such as this, OLPC has begun to attract growing criticism in contrast to the initial wave of positive support and enthusiasm. Indeed, the XO laptop itself was reported by the *New York Times* to be regarded now by some sectors of the NGO community as "the emblem of the failure of technology to achieve change for the better" (Strom 2010). The suggestion can be made, therefore, that the OLPC initiative has been thwarted by a set of mitigating issues that face any large-scale educational technology programme. These issues are therefore worth considering in more detail if we are to extend the example of OLPC to other examples of educational technology around the world.

First is the contention that the XO devices and the wider ambitions of the OLPC programme are simply inappropriate for the contexts in which they are being implemented. In particular it is argued that the XO machines have been "designed in a lab-centric rather than need-oriented paradigm", therefore failing to fit with the realities of the developing countries and poor regions where they are being implemented (Pal *et al.* 2009, p.61). It certainly could be argued that the OLPC initiative is founded upon exaggerated expectations of the vitality of laptop computing outside the developed world. As John Naughton (2005, p.6) has argued, distribution of XO devices to communities in sub-Saharan Africa raises significant questions of appropriateness, not least " … whether the folks who wrote it have any understanding of what it's like to live in a society where the average income is less than $2 a day and the notion of children's rights is as theoretical as time travel".

Taking these concerns further, it has been reasoned that machines worth over US $200 are of considerable value in most of the countries where they are being delivered. From a practical perspective, this has prompted a reticence amongst some children, young people and teachers to use the devices in fear of damaging or breaking them. As Warschauer and Ames (2010) found, some communities of XO users have also encountered difficulties in meeting the costs of running the machines and then ensuring the provision and maintenance of basic infrastructure. Indeed, in many different contexts, the XO machines have proved difficult to repair and to find replacement parts. In practice, some of the key components of the XO-1 laptop (such as the rubber membrane keyboards) have been found to quickly wear out and render the machines useless. Studies of the OLPC projects in New York City and Alabama found that large numbers of laptops were broken or otherwise unusable within the first twenty months of implementation. Similarly, in Uruguay it was reported that more than half of the XO machines that were out of commission were determined to be unusable due to breakage. As Warschauer and Ames (2010, p.41) continue, "earlier, Papert claimed that 'an eight-year-old is capable of doing 90 per cent of tech support and a 12-year-old 100 per cent'. This may well be true in theory, but in practice large numbers of XOs go unrepaired".

These practical technical limitations are compounded by a set of wider moral issues – not least the appropriateness of directing funding and resources towards what is essentially a global educational technology experiment. As Andrew Brown (2009, p.1152) concludes, "with even small amounts of money able to make a distinct difference to life chances in desperately poor parts of the world, though, for instance the provision of fresh water and vital medication, this effort is misplaced". These criticisms are especially acute with regard to the 'goodness-of-fit' between the OLPC programme and the nature of education systems in developing nations. For instance, as Larry Cuban observed, many of the guiding philosophies behind OLPC could be considered to be "naïve and innocent about the reality of formal schooling" (cited in Markoff 2006). The educational and pedagogical merits of the OLPC philosophy have therefore been challenged from a number of perspectives – not least the lack of testing and research into the educational assumptions that underpin the initiative. For instance, the philosophy of not encouraging the sharing of resources within communities has been criticised in terms of restricting any benefits of the programme to a minority of children and young people (James 2011). More broadly, as John Naughton (2005, p.6) queried at the launch of the programme:

> It is an article of faith that giving kids computers is a way of aiding their learning … [The OLPC initiative] is thus rather grandly contemptuous of mundane questions such as whether there is any evidence that giving kids

computers is educationally better than giving them books, hiring more teachers or building more schools – or even paying families to send their kids to
school. For Papert – and his MIT colleagues – technology seems to be the
answer, no matter what the question.

There are, therefore, clear divisions between the OLPC programme and the educational systems that they seek to initially work within but ultimately intend to then
work around. In particular, it could be argued that the OLPC initiative suffers from
a conceptual tension in viewing individual children as the principal sites of change
while also using the principal mechanism of change as the networked structures of
national school systems (Ananny and Winters 2007). Indeed, the deliberately pro-
vocative strategy of giving laptops to individual children and young people has
prompted considerable unease amongst those with vested interests in the continuation of formal educational institutions. As the General Secretary of the Peruvian
Unified Union of Education Workers was reported to argue, "these laptops are not
part of a comprehensive educational, pedagogical project, and their usefulness is
debatable" (Luis Muñoz Alvarado, cited in Hamm and Smith 2008).

  From all these points of view, the ambition of OLPC to import (and many would
argue impose) a homogeneous set of 'other' principles and values into a diverse range
of countries and contexts around the world has raised concerns over the programme's
cultural insensitivity and neo-colonialist approach. As William Easterly reasoned
bluntly, "it's arrogant of them. You cannot just stampede into a country's education
system and say 'Here's the way to do it'" (cited in Hamm and Smith 2008). For some
critics, then, the OLPC programme is redolent of earlier colonialist interventions into
the regions of South America and sub-Saharan Africa. As technologist Guido van
Possum has argued, "I have thought for a while that sending laptops to developing
countries is simply the twenty-first-century equivalent of sending Bibles to the
colonies" (cited in Brabazon 2010). While extreme, these criticisms are reflected in
practical aspects of XO use in local contexts – in particular the OLPC model of
open-source development of diverse 'local' content. As Linda Smith Tabb observes:

> Since most of the translators for the project are volunteers, it seems improbable
> that all of the various languages will be able to be used for the XO laptops.
> This is a concern even in countries such as Haiti – where Kreyol Aiysyen
> co-exists with French – and the Andes of Peru – where Quechua co-exists
> with Spanish – where linguistic recolonisation is at risk if laptops do not
> enable use of either language. In these cases, the Green Machine does not so
> much threaten Americanization, but cultural absorption by polities of larger
> scale in closer proximity.
>
> *(Tabb 2008, p.347)*

One final criticism is a misplaced confidence in the ability of a global technology-
project such as the OLPC to be free from political influence and interference while

still dealing with national governments and multinational corporations. From the perspective of the OLPC leadership, the decision to focus the programme on state educational systems was largely strategic and self-serving. Indeed, it has been acknowledged that focusing the OLPC programme in terms of education and learning has been a convenient means of 'translating' the XO laptop "into ways that fit with the mission" of the governments and state bureaucracies that the OLPC team needed to work with in order to achieve maximum coverage (see Luyt 2008). Indeed, Negroponte (2007) has been explicit in the role of notion of the 'educational' $100 laptop as a 'Trojan Horse' tactic to get the technology into the hands of children and young people.

Yet in taking this pathway, OLPC has shown a considerable lack of political realism in its dealings with national governments and multinational corporations. As has been suggested throughout this chapter, from its inception onwards, the OLPC initiative has been mired in the politics of international relations and of international commerce. Since its launch, the OLPC leadership has failed to find political ways of countering the continued reluctance of governments willing to commit to the required mass orders of machines. As one commentator observed four years after the high-profile launch of the initiative, "after years of deal-making and political machinations, it is still only making relatively slow progress" (Johnson 2009, p.5). This political intransigence was illustrated with the deployment of XO machines to Iraq in the aftermath of the second Gulf war. Although much heralded at the time as an instance of OLPC bringing technology and education to otherwise deprived contexts, in reality Iraqi use of the XO laptops was minimal. As Warschauer and Ames (2010, p.36) note, "the U.S. government bought 8080 XOs for donation to Iraq, but they never reached children's hands; half were auctioned off to a businessman in Basra for $10.88 each and half are unaccounted for".

Of course, political intransigence and compromise is part and parcel of international relations. Yet as far as the OLPC team seem concerned these barriers have been mostly unexpected. As Negroponte conceded in 2007, "I have to some degree underestimated the difference between shaking the hand of a head of state and having a cheque written, and, yes, it has been a disappointment". As Linda Smith Tabb (2008, p.339) reasoned in response:

> what is most striking about his statement, besides the obvious arrogance it takes to assume that a deal with a head of state could be so easily facilitated, is the disregard for the speed of a liberal democratic process, which is usually very slow. The main type of leader who might be able to make good, and fast, would be one not interested in a completely democratic process of decision making and consensus building. So, in Latin America, the traditional home of the caudillo, decisions seem to be made at a much swifter pace than in the rest of the world. The campaign at this juncture could have been renamed 'Una Computadora por Niño'.

These are certainly harsh criticisms. Yet the ease with which the OLPC programme brokered deals with world leaders such as former President Tabaré Vázquez of

Uruguay, former President Gaddafi of Libya and former President Olusegun Obasanjo of Nigeria certainly suggests a political expediency (and possible lack of concern for ethical and moral consistency) when pursuing the aim of getting the XO laptops into the hands of schoolchildren.

The political complexity of the OLPC programme's dealings with national governments is illustrated by the on-going failure of the initiative to be adopted in India. Despite placing a great deal of emphasis on the need to establish the programme in the country (Negroponte was once quoted as saying "India is the largest market for us, and I had to be there"), there have been numerous public denouncements from the Indian government to the advances of the OLPC team. Government officials argued in 2006, for example, that "India must not allow itself to be used for experimentation with children in this area" (Mukul 2006). Sudeep Banerjee, head of the Indian Ministry of Human Resources Development, branded the idea 'pedagogically suspect', and suggested that 'classrooms and teachers were more urgently needed than fancy tools'. As another official from the Human Resource Development Ministry concluded, "it would be impossible to justify an expenditure of this scale on a debatable scheme when public funds continue to be in inadequate supply for well-established needs" (Mukul 2006).

Such reactions are not attributable solely to a scepticism amongst Indian politicians about the social and educational merits of the XO laptops, but also reflect a general wariness of grand technological solutions from external Western organisations. Notably, OLPC undoubtedly suffered from Negroponte's prominent involvement in a previous project to establish a satellite 'MIT Media Lab Asia' in India, which ceased despite significant amounts of initial funding from the Indian government. Also significant has been the Indian government's desire to convey its political ambitions to be seen as an emerging superpower capable of supporting its own technology projects. As the Human Resource Development Minister stated at the launch of a proposed Indian-built $35 tablet computer, "the solutions for tomorrow will emerge from India" (Kapil Sibal, cited in BBC News 2010). Against this complex local political context, the assumed global appeal of the OLPC programme has understandably failed to take hold.

Conclusions

All these latter criticisms should not detract from the many positive outcomes that have certainly arisen from the OLPC initiative so far. These include the fore-grounding of the issue of low-cost computing onto the world political stage, as well as the many considerable advances in the technical development of low-cost computing components that have derived from the development of the XO devices. Yet, as Warschauer and Ames (2010, p.46) note, "there are important differences between a research-oriented development effort and a large-scale international campaign involving the production, distribution and use of millions of educational computers". It is here that the gulf between the grand ambitions of the educational technology community and the realpolitik of world economics and world politics are laid bare. Through its consideration of the OLPC initiative as more than a well-designed and well-intentioned technological device, this chapter has been able to further explore some of the key themes that have emerged throughout this book – not least issues of power, politics and ideology.

From even this brief discussion of the programme, the complexities of OLPC are obvious. What might appear at first glance to be an innovative and ambitious educational initiative has in fact been shaped by a number of mitigating factors. These include the professional backgrounds and beliefs of its founders; the educational, economic and ecological values driving the design of technology, hardware and software; and the complications of intervening in commercial markets and 'selling' not-for-profit technologies to state purchasers. As such, this chapter offers a rich account of the politics of educational technology. What may appear to be an uncontroversial international development project has, in practice, proved to be a site for a number of ideological conflicts. These conflicts include the privileging of the assumed power of individual actors and market forces over the governance of national governments, as well as the de-institutionalisation of public services such as schools and schooling. Far from being a benign force for 'good', the OLPC 'mission' of putting low-cost, brightly-coloured digital devices 'into the hands of children' has been driven by a complex of political struggles and conflicts. As such, OLPC highlights a number of salient issues that we should take forward into the final chapter of this book.

First and foremost, the OLPC programme highlights the need to balance any focus on the design and development of technology with consideration of social, political, cultural and economic contexts within which technology use takes place. It could be argued that many of the 'unexpected' setbacks now being faced by OLPC implementation in various local contexts relate back to the overtly technicist nature of the project and the excessive faith put into the XO technology itself. Indeed, beyond the understandable criticism of the OLPC programme that "the hackers took over" (Edith Ackermann, cited in Hamm and Smith 2008), lies a willingness amongst many people within the educational technology community – not least Negroponte himself – to approach the social issues that are supposedly being addressed through technology programmes in largely technical terms. In particular, many of the OLPC actions appear to have been informed by a prevailing view of social change as a form of programming orientated problem – i.e. as a logical series of 'bugs' in a system that needs to be fixed. As Michael Klebl (2008, p.280) reasons, OLPC, therefore, could be said to

> represent an interpretation of educational expansion solely as a technical issue to be solved like a programming mistake. An inexpensive, connected and robust laptop personally owned by every child provides the ability to learn and progress, especially for children in developing countries.

Above all, then, OLPC stands as another reminder of the tensions between global technology solutions and local contexts of implementation. Despite the technical elegance and apparent political simplicity of the OLPC business plan, it would seem that no amount of charismatic leadership, strategic lobbying and technological sophistication can impose globalised change and transformation onto whole societies or national education systems. Perhaps most importantly, OLPC reminds us that "there is no such thing as 'actor-free' dissemination or reception, lending or borrowing, export or import" (Tabb 2008, p.345). As with all the examples of educational technology discussed so far in this book, the grand global ambitions of OLPC are entwined with the mundane realities of the local educational settings and contexts in which they seek to be located (see also Cervantes *et al.* 2011). We should therefore take this thought forward as a basis of any attempt to advance the field of educational technology towards more equitable ends. It is to these issues that we now turn our attention towards the final chapter of the book.

8

EDUCATION IN A DIGITAL
WORLD – SO WHERE NOW?

Introduction

The past seven chapters have considered many forms of 'educational technology' – all being enacted in different settings for different purposes. A range of actors and interests has been implicated in these accounts, from the United Nations and Microsoft to educational policymakers and individual learners. When approached in this manner the educational use of digital technology is revealed to be a complex affair. Indeed, throughout this book educational technology has been shown to be an often inconsistent and 'messy' process. This final chapter is, therefore, unable to offer a set of straightforward conclusions or neat recommendations. Instead, educational technology continues to be an area of discussion where there will always be more conflict than clarity and consensus.

One of the guiding aims of this book was to construct a comprehensive account of education and technology from a 'relational' perspective. In this spirit the past, seven chapters have explored and exposed the inherently political nature of educational technology. We have been reminded – if reminder was needed – that educational debates about digital technology should not be framed purely in technical terms. Instead, the coming together of the educational and the digital is a predominantly social affair – based around struggles over benefit and power, equality and empowerment, structure and agency, inequality and social justice. In particular, educational technology has been shown to be a site of intense ideological conflict and shaped by a range of values, agendas and interests. As examples throughout this book have suggested, most aspects of educational technology are therefore linked (to varying degrees) with issues of economics and economy. Indeed, many forms of educational technology continue to be implemented in deliberate support of the 'learning/earning narrative' of the knowledge economy (Brown *et al.* 2011). This is perhaps most apparent in the various ways in which digital technologies are being aligned with the presumed 'twenty-first-century skill' demands of the knowledge economy and the implicit need to (re)produce the "differently literate and differently orientated workers" necessary for contemporary economic success (Apple 2010, p.32). In this sense, many aspects of educational technology provision and practice are driven by the efforts of various organisations to ensure that individual nations *and* individual citizens become and/or remain enrolled in the contemporary economic order.

Yet we should not reduce our analysis of educational technology *wholly* to an economic determinism. The past seven chapters have also suggested that the politics of educational technology are concerned with a range of issues beyond economic competitiveness and the upskilling of workforces. This book has also highlighted, for example, links between educational technology and the commercial pursuit of profit, as well as government concerns over international relations and the construction of national cultural identities. Often the influence of these factors on educational technology is less obvious than the explicit concerns of skill levels and national economic fortunes, yet is no less significant. In this sense, one of the least obvious (but certainly one of the most important) observations that has recurred throughout this book relates to the use of educational technology to 'leverage' neo-liberal dispositions and a free-market mentality into the minds and actions of national governments and individual citizens alike. It could be argued, therefore, that many of the examples considered in this book articulate closely with neo-liberal values such as self-interest, individual freedom, market individualism and meritocratic notions of aspirational action regardless of circumstance.

In all these ways, educational technology has been found to be entwined with wider societal and economic shifts that have little to do with the straightforward connections between technology, teaching and learning that usually inform discussions in this area. Instead, educational technology should be understood as an integral part of broader efforts to sustain the dominant neo-liberal project that informs so much of contemporary 'global society'. Thus while such issues are rarely considered in mainstream discussions of educational technology, it is these broader ideological connections that merit further attention and consideration. This is particularly the case with regard to the ways in which educational technology is encountered and experienced within the 'emerging' economies and commercial markets of less-wealthy countries and regions. Indeed, many of the forms of educational ICT4D reviewed in Chapters 6 and 7 are clearly predicated upon what Mosco (2009, p.9) terms the 'neo-liberal orthodoxy' which "insists that developing countries take a market-based approach with as little government intervention as possible". That these forms of technology interventions are so far "falling short of their promises and predictions in relation to actual accomplishments" should perhaps not be cause for particular surprise (ibid.).

Making Better Sense of Education, Technology and Globalisation

All of these issues lead us to the conclusion that educational technology is an integral element – for better and for worse – of the on-going 'globalisations' of education and society described in Chapter 1. This is not to say that substantial evidence has emerged in support of the 'globalist' notion of technologically transformed educational provision and practice. Indeed, it could be concluded that all of the globalist hopes and claims for technology-driven education reform reviewed in Chapter 1 have turned out to be of little or no substance. Instead, a more convincing case could be made for a 'sceptical' reading of technology acting mainly to strengthen the continuation of existing imbalances and disparities around the world. Indeed, there have been a number of occasions throughout this book which have suggested that educational technologies simply follow the logic of capital and, ultimately, serve to reinforce what Fuchs and Horak (2008, p.115) term "the unequal geography of global capitalism".

The sceptical conclusion is certainly a tempting one for us to consider. It could be observed, for example, that most mainstream forms of educational technology have done little to disrupt formal educational arrangements or challenge the ways in which education is linked to the needs of the economy and the elite interests therein. It could also be observed that most mainstream forms of educational technology appear to perpetuate a number of burgeoning global political trends of the past fifty years – not least the dominance of northern multinational corporations, and the rise of market liberalism as a preferred solution to economic problems. While it may be overly simplistic to assume that the logic of digital technology in education follows rigidly what Murdock (2004, p.19) terms "the globalisation of capitalist imperatives and its shifting relations to state logics", many of the forms of educational technology reviewed in this book would certainly seem to retain a close association with (rather than opposition to) the global *status quo*. Thus while some forms of digital technology may well be associated with significant adaptations and transformations in educational structures and forms, these are usually *not* the radical social disruptions or political rearrangements that many well-intentioned commentators assume. Instead, as Miller (2011, p.225) concludes, where substantial societal changes have taken place with regard to digital media "it is important to stress that in most cases, these are transformations that were already taking place as part of transformations under capitalist processes".

That said, we should perhaps not be *too* hasty to reach a totally sceptical and defeatist conclusion. It could be argued that there are some reasons within the pages of this book to support a 'transformationalist' reading of education and technology. Despite all of the compelling arguments just made, there *have* been occasions throughout our previous discussions where digital technology does appear to be associated with genuine disruption and change to educational arrangements around the world – albeit in an admittedly inconsistent and uneven manner. As the social shaping perspective reminds us, digital technologies are clearly not immutable forces. Accordingly, there have been points throughout this book that have detailed locally specific responses and reconfigurations of educational technology in ways that could be said to fit the needs and interests of local contexts better. Despite the appearance of educational technologies being driven simply by the logic of global capital and the hegemonic neo-liberal project, we therefore need to be careful to understand 'educational technology' within the dialectic of the global *and* the local. As Arnove (2007, p.1) reminds us, "although there are common problems – and what would appear to be increasingly similar education agendas – regional, national and local responses also vary".

Of course, it is important to note that often these local responses and rearrangements can be highly divisive and disempowering for many people. Indeed, often these local responses are part of on-going processes of struggle and friction where some people continue to win and many others continue to lose. For example, Rwanda's extensive and ambitious plans for a nationwide information and communications infrastructure do not make the country any less excluded from global power than before. The rise of teaching robots in Japan is clearly constrained by the wider industrial, cultural and gendered politics of Japanese society. Similarly, the benefits of initiatives such as the 'Hole-in-the-wall' or 'One Laptop Per Child' could not be said to extend to all individuals, despite the democratic aspirations of such projects. There are simply too many other mitigating circumstances that remain in place for educational technology to ever make a clear-cut difference to societal arrangements. Instead, it often appears that the most dominant powerful contexts are those that are more able to shape educational technology to fit their needs best. So while not being wholly defeatist when looking forward to the future, it is important to be realistic about the uneven nature of even the most localised and most 'appropriate' forms of educational technology provision and practice.

Aside from the inherent inequalities of digital technology use in education, another key issue to emerge from this book's analysis is the range of inter-related and often competing interests involved in shaping educational technology. It is therefore worth taking time to reflect further on these interests and the roles they play in the global construction of educational technology. When doing so, however, it is important to note that no one set of actors and interests could be said to dominate the shaping of educational technology. As many of this book's chapters have illustrated, power and influence is distributed unevenly throughout different sets of actors at different times and in different contexts. For example, whereas a company such as Cisco assumes an influential role in the educational technology arrangements in some sub-Saharan African school systems, this power is not consistent across all countries in the world, or even across all countries in Africa. As such, we should concur with Zygmunt Bauman's observation of contemporary society that "no decision-making agency is able to plead full (that is unconstrained, indivisible, unshared) sovereignty, let alone claim it credibly and effectively" (Bauman 2010, p.121).

So which actors and interests can be said to influence educational technology around the world? First and foremost, much of what has been reviewed in this book suggests that there are good grounds for continuing to frame educational technology within the context of the nation state. Indeed, looking back over the past seven chapters there is little evidence to suggest a dramatic decline of state sovereignty *per se*. Instead, national governments can be said to still play major roles in shaping educational technology agendas and aspirations within their borders. That said, it is clear that educational technology agendas and the changes associated with them are not driven *wholly* by nation states and national governments. In this sense, the growing importance of private sector and commercial interests has also been notable across many of the different forms of educational technology considered in this book. In contrast to the libertarian discourses of individualisation that pervade most discussions of educational technology, many of the examples highlighted in this book point to the continued corporate institutionalisation of educational technology and educational technology users. This perhaps reflects a wider paradox of contemporary society observed by Colin Crouch (2011, p.viii) that "actually existing neoliberalism, as opposed to the ideologically pure, is nothing like as devoted to free markets as is claimed. It is, rather, devoted to the dominance of public life by the giant corporation".

The diversification and multiplicity of corporate involvement in the various forms of educational technology discussed throughout this book has been striking. Aside from the supplying and selling of technology products and services, we have seen many instances of IT companies assuming roles that go well beyond their remit as technology producers and suppliers. Most notable, perhaps, are the efforts of large IT firms to position themselves as alternative authorities in the governance of educational technology systems. For example, Chapters 3 and 6 both described how multinational corporations such as Cisco and Microsoft are operating in many developing and developed countries as national educational technology authorities – providing curriculum models, teacher training resources and advice across national educational systems. We also saw how multinational firms from *outside* the IT sector are using educational technology as a means of increasing their involvement in public affairs. From the example of consultancy firms such as Ernst & Young writing educational policy blueprints for African nations to restaurant chains such as McDonald's supporting online maths tuition for Australian high school students, the past twenty years have indeed been subject to what Jane Kenway and colleagues (1994) foresaw as a coming together of markets, education and technology. As Kenway argued even before the mainstream emergence of the internet, digital technology acts as a catalyst for the increased involvement of private interests in the formulations and implementations of education policy ideas and imperatives. Looking back at Kenway's observations twenty years on, the use of digital technology in education around the world is now informed inexorably by market values (see also Spring 2012).

Of course, private interests are involved deeply in most sectors of public policy-making – not just educational technology. Yet there has been a sense throughout our preceding discussions that digital technology offers a platform from which private interests have been able to develop extensive roles in education affairs and arrangements. One key development in this respect has been the diversification of private sector actors and activities involved in educational technology – not least the growing appropriation of educational technology as a site for the enactment of what can be termed 'philanthrocapitalism' (see Bishop and Green 2008). As various chapters of the book have illustrated, this is especially noticeable within the context of low-income countries where the framing of educational technology access and use as an advanced human right has been pursued vigorously by a host of private actors in conjunction with non-government organisations. Educational technology has therefore become an important site for the activities of various forms of venture capitalists, social entrepreneurs and other strains of 'creative capitalism' – i.e. actors seeking to harness the power of the market and the use of business principles for social good (McGoey 2011). As such, educational technology in now an important arena for the various activities of edu-businesses, advocacy networks, policy entre-preneurs, social enterprises and other forms of 'new' philanthropy that increasingly inhabit public policy and the provision of public services (see Ball 2012).

Moving Beyond the Inequalities of Education, Technology and Globalisation

Having outlined the shortcomings of past and present educational technology arrangements, we now need to consider the options for future change. As Sonia Livingstone (2012, p.19) puts it, there are "three forms of critique relevant to grand claims made for the new technologies, asking in essence, what's really going on, how can this be explained, and how could things be otherwise?" We now need to turn our attention to Livingstone's suggestion of thinking 'otherwise'. Of course, even within this book's largely critical overview it has been possible to point towards some examples of educational technology 'success' that have undoubtedly enhanced the lives of individuals in a variety of ways around the world. Even an obviously flawed large-scale programme such as One Laptop Per Child could be considered a success in terms of distributing over 2 million laptops in otherwise 'technology-poor' settings. Yet as this book has pointed out, at best these forms of educational technology intervention can be judged only as partial successes, with any benefits most often being experienced in urban centres and/or by already privileged classes. In addition, these interventions are limited by the tendency of many educators, policymakers and technologists to frame the presumed benefits of educational technology around narrow criteria of economic 'success'. As Nick Couldry (2010, p.59) notes, this is a predominant notion of benefit that is "limited to the principle that everyone should have, indeed should be required to take up, the opportunity to enter the job market".

Thus one of the first ways of thinking 'otherwise' about educational technology is to reconsider dominant assumptions about why educational technology is a 'good thing' for societies and the individuals within them. In other words, we first need to challenge and problematise what are assumed to be the 'benefits' and 'outcomes' of educational technology in terms of whose interests are being benefited and advantaged. Take, for instance, the recurring theme of educational technologies leading to the acquisition of valuable and empowering 'twenty-first-century skills'. Although it is still assumed widely that employment and labour in the new knowledge economy requires higher levels of creativity, cooperation and innovation, a growing body of research now points to the 'inconvenient truth' that vast swathes of the knowledge economy in fact do not need these skills (e.g. Brown *et al.* 2011). At best, most of the 'informational' jobs of the twenty-first-century would seem to be centred around technology-based divisions of labour where most workers are no longer expected to exercise independent judgement or contribute creatively to the value-adding process. In this way, the continued implementation of educational technologies over the past twenty years can hardly be said to have led to a transformation of power relations between working classes and middle classes. Thus, as Shafiul Alam Bhuiyan (2008, p.100) concludes:

> The so-called information society is a metaphor that has been coined to hide the features of contemporary capitalism. In the information society, big corporations, which are multinational and guided by profit motives, own and control the mode of production. To generate maximum profit and maintain total control over the mode of production, they discipline the workforce. This disciplining is done through various methods.

At this point, it is perhaps useful to return to the concerns of the post-colonialist approach. As outlined in Chapter 2, this stresses the importance of taking a historical perspective on unequal power relations between different groups and different countries. Importantly, it also encourages us to explore spaces for alternative arrangements, interventions and resistance. From a post-colonialist perspective, then, much of what has been covered in the past seven chapters should warn us against viewing educational technology through an exclusively Euro-American lens, and instead consider educational technology from 'other' perspectives. As has already been implied, when educational technology is perceived from the perspective of the 'global South' it is often difficult to see it as anything less than an imperialist project designed to create markets for multinational corporations that operate at the heart of the information society – i.e. those interests that own and operate (as well as produce and sell) information technologies. This is perhaps most evident in the frequent association of educational technologies with vague notions of 'modernisation'. Of course, there is little doubt that the rapid growth of digital technologies and transfer of knowledge, skills and technologies from 'developed' to 'developing' regions has enabled considerable progress. Yet, at the same time, it is difficult to overlook the vested interests that these dominant actors have in encouraging individuals and institutions in poorer countries to engage with and adopt 'Western' ideas, practices and devices, and therefore go some way towards becoming more productive components of the global knowledge economy.

Indeed, one of the striking features of the field of 'educational ICT4D' appears to be its tendency to obscure (and often silence) a number of historical tensions within international development – not least the assumptions of less-wealthy 'developing' countries being somehow deficient and subordinate to more 'developed' countries. Many of the ICT4D examples discussed in Chapters 6 and 7 convey an implicit assumption that less-wealthy countries are stymied by a delayed access not only to digital technology devices but also to contemporary forms of knowledge and information. Of course, such thinking replicates a long history of Western concerns and ideals of the (mis)education of the new world when set against the development of other countries through more 'advanced' forms of education. Thus as Stambach and Malekela (2006, p.328) conclude:

> When it comes to ICT education policies, the absence of reflection on history is notable. New electronic and digital technologies are not new in terms of the uses to which they are to be put. The newness of information and communication technology needs to be understood in the context of an historically old and conceptually circuitous route that leads from arguments about the value of education for bridging the 'Great Divide' of oral and literate societies to, now, the value of ICT education for bridging the 'Digital Divide' that separates sub-Saharan Africa from most of the rest of the world. There is nothing new in the sense of what ICT education promises to 'do' for Africa.

The field of educational ICT4D therefore exemplifies a key concern that underpins all of the examples of educational technology considered in this book, i.e. that of power (or, more specifically, imbalances of power). It is perhaps not surprising that longstanding patterns of domination and subordination between individuals and groups of individuals are being extended (rather than being overcome) through the use of digital technologies in education. As Fuchs and Horak (2008, p.107) argue with regard to the ICT4D movement:

> Solutions to the global divide cannot be provided by Western technologies that are applied in Third World countries. Such positions are an expression of cultural imperialism that neglect that local and traditional ideas are of high cultural importance in solving the problems of the Third World. Western habits, colonialism, and post-colonial practices are part of the causes of the problems that Third World countries are facing today.

While damning in their analysis of the present, these observations do go some way towards suggesting more equitable alternative arrangements. In particular, post-colonial perspectives certainly focus our attention closer to issues of power. As McMillin (2007, p.14) reasons, "time and time again, [we] have to ask the question, 'where is power located?' before [we] can make any conclusions about global, national, or local media production and consumption". Having identified these gaps and inequalities we now need to move towards ways of 'thinking otherwise' about the power imbalances that currently beset educational technology provision and practice – i.e. conceptualising alternative models to the mainstream forms of technology arrangements that presently dominate education settings around the world.

Of course, identifying alternative arrangements that are able to affect significant transformations of power relations is an almost impossible task – although this is no reason not to try. Indeed, having spent most of our time detailing the problems of educational technology around the world, we should now turn our attention towards suggesting some potential areas of beneficial change. So how can the international inequalities that have accompanied educational technology throughout the past thirty years be resisted and disrupted? How can hitherto oppressed individuals and groups be supported to 'make their own history' and develop engaged visions of educational technology where everyone can actively participate in altering power relations? It is with these substantial questions that we shall now conclude our discussion.

Education and Technology: Looking towards Local Solutions

Constructing plausible suggestions for the reshaping of educational technology use along 'better', fairer and more equitable lines is no easy task. Inspiration can be drawn, however, from the recurring discussions throughout the book that have all pointed to increasing the role given to *local* sources of knowledge and expertise. As such, an important initial step is to scale down our language and expectations for digital technology – avoiding the hyper-narrative of a 'global educational technology' and instead developing mini-narratives and localised appeals. This involves 'relocating' the idea of educational technology away from the globalised discourses that currently dominate discussions and, instead, attempting to 'educate the local' and stress the counter-educational possibilities of more modest forms of digital technology use. Of course, in doing this we should not over-romanticise the agency of those who are located at local rather than global levels. Nevertheless, such a localised turn could involve a number of re-arrangements of educational technology that "create institutional forms that are much more responsive to oppressed and marginalised people, and that redefine what counts as legitimate knowledge all at the same time" (Apple 2010, p.198).

There are a number of ways that such localisations could be achieved. Clearly, these shifts can only be achieved if steps are taken to make educational technology a more political issue than it is at present. Much of what has been covered so far in this book relates to the limited ways that the idea of educational technology as a discursive construction have been expressed. We have seen, for example, how educational technology remains an area of society that is generally unchallenged, un-critiqued and un-problematised. Behind the broad slogans of 'twenty-first-century skills', 'digital-natives' and so on, popular debates and public understandings move very rarely beyond what Vincent Mosco (2004) termed 'the digital sublime' – i.e. the commonly accepted myths concerning the revolutionary potential of technologies in bringing social progress. Very little is acknowledged publicly about the clear inequalities associated with technology use in education, or the exploitative power relations that underpin much of the implementation of educational technologies around the world. Even the language that is used to discuss education and technology is often overly technicist and far removed from the language that is used often to discuss people's 'real-life' engagements with education. Seldom are alternative opinions voiced from those who are being educated or those who are educating.

Following this line of reasoning, coordinated attempts should be made to 'capture' the common-sense understandings that surround education and technology, and to enable an enhanced critical public awareness. An initial step in this respect would be to encourage as many people in as many contexts as possible to get involved in the shaping of educational technology through the development and the stimulation of a democratised discourse about the capabilities and purpose of digital technology in education. Just as there are growing calls for the development of 'public under-standing of science' or a 'public understanding of the past' given the increasing importance of science and history in people's lives, so, too, there should be increased public engagement with issues surrounding education and technology. There are many aspects of educational technology that are currently under-publicised and under-discussed but need to be brought into mainstream discussions. These conversations should be expanded to encompass a host of contemporary questions that surround the moral philosophy and ethics of educational technology. As Keri Facer (2011) has pointed out, educational technology discussion and debate usually overlooks long-term issues such as the educational implications of fast-aging populations, the technological implications of ecological and environmental change, or the societal implications of the collapse of industrial models based on oil con-sumption and the internal combustion engine. In Foucauldian terms, then, support needs to be given to the production of 'counter-narratives' about education and technology – critiquing dominant discourses by revealing the partiality, inadequacy and provisionality of overarching grand theories of educational technology, and making transparent the relations of power behind specific claims to the 'truth' about educational technology.

Much of this discursive politicisation of educational technology would involve reframing and repurposing the ideas, language and values that have been attached to educational technologies over the past thirty years. This 'ideological cleansing' could involve, for example, finding new ways of 'de-scribing' what are rather tightly scripted products – for example, the currently popular description of 'Technology Enhanced Learning' which offers a highly bounded and partial account of the rela-tionship between technology and education. Even the simple act of encouraging a more diverse vocabulary for describing technology use in education could work to introduce alternative values in educational technology provision and practice (e.g. using language that reflects the right to participate, income equality, full public participation in production). There is also scope for an 'intellectual cleansing' of educational technology in many countries and contexts. Most educational technology theorising, for example, comes from a very limited and decontextualised set of sources – as can be seen in the continued bearing of twentieth-century Russian learning theory over our conceptions of how digital technologies are used all over the world. What would a twenty-first-century Confucian or Islamic theory of digital learning look like? How can we challenge the Euro-American dominance of the field of educational technology, and create expectations of the 'expert South' providing readymade answers to the 'lay North'?

A further form of political action would be supporting local communities and groups to (co)produce their own 'appropriate' educational technologies. This area of intervention has certainly become more practically achievable with the shift in the ownership of the means of technology production associated with 'open source' practices – moving the production of software and hardware artefacts from closed, centralised and commercially-controlled models to more open, decentralised and collectively governed models. These shifts are not necessarily restricted to the production of new technologies *per se*, as much as the reconfiguration of existing technologies into new forms. Inspiration can perhaps be taken from de Laet and Mol's (2000) description of the relatively successful adoption of the Zimbabwe Bush Pump throughout different communities and contexts in the country. Here the success of a particular water pump was associated with the variability of the artefact – what could be termed its mutability and variability in terms of its material and social forms. As Law and Mol (2001, p.613) explain, this technology was successful because of its 'configurable variance', i.e.:

> because it changes shape. Of this pump and everything that allows it to work, nothing in particular necessarily holds in place. Bits break off the device and are replaced with bits which don't seem to fit. And other components – we're talking here both of parts of the 'machine itself', and the social relations embedded in it – are added to it, components which were not in the original design itself.

As the example of the Zimbabwe Bush Pump suggests, more consideration needs to be given to alternative ways of imagining and then producing educational technologies that are not imposed with rigid designs and discourses, but can be gradually adapted and co-constructed by the local communities which wish to make use of them.

Means of Politicising Education and Technology Around the World

In many ways, the likely actions that are required to support the emergence of these alternative 'other' forms of educational technology are highly idealistic in nature. Of course, if any shifts of this nature are to take place, then fundamental changes need to take place across all levels of educational technology interest and activity. In particular, much of what has been just outlined relates to enhancing the agency of currently less-powerful individuals and local groups of educational technology 'receivers' at the expense of more dominant groups and interests. Of course, engineering any such recalibration of agency within society is a difficult task. As Wallerstein (1986, p.335) notes, as "any structural analysis implies that an individual, a group is caught in some web not of their own making and out of their control". As such, any attempt to achieve the types of change being suggested here would require sustained interventions with those individuals and groups who are weak in terms of their ability to exercise power, as well as sustained interventions with those individuals and groups who are stronger. As such, for any re-alignments to occur then action is required at all levels. As Mohan and Stokke (2000, p.249) concur, care must be taken not to "view 'the local' in isolation from broader economic and political structures". So what aspects of top-down *and* bottom-up change would be required to support the construction of more appropriate and fitting arrangements for educational technology around the world? In the few remaining pages of this chapter we can consider four areas of possible change – from the recasting of the role of the state, to reimagining the role of the academic research community.

Re-orienting State Involvement in Educational Technology

Perhaps the most immediate area for change is enhancing the role that nation-states play in engaging actively with educational technology. As described in Chapter 4, while states continue to devote considerable amounts of time and resourcing towards educational technology, this takes place on an ultimately uncommitted basis. Beyond the symbolic policy statements and directing of funding, most nation states remain noticeably un-involved in educational technology arrangements 'on the ground'. As Leonard Waks (2011) argues, states have little impetus to get involved in the use of technology in education, beyond ensuring the maintenance of state control and state legitimacy. Yet it could be argued (perhaps naïvely) that nation states have a duty to remain involved actively at all stages of educational technology implementation and use. In particular, it would seem desirable that nation states continue to work on behalf of disadvantaged and peripheral popula-tions long after the policy statements have been announced and the funding dis-pensed. As Divya McMillin (2007, p.190) reasons, "the nation-state is a crucial entity to ensure basic human rights, when it works as it is supposed to".

So how could nation states (assuming that they are working as they are supposed to) work more effectively as long-term systems of support and social welfare where educational technology is concerned? One possible role is the nation state acting to mediate and adapt 'incoming' forms of educational technology. We have seen throughout this book that the local context is key to educational technology initiatives being implemented effectively. It is here, then, that national governments can be seen to have a vital role to play as local interpreters and 'cleansers' of incoming global models of educational technology provision and practice. Instead of simply acting as conduits for global agendas and imperatives, nation states could attempt to reconstruct them first from a national perspective, and then to fit in with local social needs.

There are also a number of other practical interventions that nation states could make in the construction of educational technology 'on the ground' with regard to increasing equality of opportunity. For instance, states could be more involved in the establishment and control of adequate telecommunications infrastructures across *all* regions of a country. States could also work harder to encourage a heightened social consciousness on the part of usually profit-hungry private telecommunications companies. There is also clear scope for nation states and governments to support democratic forms of governance of educational technology. By projecting a unified notion of consensual educational technology use through the production of national strategies and policies, it could be argued that states currently act in ways that suppress the needs and wishes of dissenting publics. Rather than seeking to promote top-down strictures on 'national' educational technology use, the role of states could be reoriented so that they become what Shafiul Alam Bhuiyan (2008, p.113) terms "the states of the subaltern classes".

Here, then, states can assume a role as a key driver of democratic forms of educational technology provision and practice within national contexts. As Michael Burawoy reasons, there can be many benefits that arise from a state that is engaged in this manner, i.e. "democratically self-governing, responsive to multiple interests, and ... responsive to civil society, facilitating, promoting and protecting the conditions of participatory democracy" (Burawoy 2005, p.324–5). There is clear room here, therefore, for states to act as stimulators rather than suppressors of democratic engagement with educational technology. This would certainly require states to move beyond the notion of 'skills' as an economic or social panacea, and focus instead on the wider issues underlying educational technology – such as social justice, ethics and other currently obscured issues (Keep and Mayhew 2010).

Challenging Corporate Involvement in Educational Technology

The second aspect of educational technology governance that needs to be addressed is that of the corporations that own and operate the information technologies, as well as the corporate interests who effectively own and operate the global knowledge economy. At present, corporate involvement in the field of educational technology is driven primarily by profit making motivations – albeit increasingly in the guise of 'cool capitalism' where corporate interests pursue market-orientated activities under the veneer of being involved in worthy, sustainable and socially-minded action (see McGuigan 2009). As has been observed throughout this book, in most instances, these corporate actions nevertheless remain centred around the ultimate establishment of privatised and liberalised markets for digital technology products, and the enrolment of individuals and countries into the digital economy (as consumers, as employers and so on).

So what scope is there to re-orientate the actions and activities of commercial actors away from self-interest and market-building and, instead, towards engaging with educational technology primarily for the benefit of others? Many people would argue that these shifts can only be achieved by publicly problematising the educational technology activities of companies and corporations around the world. As such, civil society and non-profit interests need to confront and challenge the educational technology activities of corporations such as Cisco, Microsoft, Dell, Apple and so on. Conversely, civil society and non-profit interests also need to work with corporations to construct more democratic and less commercially interested forms of educational technology. Transnational corporations need to be made accountable for the limited effects of their past and present actions, and to be persuaded and cajoled into pursuing fairer and more appropriate forms of truly 'socially responsible' corporate action. As Colin Crouch (2011, n.p.) concludes:

> hope for the future, therefore, cannot lie in suppressing the power of corporations in order to attain either an economy of pure markets or a socialist society. Rather it lies in dragging the giant corporation fully into political controversy.

The nature of these new actions can be broad and far reaching. For example, we could revisit the suggestion made by the Senegalese government during the 2000s that multinational IT firms contribute to a 'digital solidarity fund' for less-wealthy countries to draw upon. If managed appropriately, such redistributive actions could allow national governments and local communities to purchase (or even produce) forms of educational technology that they consider to best fit their circumstances. Alternatively, commercial interests could be encouraged to think more radically about the ways in which their IT products are distributed. For instance, it could be argued that the most effective way of interrupting the social inequalities of the commercial market for digital technology in developing countries involves bypassing the logic of market forces altogether. This could see, for instance, the distribution of *no*-cost rather than *low*-cost computers. As Fuchs and Horak suggest, in contrast to the low-specification $100 laptop approach of OLPC, the Simputer and Classmate:

> what is needed are not new business strategies, but solutions to the material and social causes of the global digital divide as well as free advanced hardware, infrastructure, and software that are based on open standards and copy-left licenses. ... Open source technologies have a potential to transcend market logic, what is needed is an advanced $0 laptop with free software for people in developing countries as well as criticism of the capitalist logic that has caused the divide between developing and developed countries and solutions to the social, economic, political, and cultural inequalities that underpin the global digital divide.
>
> *(Fuchs and Horak 2008, p.113)*

As this argument implies, such moves beyond the market could perhaps be achieved through the increased involvement of transnational corporations in open-source and community-led actions. It could well be, for instance, that the imperatives of what Nissenbaum (2004, p.201) terms the "commercial marketplace and supporting institution of private property" could be reduced if companies were encouraged to view the field of educational technology not as a site of immediate profit-making, but as a site to exercise genuine corporate social responsibility. This would shift the basis for making decisions away from concerns of what profits can be gleaned from educational technology 'customers'. Instead, firms would be motivated by the longer-term societal and educational consequences of their activities. Although idealistic, these suggestions certainly begin to address the need for those in non-profit positions to work with industry and corporate actors. As Michael Apple (2007) argues, those seeking to engineer fairer forms of education provision should give serious consideration to the possibility of finding spaces where it is possible to *use* rather than *reject* dominant organisations such as IT corporations. From this perspective, we should at least consider the possibility of thinking strategically about the possibilities of interrupting the dominant priorities and practices of commercial IT firms and steering them towards social democratic educational goals.

Expanding the Publics of Educational Technology

Aside from the sustained re-engagement of state, private and commercial interests, there is also a clear need to involve more closely all of the potential 'publics' of education and technology – first by raising mutual awareness, and then by increasing dialogue and debate. These concerns are linked to the interest being shown elsewhere in the fields of 'critical participative democracy' and 'participatory politics'. These areas are concerned with enhancing citizens' participation in making decisions that affect their lives, especially with regard to public policy (Barber 2003). In this respect, these fields of work start from an acknowledgement that dialogue amongst citizens is essential for the democratic improvement of any area of society (Price 2009). As such, it would seem sensible – if not desirable – that any expert decisions about educational technology should take place within the context of broader public deliberation and scrutiny leading to the production of more robust and legitimate decisions. This would require the genuine inclusion of the perspectives and interests of disinterested 'lay-citizens' at all stages of educational technology implementation.

Encouraging wider debate and engagement amongst non-expert groups about educational technology is no easy task. At present, education and technology is simply not a topic that many people talk openly about, let alone get impassioned or angry over. However, there are a number of participative democratic mechanisms that may be used to increase the range of people who are able to contribute to the expert debates that shape educational technology. This is particularly important with regard to the 'political' phases of debates about education and technology, as distinct from the earlier 'technical' phases. As Collins and Evans (2002) describe, while the technical phases of any debate around technology are value-driven and certainly require the involvement of a full range of experts, it is the subsequent democratic phases that benefit most from the full range of non-expert citizens. These are debates that are

> concerned with the development of the policies and regulatory frameworks within which technical debates are permitted to take place and through which they are held accountable. [Their] outcome is thus a strategy for action that sets out what should be done.
>
> *(Evans and Plows 2007, p.833)*

Of course, as these authors acknowledge, "the challenge for the democratic/ political phase is to find some way of assessing the response of non-expert citizens to expert debates about which they will, almost by definition, be largely unaware" (Evans and Plows 2007, p.842). There are a number of mechanisms that could allow for non-expert inclusion in democratic debates over educational technology. For instance, other areas of the public engagement in science (such as debates over GM food) have seen growing use of mechanisms such as 'public debates' selected to include a range of social and demographic groups – i.e. series of local and national public meetings, feedback forms, websites, and 'citizen juries'. While by no means completely inclusive, the application of these ideas to the area of educational technology would seem a useful first step to the re-constitution of the field and of its practices along more democratic and participatory lines – especially during the formation of new and emerging educational technology policies.

Altering the Nature of Academic Involvement in Educational Technology

This latter set of suggestions raises the question of who assumes the role of coordinator and arbiter of such democratising activities. While there is no reason why state, community *and* private actors could not assume such roles, the case can certainly be made for these participative and democratic activities to be also pursued through the work of academic researchers and writers. It could be argued that the (supposedly) expert, unattached and disinterested position of the academic educational technologist is an ideal position from which to support and sustain the critical scrutiny of educational technology in society. This would certainly bring educational technology scholarship in line with wider trends within the academic social sciences, not least recent calls for forms of 'public sociology' that respond to "the necessity and possibility of moving from interpretation to engagement, from theory to practice, from the academy to its publics" (Burawoy 2005, p.324). This also introduces the possibility for educational technology scholars to cultivate stronger roots in their communities and to work to maintain links with local issues and struggles that connect to people and their experiences.

If we take these suggestions seriously, then academic educational technologists could clearly be doing more throughout the course of their work than is often the case at present. It could be argued that it is not good enough to do what this book has done and simply document the inequalities of education and technology. Instead, more effort could be made by academics to work actively on behalf of those who are disadvantaged – what Michael Apple describes as acting as 'secretaries' for the interests of the disadvantaged. As such, there is also clear room for academics to engage in more critical and disruptive forms of educational technology scholarship – providing "a disruptive but necessary voice in democratic debate" (Lauder *et al.* 2009, p.580). While these latter suggestions may appear either hopelessly romantic or overly self-important, they do touch upon the possibility that academia offers a ready 'way out' of the hyperbole and a ready 'way into' the complicated questions that need to be asked of educational technology. Because the fields of education and technology are so bound up with the networks of information, logistical imperatives and relationships that make up globalisation, then there are perhaps few alternative spaces for those of us involved with educational technology to think or act 'outside' the global system. From this perspective, then, more work could be pursued within the academic study of educational technology that challenges and tests the divisions between research and action. There is certainly space, therefore, for academics to undertake their educational technology activities in a more critical manner – acting on a desire to foster and support issues of empowerment, equality, social justice and participatory democracy (see Selwyn 2010, Selwyn and Facer 2013).

Conclusions

All of these suggestions point towards the need for a profound politicisation of educational technology, and this is as good a place as any to conclude our analysis. Suffice to say, educational technology is not something that should simply be 'done' to people around the world. Instead, everyone involved in the use of technology in education (not just those who stand to gain most from it) needs to play active roles in comprehending the limits *and* the possibilities of technology in education. Moreover, everyone involved in the use of digital technology in education needs to be involved in deciding what forms of educational technology take place, and for what reasons. Educational technology the world over therefore needs to be reimagined and re-appropriated as an integral element of what Shafiul Alam Bhuiyan (2008, p.114) describes as "an inclusive information society, which fosters equality and participation and functions according to the need of human well-being [rather than] the logic of commodification". It is important that the alternative perspectives, beliefs and values of those involved at the grass roots of education are more prominently included in the development and implementation of educational technologies around the world. It is therefore crucial that the voices of *all* individuals in *all* countries are heard.

These are certainly wildly ambitious sentiments. What has been suggested over the past few pages of this chapter would involve a reorientation of the field of educational technology away from the logics of neoliberalism and the self-interested actions of dominant actors in the global knowledge economy. This would involve readjusting dominant understandings of the educational technology 'market' and fostering a shared understanding that "in a democracy, individuals do not only express personal preferences – they also make public and collective choices related to the common good" (Carr and Hartnett 1996, p.192). Put simply, then, what we have suggested in this final chapter would involve a fundamental reorientation of social relations as well as educational technology arrangements. Even then, it is highly likely that if all the suggestions in this chapter were followed to the letter, any resulting change would be slight. Yet the difficulty of addressing the wrongs of global capitalism is to be expected, and is certainly no reason to give up on attempts to make educational technology a more democratically empowering process around the world. As Michael Apple (2010, p.20) concludes, "the on-going relations between education and dominance/subordination and the struggles against the relations are exactly that, the subject of struggles". As such it is worth reminding ourselves that there are *no* grand solutions to the issues highlighted throughout this book, only continued struggles and occasional success.

REFERENCES

Akubue, A. (2000). 'Appropriate technology for socioeconomic development in third world countries'. *The Journal of Technological Studies*, 26, 1, pp.33–43.

Álvarez, C. (2006). 'ICT as part of the Chilean strategy for development' in Castells, M. and Cardoso, G. (eds). *The network society: from knowledge to policy'*. Washington, DC, John Hopkins Centre for Transatlantic Relations (pp.381–404).

Amen, M. (2008). 'NGOs and educational reform in Egypt: shared and contested views', unpublished PhD thesis, Case Western Reserve University.

Amin, A. and Thrift, N. (2005). 'What's left? Just the future'. *Antipode*, 37, pp.220–38.

Ananny, M. and Winters, N. (2007). 'Designing for development: understanding one laptop per child in its historical context'. *Proceedings of the IEEE/ACM International Conference on Information and Communication Technologies and Development*, Bangalore (pp.107–18).

Anderson, W. (2005). 'New Zealand: is online education a highway to the future?' in Carr-Chellman, A. (ed.). *Global perspectives on e-learning*. Thousand Oaks, CA, Sage (pp.163–78).

Andreoni, J. (1989). 'Giving with impure altruism: applications to charity and Ricardian equivalence'. *Journal of Political Economy*, 97, 6, pp.1447–58.

Anheier, H. and Daly S. (2004). 'The future of global philanthropy' in Kaldor, M., Anheier, H., and Glasius, M. (eds). *Global Civil Society Yearbook*. London, Sage.

Appadurai, A. (1990). 'Disjuncture and difference in the global cultural economy'. *Public Culture* 2, 2, pp.1–24.

Apple, M. (2007). 'Markets, standards, God, and inequality' seminar given at the Institute of Education, London, June 5th.

——(2010). *Global crises, social justice, and education*. London, Routledge.

Arnove, R. (2007). 'Introduction: reframing comparative education' in Arnove, R. and Torres, C. (eds). *Comparative education: the dialectic of the global and the local'* (third edition). Lanham MA, Rowman and Littlefield (pp.1–20).

Arora, P. (2010). 'Hope-in-the-wall? A digital promise for free learning'. *British Journal of Educational Technology*, 41, 5, pp.689–702.

Baker, K. (1993). *The turbulent years: my life in politics*. London, Faber and Faber.

Balasubramanian, K., Thamizoli, P., Umar, A. and Kanwar, A. (2010). 'Using mobile phones to promote lifelong learning among rural women in Southern India'. *Distance Education*, 31, 2, pp.193–209.

Ball, S. (1998). 'Big policies/small world: an introduction to international perspectives in educational policy'. *Comparative Education*, 34, 2, pp. 119–30.

——(2006). *Educational policy and social class*. London, Routledge.

——(2007). *Education plc: understanding private sector participation in public sector education* London, Routledge.

——(2008). 'New philanthropy, new networks and new governance in education'. *Political Studies*, 56, 4, pp.747–65.

——(2012). *Global education Inc.: new policy networks and the neoliberal imaginary*. London, Routledge.

Ball, S., Maguire, M. and Braun, A. (2012). *How schools do policy: policy enactments in secondary schools*. London, Routledge.

Barber, B. (2003). *Strong democracy: participatory politics for a new age*. Berkeley, CA, University of California Press.

Bauman, Z. (2010). *Forty-four letters from the liquid modern world*. Cambridge, Polity.

BBC News (2010). 'India unveils prototype for $35 touch-screen computer'. *BBC News Online*, July 23rd.

Beatham, M. (2008). 'Technological literacy' in Gabbard, D. (ed.). *Knowledge and power in the global economy* (second edition). New York, Lawrence Erlbaum (pp.511–24).

Becker, G. (1975). *Human capital: a theoretical and empirical analysis*. Chicago, University of Chicago Press.

Bell, D. (1980). 'The social framework of the information society' in Forester, T. (ed.). *The microelectronics revolution*. Oxford, Blackwell.

Benson, L. and Harkavy, I. (2002). 'Saving the soul of the university: what is to be done?' in Robins, K. and Webster, F. (eds). *The virtual university: knowledge, markets and management*. Oxford, Oxford University Press (pp.169–209).

Bergeron, S. (2008). 'Shape-shifting neoliberalism and World Bank education policy'. *Globalisation, Societies and Education*, 6, 4, pp.349–53.

Bijker, W., Hughes, T. and Pinch, T. (1987). *The social construction of technological systems*. Cambridge MA, MIT Press.

Bishop, M. and Green, M. (2008). *Philanthrocapitalism*. London, A & C Black.

Blunkett, D. (2000). Speech on higher education, Greenwich University, London, February 15th.

Brabazon, T. (2010). 'The Finns have got it right'. *Times Higher Education Supplement*, August 11th.

Bromley, H. (1997). 'The social chicken and the technological egg: educational computing and the technology/society divide'. *Educational Theory*, 47, 1, pp.51–65.

Brown, A. (2009). 'Digital technology and education: context, pedagogy and social relations' in Cowen, R. and Kazamias, A. (eds). *International handbook of comparative education*. Berlin, Springer (pp.1159–72).

Brown, P., Lauder, H. and Ashton, D. (2008). 'Education, globalisation and the future of the knowledge economy'. *European Educational Research Journal*, 7, 2, pp.131–56.

——(2011). *The global auction: the broken promises of education, jobs and incomes*. Oxford, Oxford University Press.

Buchanan, R. (2011). 'Paradox, promise and public pedagogy'. *Australian Journal of Teacher Education*, 36, 2 [http://ro.ecu.au/ajte/vol36/iss#2/6/].

Burawoy, M. (2005). 'The critical turn to public sociology'. *Critical Sociology*, 31, 3, pp.313–26.

Busch, A. (2000). 'Unpacking the globalisation debate' in Hay, C. and Marsh, D. (eds). *Demystifying globalisation*. Basingstoke, Palgrave (pp.21–48).

Carey, B. and Markoff, J. (2010). 'Reading, writing and robots'. *New York Times*, international edition, July 18th, pp.1–4.

Carmichael, P. and Honour, L. (2002). 'Open source as appropriate technology for global education'. *International Journal of Educational Development*, 22, 1, pp.47–53.

Carr, W. and Hartnett A. (1996). *Education and the struggle for democracy*. Buckingham, Open University Press.

Carr-Chellman, A. (2005). *Global perspectives on e-learning*. Thousand Oaks, CA, Sage.

Carstens, R. and Pelgrum, W. (2009). 'Second information technology in education study: SITES 2006 technical report'. Hamburg, International Association for the Evaluation of Educational Achievement.

Castells, M. (1996). *The rise of the network society*. Oxford, Blackwell.

——(2000). 'Materials for an exploratory theory of the network society'. *British Journal of Sociology*, 51, 1, pp. 5–24.

——(2006). 'The network society: from knowledge to policy' in Castells, M. and Cardoso, G. (eds). *The network society: from knowledge to policy*. Washington DC, John Hopkins Centre for Transatlantic Relations (pp.3–22).

Cervantes, R., Warschauer, M., Nardi, B. and Sambasivan, N. (2011). 'Infrastructures for low-cost laptop use in Mexican schools' in *Proceedings of the 29th International Conference on Human Factors in Computing Systems*, CHI 2011 (pp.945–54).

Chai, C., Hong, H. and Teo, T. (2009). 'Singaporean and Taiwanese pre-service teachers' beliefs and their attitude towards ICT use: a comparative study'. *The Asia-Pacific Education Researcher*, 18, 1, pp. 117–28.

Chakravartty, P. and Sarikakis, K. (2006). *Media policy and globalisation*. Edinburgh, Edinburgh University Press.

Clarke, J. (2004). 'Dissolving the public realm? The logics and limits of neo-liberalism'. *Journal of Social Policy*, 33, 1, pp.27–48.

Colle, R. and Roman, R. (2003). 'ICT4D: a frontier for higher education in developing nations'. *African and Asian Studies*, 2, 4, pp. 381–420.

Collins, H. and Evans, R. (2002). 'The third wave of science studies: studies of expertise and experience'. *Social Studies of Sciences*, 32, 2, pp.235–96.

Collis, B. (2006). 'E-learning and the transformation of education for a knowledge economy' in Castells, M. and Cardoso, G. (eds). *The network society: from knowledge to policy*. Washington, DC, John Hopkins Centre for Transatlantic Relations (pp.215–24).

Conole, G. (2012). *Designing for learning in an open world*. New York, Springer.

Considine, M. (2005). *Making public policy*. Cambridge, Polity.

Couldry, N. (2010). *Why voice matters: culture and politics after neoliberalism*. London, Sage.

Cowen, R. (2006). 'Acting comparatively upon the educational world: puzzles and possibilities'. *Oxford Review of Education*, 32, 5, pp.561–73.

Crouch, C. (2011). *The strange non-death of neoliberalism*. Cambridge, Polity.

Cummings, W. (1989). 'The American perception of Japanese education' *Comparative Education*, 25, 3, pp.293–302.

Dale, R. (2005). 'Globalisation, knowledge economy and comparative education'. *Comparative Education*, 41, 2, pp.117–49.

Dale, R. and Robertson, S. (2002). The varying effects of regional organizations as subjects of globalization of education. *Comparative Education Review*, 46, 1, pp.10–36.

——(2002). 'Open learning: transforming education for development' speech to *Pan-Commonwealth Forum on Open Learning* Durban, South Africa, July 29 to August 2 [www.col.org/pcf2/papers/Sir John Daniel speech.pdf].

——(2009). 'The expansion of higher education in the developing world' in Vrasidas, C., Zembylas, M. and Glass, G. (eds). *ICT for education, development and social justice*. Charlotte, NC, Information Age (pp.53–63).

——(2010). *Mega-schools, technology and teachers*. London, Routledge.

Davis, N. (2008). 'Foreword' in Law, N., Pelgrum, W. and Plomp, T. (eds). *Pedagogy and ICT use in schools around the world*. Rotterdam, Springer (pp.xxxiii–xxxvi).

Davison, R., Vogel, D., Harris, R. and Jones, N. (2000). 'Technology leapfrogging in developing countries – an inevitable luxury?'. *Electronic Journal of Information Systems in Developing Countries*, 1, 5, pp.1–10.

de Bastion, G. and Rolf, T. (2008). 'Low-cost ICT devices – new solutions for development?'. *Rural 21*, June, pp.30–1.

de Laet, M. and Mol, A. (2000). 'The Zimbabwe bush pump: mechanics of a fluid technology'. *Social Studies of Science, 30*, pp.225–63.

Dean, J. (2002). *Publicity's secret: how technoculture capitalised on democracy*. Ithaca NY, Cornell University Press.

Dearing, R. (1993). *The National Curriculum and its assessment*. London, Schools Examinations and Assessment Council.

DfEE (1998). *The learning age: a renaissance for a new Britain*. London, Stationery Office.

Dillon, P., Bayliss, P., Stolpe, I. and Bayliss, L. (2008). 'What constitutes 'context' in sociocultural research? How the Mongolian experience challenges theory'. *Transtext(e)s Transcultures* 跨文本跨文化, 4, pp.18–31.

Escobar, A. (1995). *Encountering development*. Princeton, NJ, Princeton University Press.

——(2000). 'Beyond the search for a paradigm? Post-development and beyond'. *Development, 43*, 4, pp.11–14.

Evans, R. and Plows, A. (2007). 'Citizen listening without prejudice? Re-discovering the value of the disinterested'. *Social Studies of Science*, 37, 6, pp.827–53.

Facer, K. (2011). *Learning futures: education, technology and social change*. London, Routledge.

Fang, X. and Warschauer, M. (2004). 'Technology and curricular reform in China: a case study'. *TESOL Quarterly*, 38, 2, pp.301–23.

Fidalgo-Neto, A., Tornaghi, A., Meirelles, R., Berçot, F, Xavier, L., Castro, M. and Alves, L. (2009). 'The use of computers in Brazilian primary and secondary schools'. *Computers and Education, 53*, 3, pp. 677–85.

Foucault, M. (1981). *The history of sexuality: an introduction*. London, Penguin.

Fraser, N. and Honneth, A. (2003). *Redistribution or recognition? A political-philosophical exchange*. New York, Verso.

Friedman, T. (2007). *The world is flat* (third edition). New York, Farrar, Straus and Giroux.

Fu, G. (2010). Speech to the Microsoft Regional Asia Pacific Innovative Education Forum, 9th March.

Fuchs, C. and Horak, E. (2008). 'Africa and the digital divide'. *Telematics and Informatics*, 25, 2, pp.99–116.

Gabriel, Y. and Sturdy, A. (2002). 'Neo-imperialism and global consumerism' in Robins, K. and Webster, F. (eds). *The virtual university: knowledge, markets and management*. Oxford, Oxford University Press (pp.148–68).

Garnham, N. (2000). 'Information society as theory or ideology?'. *Information, Communication and Society*, 3, 2, pp. 139–52.

——(2002). 'Information society: theory or ideology?' in Dutton, W. and Loader, B (eds). *Digital academe*. London, Routledge.

Gates, W. (2005). Speech to Microsoft Government Leaders Forum – Washington, DC, April 27th.

George, C. (2005). 'The internet's political impact and the penetration/participation paradox in Malaysia and Singapore'. *Media Culture Society*, 27, 6, pp. 903–20.

Grant, N. (2000). 'Tasks for comparative education in the new millennium'. *Comparative Education*, 36, 3, pp. 309–17.

Green, A. (1997). 'Core skills, general education and unification in post-16 education' in Hodgson, A. and Spours, K. (eds). *Dearing and beyond: 14–19 qualifications, frameworks and systems*. London, Kogan Page (pp.88–104).

——(2003). 'Education, globalisation and the role of comparative research'. *London Review of Education*, 1, 2, pp.84–97.

Hale, T. and Held, D. (2011). *Handbook of transnational governance*. Cambridge, Polity.

Halls, W. (1990). *Comparative education: contemporary issues and trends*. London, Jessica Kingsley Publishers.

Halpin D. and Troyna B. (1995). 'The politics of education policy borrowing'. *Comparative Education*, 31, 3, pp.303–10.

Ham, S. and Cha, Y. (2009). 'Positioning education in the information society: the transnational diffusion of the information and communication technology curriculum'. *Comparative Education Review*, 53, 4, pp.535–57.

Hamm, S. and Smith, G. (2008). 'One laptop meets big business'. *Business Week*, June 5th.

Hardt, M. and Negri, A. (2005). *Multitude*. London, Penguin.

Harvey, F. (2002). 'Computers for the third world'. *Scientific American*, 287, 4, pp.100–2.

Hay, C. and Rosamond, B. (2002). 'Globalization, European integration and the discursive construction of economic imperatives'. *Journal of European Public Policy*, 9, 2, pp.147–67.

Hazeltine, B. and Bull, C. (1999). *Appropriate technology: tools, choices, and implications*. San Diego, CA, Academic Press.

Heeks, R. (2008). 'ICT4D 2.0: the next phase of applying ICT for international development'. *Computer*, June, pp. 26–33.

——(2010). 'Do information and communication technologies contribute to development?'. *Journal of International Development*, 22, 5, pp.625–40.

Held, D. and McGrew, A. (2000). *The global transformations reader: an introduction to the globalization debate*. Cambridge, Polity.

Held, D., McGrew, A., Goldblatt, D. and Perraton, J. (1999). *Global transformations*. Stanford, CA, Stanford University Press.

Hinostroza, J., Labbé, C. Brun, M. and Matamala, C. (2011). 'Teaching and learning activities in Chilean classrooms: is ICT making a difference?' *Computers and Education*, 57, 1, pp.1358–67.

Hirst, P., Thompson, G. and Bromley, S. (2009). *Globalisation in question* (third edition). Cambridge, Polity.

Hlynka, D. and Belland, C. (1991). *Paradigms regained*. Englewood Cliffs, NJ, Educational Technology Publications.

Hollow, D. (2009). 'Radio for education' in Unwin, T. (ed.). *ICT4D: information and communication technology for development*. Cambridge, Cambridge University Press (pp.102–3).

Hoogvelt, A. (1997). *Globalisation and the postcolonial world: the new political economy of development*. Basingstoke, Macmillan.

Huntington, S. (2003). 'The clash of civilizations?'. *Foreign Affairs*, 72, 3, pp.22–49.

Information Infrastructure Task Force (1993). *The national information infrastructure: agenda for action*. Washington, DC, ITAF.

James, J. (2011). 'Low-cost computers for education in developing countries'. *Social Indicators Research*, 103, 3, pp.399–408.

Jarvis, P. (2000). 'Globalization, the learning society and comparative education'. *Comparative Education*, 36, 3, pp.343–56.

Jensen, C. and Lauritsen, P. (2005). 'Reading digital Denmark: IT reports as material-semiotic actors'. *Science, Technology and Human Values*, 30, 3, pp.352–73.

Jenson, J., Lewis, B., Rose, C. and Smith, R. (2007). *Policy unplugged: dis/connections between technology policy and practices in Canadian schools*. Montreal, McGill-Queen's University Press.

Jenson, J. and Santos, B. (2000). *Globalizing institutions: case studies in social regulation and innovation*. Aldershot, Ashgate.

Johnson, B. (2009). 'PlayPower: 1980s computing for the 21st century'. *The Guardian*, Technology section November 5, p.5.

Johnson, J. (2002). 'Open source software: private provision of a public good'. *Journal of Economics and Management Strategy*, 11, 4, pp.637–62.

Jones, P. (2009). *World Bank financing of education: lending, learning and development* (second edition). London, Routledge.

Keep, E. and Mayhew, K. (2010). 'Moving beyond skills as a social and economic panacea'. *Work, Employment and Society*, 24, pp.565–77.

Kelly, K. (2010). 'My bright idea: technology is as great a force as nature'. *The Observer*, Review section, October, 24th, p.22.

Kenway, J., Bigum, C., Fitzclarence, L, Collier, J. and Tregenza, K. (1994). 'New education in new times'. *Journal of Education Policy*, 9, 4, pp.317–33.

King, N. (2002). 'Security, disease, commerce: ideologies of post-colonial global health'. *Social Studies in Science*, 35, 5–6, pp.763–89.

Klebl, M. (2008). 'Explicating the shaping of educational technology: social construction of technology in the field of ICT and education' in *Readings in education and technology: proceedings of ICICTE 2008* (pp.278–89).

Kobayashi, H. (2009). cited in Demetriou, D. 'Robot teacher conducts first class in Tokyo school'. *Telegraph*, May 12th.

Kozma, R. (2005). 'National policies that connect ICT-based education reform to economic and social development' *Human Technology*, 1, 2, pp.117–56.

——(2008). 'Comparative analysis of policies for ICT in education' in *International hand-book of information technology in primary and secondary education: volume nineteen*. Berlin, Springer.

Latchem, C. and Jung, I. (2010). *Distance and blended learning in Asia*. London Routledge.

Latzer, M. (1995). 'Japanese information infrastructure initiatives: a politico-economic approach'. *Telecommunications Policy*, 19, 7, pp.515–29.

Lauder, H., Brown, P. and Halsey, A. (2009). 'Sociology of education: a critical history and prospects for the future'. *Oxford Review of Education*, 35, 5, pp.569–85.

Lauwerys, J. and Taylor, G. (1973). *Education at home and abroad*. London, Kogan Page.

Law, J. and Mol, A. (2001). 'Situating technoscience: an inquiry into spatialities'. *Society and Space*, 19, pp.609–21.

Law, N., Pelgrum, W. and Plomp, T. (2008). *Pedagogy and ICT use in schools around the world*. Berlin, Springer.

Leach, J. (2008). 'Do new information and communications technologies have a role to play in the achievement of education for all?' *British Educational Research Journal*, 34, 6, pp.783–805.

Leadbeater, C. (2008). *We-think*. London, Profile.

Levidow, L. (2002). 'Marketising higher education' in Robins, K. and Webster, F. (eds). *The virtual university: knowledge, markets and management*. Oxford, Oxford University Press (pp.227–48).

Li, L., Chang, C. and Chen, G. (2009). 'Researches on using robots in education' in Chang, M. (ed.) *Learning by playing: game-based education system design and development*. Lecture Notes in Computer Science, 5670 pp.479–82.

Lim, C. (2007). 'Effective integration of ICT in Singapore schools: pedagogical and policy implications'. *Educational Technology Research and Development*, 55, pp.83–116.

Lim, C. and Hedberg, J. (2009). 'School-community ICT-mediated linkages' in Vrasidas, C., Zembylas, M. and Glass, G. (eds). *ICT for education, development and social justice*. Charlotte, NC, Information Age (pp.169–79).

Lingard, B., Rawolle, S. and Taylor, S. (2005). 'Globalizing policy sociology in education'. *Journal of Education Policy*, 20, 6, pp.759–77.

Livingstone, S. (2012). 'Critical reflections on the benefits of ICT in education'. *Oxford Review of Education*, 38, pp.9–24.

Luyt, B. (2008). 'The One Laptop Per Child project and the negotiation of technological meaning'. *First Monday*, 13, 6.

Lyon, D. (1988). The information society. Cambridge, Polity.

Macfadyen, L. (2011). 'Perils of parsimony: the problematic paradigm of "national culture"'. *Information, Communication and Society*, 14, 2, pp.280–93.

Mansell, R. (2004). 'Political economy, power and new media'. *New Media and Society*, 6, 1, pp.96–105.

Marginson, S. (1999). 'After globalisation'. *Journal of Education Policy*, 14, 1, pp.19–31.

Markoff, J. (2005). *What the dormouse said: how the sixties counterculture shaped the personal computer*. London, Penguin.

——(2006). 'For $150, third-world laptop stirs big debate'. *New York Times*, November 30th [www.nytimes.com/2006/11/30/technology/30laptop.html].

Masschelein, J. and Quaghebeur, K. (2005). 'Participation for better or for worse?' *Journal of Philosophy of Education*, 39, 1, pp. 52–65.

Massey, D. (1993). 'Power-geometry and a progressive sense of space' in Bird, J. (ed.). *Mapping the futures: local cultures, global change*. London, Routledge (pp.60–70).

McBurnie, G. and Ziguras, C. (2010). *Transnational education: issues and trends in offshore higher education*. London, Routledge.

McGoey, L. (2011). 'Philanthropolitics and the commodification of self-interest' paper presented to the British Sociological Association annual conference, London, April.

McGuigan, J. (2009). *Cool capitalism*. London, Pluto.

McLaughlin, R. (1999). 'The internet and Japanese education: the effect of globalisation on education policies and government initiatives'. *Aslib Proceedings*, 51, 7, pp.224–32.

McMillin, D. (2007). *International media studies*. Oxford, Blackwell.

Meiksins Wood, E. (1997). 'Globalization or globaloney?' *Monthly Review*, 48, 9, pp.21–33.

Menchik, D. (2004). 'Placing cyber-education in the UK classroom'. *British Journal of Sociology of Education*, 25, 2, pp.193–213.

Miller, V. (2011). *Understanding digital culture*. London, Sage.

Ministry of Education (1998). *Learning to think, thinking to learn: towards thinking schools, learning nations*. Singapore, Ministry of Education.

Ministry of International Trade and Industry (1994). *Program for advanced information infrastructure*. Tokyo, Ministry of International Trade and Industry.

Mitra, S. (2010). 'Give them a laptop and a group of pupils will teach themselves'. *Guardian*, Educational Supplement, October 19th.

Mohan, G. and Stokke, K. (2000). 'Participatory development and empowerment: the dangers of localism'. *Third World Quarterly*, 21, 2, pp.247–68.

Mok, J. and Lee, M. (2003). 'Globalization or glocalization? Higher education reforms in Singapore'. *Asia Pacific Journal of Education*, 23, 1, pp.15–42.

Moore, N. (1998). 'Confucius or capitalism? Policies for an information society' in Loader, B. (ed.). *Cyberspace divide: equality, agency and policy in the information society*. London, Routledge (pp.149–60).

Mosco, V. (2004). *The digital sublime: myth, power and cyberspace*. Cambridge MA, MIT Press.

——(2009). *The political economy of communication* (second edition). London, Sage.

Mosse, D. (2005). 'Global governance and the ethnography of international aid' in Mosse, D. and Lewis, D. (eds). *The aid effect: giving and governing in international development*. London, Pluto Press (pp. 1–36).

Mukul, A. (2006). 'HRD rubbishes MIT's laptop scheme for kids'. *Times of India*, July 3rd.

Munro-Smith, N. (2002). 'A tale of two cities: computer mediated teaching and learning in Melbourne and Singapore' paper presented to *ASCILITE 2002 conference*, December, Auckland.

Murata, S. and Stern, S. (1993). 'Technology education in Japan'. *Journal of Technology Education*, 5, 1, pp.29–37.

Murdock, G. (2004). 'Past the posts: rethinking change, retrieving critique'. *European Journal of Communication*, 19, 1, pp. 19–38.

Naughton, J. (2005). 'The $100 laptop question'. *The Observer*, Business supplement December 4th, p.6.

Negroponte, N. (2007). Keynote address to Internet and Society conference – 'University – knowledge beyond authority' May 31st to June 1st, Cambridge, MA, Berkman Centre for Internet and Society at Harvard Law School.

——(2009). 'Lessons learned and future challenges' speech given to Reinventing the classroom: social and educational impact of information and communications technologies in education seminar, September, Washington, Inter-American Development Bank.

Ng, P. (2010). 'Educational technology management approach: the case of Singapore's ICT Masterplan Three'. *Human Systems Management*, 29, 3, pp.177–87.

Ngimwa, P. and Wilson, T. (2013). 'Is Africa ready to adopt OER? An assessment of practicalities and benefits'. *Learning, Media and Technology*, 38, 3 [forthcoming].

Ngo, T., Lingard, B. and Mitchell, J. (2006). 'The policy cycle and vernacular globalization'. *Comparative Education*, 42, 2, pp.225–42.

Nisbett, R. (2003). *The geography of thought: how Asians and Westerners think differently, and why*. New York, Free Press.

Nissenbaum, H. (2004). 'Hackers and the contested ontology of cyberspace'. *New Media and Society*, 6, 2, pp.195–217.

Nordtveit, B. (2010). 'Towards post-globalisation? On the hegemony of western education and development discourses'. *Globalisation, Societies and Education*, 8, 3, pp.321–37.

Novoa, A. and Yariv-Mashal, T. (2003). 'Comparative research in education: a mode of governance or a historical journey'. *Comparative Education*, 39, 4, pp.423–38.

Nye, D. (2007). *Technology matters: questions to live with*. Cambridge, MA, MIT Press.

OECD (2005). *Are students ready for a technology-rich world: what PISA studies tell us*. Paris, Organisation for Economic Co-operation and Development.

——(2010). *Are the new millennium learners making the grade? Technology use and educational performance in PISA*. Paris, Organisation for Economic Co-operation and Development.

Oliver, M. (2011). 'Technological determinism in educational technology research: some alternative ways of thinking about the relationship between learning and technology'. *Journal of Computer Assisted Learning*, 27, 5, pp.373–84.

OLPC (One Laptop Per Child]) (2010). 'One Laptop Per Child – mission statement'. [www.laptop.org/vision].

Ozga, J. (2011). 'Researching the powerful: seeking knowledge about policy'. *European Educational Research Journal*, 10, 2, pp.218–24.

Pal, J, Patra, R., Nedevschi, S., Plauche, M. and Pawar, U. (2009). 'The case of the occasionally cheap computer: low-cost devices and classrooms in the developing world'. *Information Technologies and International Development*, 5, 1, pp.49–64.

Pantzar, E. (2001). 'European perspectives on lifelong learning environments in the information society'. in Karvonen, E. (ed.). *Informational societies*. Tampere, Tampere University Press (pp.240–58).

Paton, G. (2007). 'Google aims to net teenagers for life'. *The Telegraph*, June 13th, p.11.

Peeraer, J. and Tran, N. (2009). *Policy analysis integration of ICT in higher education in Vietnam* paper presented to the UNESCO-APEID Conference ICT Transforming Education, Hangzhou, November 15th to 17th.

Pelgrum, W. and Plomp, T. (1993). *The IEA study of computers in education: implementation of an innovation in twenty-one education systems*. Oxford, Pergamon.

Pelgrum, W., Reinen, I. and Plomp, T. (1993). *Schools, teachers, students and computers: a cross-national perspective*. Enschede, University of Twente.

Perkins, R. and Neumayer, E. (2011). 'Is the internet really new after all? The determinants of telecommunications diffusion in historical perspective'. *The Professional Geographer*, 63, 1, pp.55–72.

Phillips, D. and Ochs, K. (2007). 'Processes of policy borrowing in education: some explanatory and analytical devices' in Crossley, M., Broadfoot, P. and Schweisfurth, M. (eds). *Changing educational contexts, issues and identities*. London, Routledge (pp.370–82).

Phillips, D. and Schweisfurth, M. (2008). *Comparative and international education*. London, Continuum.

Potts, J. (2008). 'Who's afraid of technological determinism? Another look at medium theory'. *Fibreculture* [http://journal.fibreculture.org/issue12/issue12_potts.html].

Price, V. (2009). 'Citizens deliberating online: theory and some evidence' in Davies, T. and Gangadharan, S. (eds). *Online deliberation: design, research, and practice*. Chicago, University of Chicago Press (pp. 37–58).

Qablan, A., Abuloum, A. and Al-Ruz, J. (2009). 'Effective integration of ICT in Jordanian Schools: an analysis of pedagogical and contextual impediments in the science classroom' *Journal of Science Education and Technology*, 18, pp.291–300.

Qi, J (2005). 'The gap between e-learning availability and e-learning industry in Taiwan' in Carr-Chellman, A. (ed.). *Global perspectives on e-learning: rhetoric and reality*. Thousand Oaks, CA, Sage (pp.33–51).

Readings, W. (1996). *The university in ruins*. Cambridge, MA, Harvard University Press.

Richards, C. (2004). 'From old to new learning: global imperatives, exemplary Asian dilemmas and ICT as a key to cultural change in education'. *Globalisation, Societies and Education*, 2, 3, pp.337–53.

Rizvi, F. and Lingard, R. (2010). *Globalising education policy*. London, Routledge.

Robertson, J. (2010). 'Gendering humanoid robots: robo-sexism in Japan'. *Body and Society*, 16, 1, pp.1–36.

Robertson, S., Novelli, M., Dale, R., Tikly, L., Dachi, H. and Alphonce, N. (2007). *Globalisation, education and development: ideas, actors and dynamics*. London, Department for International Development.

Robins, K. and Webster, F. (1989). *The technical fix: education, computers and industry*. London, Macmillan.

——(2002). 'The virtual university?' in Robins, K. and Webster, F. (eds). *The virtual university: knowledge, markets and management*. Oxford, Oxford University Press (pp.3–19).

Rowell, L. (2007). 'Can the $100 Laptop Change the World?' *eLearn Magazine* [http://elearnmag.acm.org].

Rubagiza, J., Were, E. and Sutherland, R. (2011). 'Introducing ICT into schools in Rwanda'. *International Journal of Educational Development*, 31, 1, pp.37–43.

Rybczynski, W. (1980). *Paper heroes: a review of appropriate technology*. Garden City, Anchor Books.

Samoff, J. (2007). 'Institutionalising international influence' in Arnove, R. and Torres, C. (eds). *Comparative education: the dialectic of the global and the local*. Lanham, MA, Rowman and Littlefield (pp.47–78).

Sánchez, J. and Salinas, A. (2008). 'ICT and learning in Chilean schools: lessons learned'. *Computers and Education*, 51, 4, pp.1621–33.

Schirato, A. and Webb, J. (2003). *Understanding globalisation*. London, Sage.

Selinger, M. (2009). 'ICT in education: catalyst for development' in Unwin, T. (ed.) *ICT4D: Information and communication technology for development*. Cambridge, Cambridge University Press (pp.206–48).

Selwyn, N. (2002). 'Learning to love the micro: the discursive construction of "educational computing" in the UK, 1979–89'. *British Journal of Sociology of Education*, 23, 3, pp.427–43.

——(2010). 'Looking beyond learning: notes towards the critical study of educational technology'. *Journal of Computer Assisted Learning*, 26, 1, pp.65–73.

——(2011). 'Digitally distanced learning: a study of international distance learners' (non) use of technology'. *Distance Education*, 32, 1, pp.85–99.

Selwyn, N. and Facer, K. (2013). *The politics of education and technology*. Basingstoke, Palgrave Macmillan.

Shafiul Alam Bhuiyan, A. (2008). 'Peripheral view: conceptualizing the information society as a post-colonial subject'. *International Communication Gazette*, 70, 2, pp.99–116.

Shields, R. (2011). 'ICT or I see tea? Modernity, technology and education in Nepal'. *Globalisation, Societies and Education*, 9, 1, pp.85–97.

Shohel, M. and Kirkwood, A. (2013). 'Using technology for enhancing teaching and learning in Bangladesh'. *Learning, Media and Technology*, 38, 3.

Simba (2010). *Moving online: K-12 distance learning market forecast.* Rockville, MD, Simba Information.

Spring, J. (2009). *Globalisation of education,* London, Routledge.

——(2012). *Education networks: power, wealth, cyberspace and the digital mind,* London, Routledge.

Stambach, A. and Malekela, G. (2006). 'Education, technology, and the "new" knowledge economy: views from Bongoland'. *Globalisation, Societies and Education,* 4, 3, pp.321–36.

Starke-Meyerring, D. and Wilson, M. (2008). *Designing globally networked learning environments: visionary partnerships, policies, and pedagogies.* Rotterdam, Sense.

Stiegler, B. (2010). *For a new critique of political economy* (trans. Daniel Ross). Cambridge, Polity.

Streeck, W. (1992). *Social, institutional and economic performance.* London, Sage.

Streicher-Porte, M., Marthaler, C., Boni, H., Schuep, M, Camacho, A. and Hilty, L. (2009). 'One laptop per children, local refurbishment or overseas donations? Sustainability assessment of computer supply scenarios for schools in Colombia'. *Journal of Environmental Management,* 90, 11, pp. 3498–3511.

Strom, S. (2010). 'Non-profits review technology failures'. *New York Times,* August 16th.

Stronach, I. (2010). *Globalizing education, educating the local: how method made us mad.* London, Routledge.

Stubbs, R. and Underhill, G. (2006). *Political economy and the changing global order.* Oxford, Oxford University Press.

Tabb, L. (2008). 'A chicken in every pot – One Laptop Per Child: the trouble with global campaign promises'. *E-Learning and Digital Media,* 5, 3, pp.337–51.

Takayama, K. (2011). 'A comparativist's predicaments of writing about "other" education: a self-reflective, critical review of studies of Japanese education'. *Comparative Education,* 47, 4, pp.449–70.

Telecommunications Council (1994). *Reforms towards the intellectually creative society of the 21st century.* Tokyo, Telecommunications Council.

Teo, T. and Lim, V. (1998). 'Leveraging information technology to achieve the IT2000 vision: the case study of an intelligent island'. *Behaviour and Information Technology,* 17, 2, pp.113–23.

Toh, Y. and So, H. (2011). 'ICT reform initiatives in Singapore schools: a complexity theory perspective'. *Asia Pacific Educational Review* 12, 3, pp.349–57.

Traore, K. (2008). 'Are ICTs a new revolution in rural areas?' *Rural 21,* June, pp.8–10.

Turkle, S. (2011). *Alone together: why we expect more from technology and less from each other.* New York, Basic Books.

UK Race Online (2010). *Manifesto for a networked Britain.* London, UK Race Online.

UNESCO (2010). *UNESCO Institute for Information Technologies in Education Medium-Term Strategy 2008–2013.* Moscow, UNESCO Institute for Information Technologies in Education.

United Nations (2003). 'E-schools and communities initiative launched today at information summit: will connect pupils, villagers across developing world' press release PI/1548, December.

Unwin, T. (2009a). 'Development agendas and the place of ICTs' in Unwin, T. (ed.). *ICT4D: information and communication technology for development.* Cambridge, Cambridge University Press (pp.7–38).

——(2009b). 'ICT4D implementation: policies and partnerships' in Unwin, T. (ed.). *ICT4D: information and communication technology for development.* Cambridge, Cambridge University Press (pp.125–76).

——(2009c). 'The technologies: identifying appropriate solutions for development needs' in Unwin, T. (ed.). *ICT4D: information and communication technology for development.* Cambridge, Cambridge University Press (pp.76–124).

——(2009d). 'Introduction' in Unwin, T. (ed.). *ICT4D: information and communication technology for development.* Cambridge, Cambridge University Press (pp.1–6).

Urry, J. (2002). 'Globalising the academy' in Robins, K. and Webster, F. (eds). *The virtual university: knowledge, markets and management*. Oxford, Oxford University Press (pp.20–30).

USAID (2011). *Education opportunity through learning: USAID education strategy*. Washington, DC, USAID.

US Department of Education (1996). *Getting America's students ready for the 21st century: meeting the technology literacy challenge*. Washington, DC, US Department of Education.

——(2010). *Transforming American education: learning powered by technology*. Washington, DC, US Department of Education.

Usun, S. (2004). 'Undergraduate students' attitudes on the use of computers in education'. *Turkish Online Journal of Educational Technology*, 3, 2.

Waks, L. (2011). 'Transforming American education: revolution or counter-revolution?'. *E-learning and Digital Media*, 8, 2, pp.145–53.

Wallerstein, I. (1986). 'Walter Rodney: the historian as spokesman for historical forces'. *American Ethnologist*, 13, 2, pp. 330–7.

Warschauer, M. (2001). 'Singapore's dilemma: control vs. autonomy in IT-led development' *The Information Society*, 17, 4, pp.305–11.

——(2004). *Technology and social inclusion: rethinking the digital divide*. Cambridge, MA, MIT Press.

Warschauer, M. and Ames, M. (2010). 'Can one laptop per child save the world's poor?'. *Journal of International Affairs*, 64, 1, pp.33–51.

Waters, J. and Brooks, R. (2011). 'International/transnational spaces of education' *Globalisation, Societies and Education*, 9, 2, pp.155–60.

Webster, F. (2006). *Theories of the information society* (third edition). London, Routledge.

White House (2009). *Federal open government directive*. Washington, DC, Executive Office of the President.

Williams, R. (1981). *Keywords: a vocabulary of culture and society*. London, Fontana.

Willinsky, J. (2009). 'Forward' in Vrasidas, C., Zembylas, M. and Glass, G. (eds). *ICT for education, development and social justice*. Charlotte, NC, Information Age (pp.xi–xiv).

Willsher, K. (2011). 'Rupert Murdoch uses eG8 to talk up net's power to transform education'. *Guardian* May 24th.

Wilson, M. (2010). 'The impact of globalization on higher education: implications for globally networked learning environments'. *E-Learning and Digital Media*, 7, 2, pp.182–7.

Wims, P. and Lawler, M. (2007). 'Investing in ICTs in educational institutions in developing countries: an evaluation of their impact in Kenya'. *International Journal of Education and Development using Information and Communication Technology*, 3, 1, pp.5–22.

Winner, L. (1993). 'Upon opening the black box and finding it empty: social constructivism and the philosophy of technology'. *Science, Technology and Human Values*, 18, 3, pp.362–78.

Witchalls, C. (2005). 'Bridging the digital divide'. *The Guardian* 'Online' supplement, February 17th, p.23.

Wyatt, S. (2008). 'Technological determinism is dead: long live technological determinism' in Hackett, E., Amsterdamska, O., Lynch, M. and Wajcman, J. (eds). *The handbook of science and technology studies*. Cambridge MA, MIT Press (pp.165–81).

Yamada, M. (1999). *Parasaito singuru no jidai*. Tokyo, Chikuma Shinsho.

Yeates, N. (2001). *Globalization and Social Policy*. London, Sage.

You, Z., Shen, C., Chang, C., Liu, B. and Chen, G. (2006). 'A robot as a teaching assistant in an English class'. *Sixth International Conference on Advanced Learning Technologies*, 5–7 July, pp.87–91.

Yujuico, E. and Gelb, B. (2011). 'Marketing technological innovation to LDCs: lessons from one laptop per child'. *California Management Review*, 53, 2, pp. 50–68.

Zembylas, M. (2009). 'ICT for education, development and social justice' in Vrasidas, C., Zembylas, M. and Glass, G. (eds). *ICT for education, development and social justice*. Charlotte, NC, Information Age (pp.3–16).

Zhang, C. (2008). 'The institutional framework of the United Nations Development Programme – Ministry of Science and Technology telecentre project in rural China'. *Journal of Information Technologies and International Development*, 4, 3.

Zhang, J. (2007). 'A cultural look at information and communication technologies in Eastern education' *Education Technology Research and Development*, 55, pp.301–14.

Zhao, Y., Lei, J. and Conway, P. (2006). 'A global perspective on political definitions of e-learning' in *International handbook of virtual learning environments*. Netherlands, Kluwer (pp.673–97).

Zhao, Y., Lei, J., Li, G., He, M., Okano, K., Megahedn N., Gamage, D. and Ramanathan, H. (2011). *Handbook of Asian education: a cultural perspective*. London, Routledge.

Žižek, S. (1996). *The indivisible remainder: an essay on Schelling and related matters*. London, Verso.

INDEX

robots/robotics 53, 99–102, 150

Simputer 131, 160
Singapore 70–1, 75, 76, 77, 78, 81, 88,
91, 92, 97–9
skills 4–5, 46, 49, 52, 58–60, 65, 75–7, 88,
153, 159; twenty-first-century skills
57–60, 61, 76, 85, 148, 153, 155
South Korea 6, 89, 98, 99
Spring, Joel 48, 52, 93, 102
sub-Saharan Africa 33, 64, 87, 91–2, 105,
111–13, 119, 120, 150, 154
supranational organisations 24, 29, 40–1,
44, 49, 58, 61

technical fix 36, 105, 125
technological determinism 35–8, 41, 148
technology, social shaping of 38–40, 86,
136, 149
TIMSS 13, 87
topography *see* geography (physical)
Turkey 49, 89, 91, 95
Twenty-first-century skills *see*
under skills

UNESCO *see* United Nations
Educational, Scientific and Cultural
Organization
United Kingdom 66, 72, 73, 81, 92, 96,
111–12
United Nations 46, 47–8, 110, 147
United Nations Educational,
Scientific and Cultural Organization
47, 48, 50, 58, 61
United States 11, 67–8, 112
Unwin, Tim 56, 91, 107,
120, 122
Uruguay 96, 135, 141, 144
US Department of Education 59, 74

virtual schooling 74, 96–7, 111

'War on terror' *see* 9/11
Warschauer, Mark 70, 98, 121, 141
Washington Consensus 11, 107
Western thought/values 33, 35, 45, 93–5,
101, 102, 103, 122, 153–4
World Bank 24, 32–4, 44–7, 49–50,
117, 118